# When Nature Strikes

# When Nature Strikes

## Weather Disasters and the Law

*Marsha L. Baum*

Westport, Connecticut
London

**Library of Congress Cataloging-in-Publication Data**

Baum, Marsha L.
    When nature strikes : weather disasters and the law / Marsha L. Baum.
        p.   cm.
    Includes bibliographical references and index.
    ISBN 978–0–275–22129–4 (alk. paper)
    1. Natural disasters—Law and legislation—United States.
    2. Disaster relief—Law and legislation—United States.   3. Crime and
    weather.   I. Title.
    KF3750.B38    2007
    344.7305′3492—dc22        2007014271

British Library Cataloguing in Publication Data is available.

Library of Congress Catalog Card Number: 2007014271
ISBN-13: 978–0–275–22129–4
ISBN-10: 0–275–22129–6

First published in 2007

Praeger Publishers, 88 Post Road West, Westport, CT 06881
An imprint of Greenwood Publishing Group, Inc.
www.praeger.com

Printed in the United States of America

The paper used in this book complies with the
Permanent Paper Standard issued by the National
Information Standards Organization (Z39.48–1984).

10  9  8  7  6  5  4  3  2  1

*To Richard Klingler
and to our daughters, Elise and Amanda Klingler*

# Contents

# Contents

# Acknowledgments

I want to express my appreciation to all of the people who made this book a reality.

My research assistants from the University of New Mexico Law School—Brian Grayson, Amber Chavez, Shela Young, Keith Blake, Ben Sherman, Karl Reifsteck, and Alex Beattie—for their thoroughness and creativity in locating materials and for offering ideas. A very special thank you to Brian Grayson, my long-term research assistant, who was involved in this project from its inception and who worked diligently to locate and organize massive amounts of information. This book would not have been possible without his efforts.

The librarians and library staff at the University of New Mexico Law Library, whose fantastic service and enthusiasm for this topic made my life so much easier: Barbara Lah, Alexandra Siek, and the students in the research pool (Tyler Atkins, Brooke Nowak Neely, Rebecca Shreve, Renee Ruybal, Vanessa Chavez, Anthony Apodaca, Marcos Perales, Daniel Marquez, Kerry Cait Winkless-Hall, and Juliet Keene), who worked continuously on research projects that required special efforts and training; Lorraine Lester, who, with persistence and an amazing ability to locate the most esoteric materials, identified some incredible items on topics from lighthouses to cannibalism; Eileen Cohen, who can locate materials almost before you ask for them; Jeanette Hennie, who handled all the

# Acknowledgments

hundreds (literally) of interlibrary loan requests required to research this topic; Moses Moya, the library's extraordinary student employee who collected materials from other libraries on campus so quickly I never noticed a time lag; Robert Flinkman and Carolyn Kelly, who were so responsive to requests for purchases and kept the materials coming in every week; and, Carol Parker, Michelle Rigual, and the rest of the outstanding staff who never complained about the amount of time my numerous requests required. And, to Ron Wheeler, formerly on the UNM Law Library faculty, who supervised research until he left us for Georgia State.

The administration of the UNM Law School, particularly Dean Suellyn Scarnecchia and Assistant Dean Susan Mitchell, who provided support for the incredible number of student research assistant hours I needed to complete this project.

The staff of the UNM University Libraries Zimmerman Library, the Science and Engineering Library, and the Government Documents unit for maintaining a collection of materials, both print and electronic, that made research on the history of law and policy related to weather and disasters possible.

My colleagues on the UNM Law School faculty who were so incredibly supportive and encouraging during the process of researching and writing this book, especially Jim Ellis, who seems to read everything printed and who forwarded great news items and books, Chris Fritz, who was kind enough to buy a book on weather that he saw and thought I might find of interest and, unknowingly, provided me with the perfect source to fill a gap in my research, and Sherri Burr, who read an early version and offered suggestions and insights.

My family and friends who read and edited and provided input on many drafts of this work—Alice Ann Klingler, Shirley Baum, Warren Baum, Ed Baum, Marianne Chiafery, Sandra Stringer, Jessi Baum, and, of course, my co-author on *Internet Surf and Turf* and editorial guru, Barbara M. Waxer.

My editor at Praeger Publishers, Hilary Claggett, whose patience and candor made this foray into solo authorship more workable.

Author David Laskin, whose book, *The Children's Blizzard*, inspired this research.

And, finally but most importantly, my husband, Richard Klingler, who spent months taking care of our daughters virtually single-handedly to allow me to undertake this project. His overall support, patience, and understanding, along with his willingness to read drafts and help me figure out how to approach topics, made this book possible. Thank you, Richard.

# Introduction: Why Weather and Law

As I researched and wrote this book, people frequently asked me the topic. When I said "Weather Law" or "Law and Weather," the next question invariably was "What is that?!" As I explained the topics I would be covering in the book, people generally responded that they had never seen the connection between the two topics before.

Most people do not recognize the intersection of weather events and the law. Even though both law and weather affect us every day of our modern lives, we do not know how the weather has affected developments in the law and how the law has attempted to develop ways to affect the weather. This book is the first effort to publish a description of various areas in which law and weather meet and affect each other.

The law related to weather includes the full spectrum of legal topics. If you were to take a law school curriculum and superimpose it over the topics covered in this book, you would find it difficult to identify a law school subject area not affected by weather. Through legislative and administrative action, federal and state governments have been involved in the evolution of our weather services from simple weather recording into weather forecasting and warning systems. Harm from weather events, from a slip on the ice to the horrible devastation wrought by a deadly hurricane, is addressed by legal remedies in tort law and contract law. Inventions of devices to increase safety from weather events are protected by patent law.

Weather can be the means to commit a crime or the factor that creates a deadly result that turns an event from a terrible accident into a criminal act. Weather can be used as defense to liability in both civil claims and criminal claims. The necessity defense applies in situations where the defendant chose to break the law to survive or to ensure survival of other people. The natural accumulation defense or the open and obvious defense (which has also been called the "watch where you're going" defense) can protect homeowners from liability for injury to people who slip on the ice.

The operation of the courts and the criminal justice system can be affected by weather events that prevent physical access to the buildings or that destroy evidence or records needed for prosecution or to allow release of prisoners. Governments can defend against claims for injuries through the doctrine of sovereign immunity. Homeowners and other property owners affected by flooding or hail or wind damage look to insurance law and contract law for relief.

To attempt to prevent future disasters, the government drafts legislation and creates regulations to identify emergency management programs for prevention and mitigation of future disasters and for relief in the aftermath of major weather events. Some of those efforts include traditional legal steps such as changes in communications law, insurance law, zoning and property law, and criminal law to provide broader protections or new systems of remedies. Other efforts relate to attempts to change the weather such as creation of treaties to stop global warming and federal funding for research into weather modification.

The wide range of legal topics that touch upon weather events is fascinating and, at times, overwhelming. In a book of limited length, decisions about coverage had to be made. Not all topics could be covered in depth; some topics are not covered at all or mentioned only in an endnote. Furthermore, some nuances of the law will be foregone in favor of brevity and understandability but the extensive endnotes offer some compensation for the loss of fine distinctions in various legal concepts and among various jurisdictions.

This book describes the law related to weather in the United States in the context of specific cases, legislation, and administrative legal action. The public policy issues and the non-legal aspects of weather disasters are left for another book or another author. And, of course, given the massive number of cases and the frequency of weather events, this book can cover only a sampling of cases and is limited to a select few weather events representing the two hundred years of U.S. history.

The focus of the book is on three areas: the history and role of the government in weather reporting, forecasting, and warning systems; human attempts to affect the weather and governmental regulation of those efforts; and, liability for harm resulting from weather-related incidents that affect individuals. While emergency management and relief efforts show the law in relation to disasters affecting a region, a town, a large population in which people are killed and massive amounts of property are lost or destroyed, the individual can also be harmed by the more specific event such as a "slip and fall" case, an auto accident, loss of a loved one when a car is washed away by localized flood waters, or financial losses due to airline or train or ship carrier error. These individual events can be as disastrous for the specific family, person, or business struck by that storm as the widespread devastation of a hurricane, massive flooding, a blizzard, tornadoes, or forest fires is for the larger population of a region struck by a weather disaster.

The continued unpredictability of weather events and the potential for harm place a burden on the legal system to offer relief. Weather can never be held legally accountable but the law can attempt to provide justice and protection from harm.

# CHAPTER 1

# Weather Forecasting and Warning Systems

*In January 1888, on the first warm day in several months, a cold front moved down from Canada and hit the warm air in the Midwestern states and territories in the U.S., catching a large number of people unprepared for a major winter storm. In uncharacteristic manner for January in the Dakota Territory, Montana, and Minnesota, children had gone to school without their winter coats, farmers left the safety of their houses and went out into fields far from buildings, and people who would not have considered taking such a trip during normal winter weather took off on foot or horseback for other towns to conduct business.*

*When the cold front from the north met the warm air which had raised the temperature to 74° F, the skies filled with lightning and blowing snow with winds of up to 80 mph. In three minutes, the temperature dropped 20 degrees. During the next 24 hours, temperatures dropped to −28° F ... Reportedly hundreds of people were caught in the freezing air and blowing snow, including approximately 500 school children who lost their lives.[1]*

In 1888, the United States had a system for recording temperatures and weather events and for transmitting the data from the outlying states back to Washington, DC, but had no established system for forecasting the weather or issuing warnings. Even if a reliable system for weather forecasts had existed in 1888, no effective method was available for relaying warnings and weather information to the residents of communities who would be affected by incoming weather. While telegraph lines could relay information from station to station, people out on the plains, miles from their nearest neighbors, did not have ready and timely access to any warnings of extreme weather that might be transmitted.

## RECORDING WEATHER DATA

How did the system for recording weather data start? Records of information about weather and major weather events have existed for a long time. The Native Americans recorded weather events as part of their histories. For example, the Sioux maintained records of the major event of each year by drawing pictographs on animal skins. One such record, The Big Missouri Winter Count, which can be found in the Sioux Indian Museum in Rapid City, South Dakota, includes information about winter weather and its effect on the Indian nation. One recorded event from 1827 shows that the ground was so icy that hunters went out on foot rather than on horseback and carried game home by dragging the game in its own skin. Other recorded events illustrate the desperate measures that Native American children would take to get away from their boarding schools. The Winter Count shows that, on a cold day in 1919, two Indian girls deserted the Saint Francis School on the Rosebud Reservation in South Dakota; one froze to death and the other's feet had to be amputated. In 1921, one of two boys who left the same school on a very cold day froze to death.[2]

To record weather data, it is necessary to have both devices to measure meteorological variables such as temperature and barometric pressure[3] and people to collect information. In prior decades, it was always necessary to have people with the equipment to take the measurements. Without balloons and satellites to lift equipment and without communication technologies to provide easy ways to relay information, recording was limited to reachable areas and centers of population, leaving out the oceans and large areas of uninhabited land.

While much of the recording of weather data is now accomplished using remote sensing equipment, satellites, and computers, the need for people to take measurements and record data still exists. Even though the modern equipment is certainly less costly than labor-intensive human data collection, the cost of the equipment limits the number of recording systems that can be provided around the country. As a result, to ensure comprehensive data collection, the tried and true manual collection methods are still needed, with both paid and volunteer weather observers helping to gather information about the weather.

Many people have collected weather data on their own initiative, including George Washington and Thomas Jefferson. Thomas Jefferson reportedly bought his first thermometer and his first barometer while in Philadelphia in 1776,[4] recording temperature data for July 4th in his weather diary.[5] The Weather Bureau's "cooperative observers" of the 1920s made daily observations of weather conditions on a volunteer basis, making it possible for the Bureau to continue operations without adding new staff.[6] The fascination with the weather has continued to the present day with volunteer weather observers, both "cooperative observers" who record daily temperature and rainfall and "storm spotters" who are specially trained to serve as extra "eyes and ears in the field,"[7] providing data and storm information to the National Weather Service.

The government's ability to collect data has improved dramatically with advances in satellite and computer technology that allows remote and rapid assembly of information. In 1960, the first of a series of weather satellites known as Television and Infrared Observation Satellites (TIROS) was launched by the National Aeronautics and Space Administration (NASA).[8] In 1972, NASA launched the Earth Resources Technology Satellite (ERTS), later known as Landsat 1. ERTS set the stage for the move toward systematic collection of land images from space.[9] Since that first launch, NASA and the National Oceanic and Atmospheric Administration (NOAA) have worked together to develop near-real-time imagery collected by satellites. NASA's Earth Observation System (EOS) can be used to assess litigated matters such as water use or environmental compliance[10] while NOAA's Geostationary Orbiting Environmental Satellites (GOES) provide the capability for observing rapidly changing weather and environmental events such as floods, dust storms, hurricanes, and forest fires.[11] Being able to see clearly the course of a weather event provides a better opportunity to mitigate the losses of life and property and to provide warnings sooner than in the past.

## THE DEVELOPMENT OF THE NATIONAL WEATHER SERVICE

The present National Weather Service (NWS) bears little resemblance to the service officially started by the U.S. government in 1870. Weather observation, reporting, forecasting, and warning systems have grown and developed over the past 130-plus years, from a simple system for recording and reporting data from around the country to benefit agriculture and commercial interests to international cooperation on forecasting and warning about major weather events.

The first federal entity with official weather recording responsibilities was the War Department. On February 9, 1870, President Grant approved a joint resolution of Congress establishing the responsibility for weather observation and storm warnings within the Army Signal Service. The initial charge was to provide notice of storms on the Great Lakes and along the seacoast. The text of the resolution reads:

> Be it resolved by the Senate and House of Representatives of the United States of America in Congress assembled, That the Secretary of War be, and he hereby is, authorized and required to provide for taking meteorological observations at the military stations in the interior of the continent, and at other points in the States and Territories of the United States, and for giving notice on the northern lakes and on the sea-coast, by magnetic telegraph and marine signals, of the approach and force of storms.[12]

The goals of the service were expanded in 1872 to provide information to farmers and to businesses to aid in commerce.

> The Secretary of War shall provide, in the system of observations and reports in charge of the Chief Signal Officer of the Army, for such stations, reports and signals as may be found necessary for the benefit of agriculture and commercial interests.[13]

During the War of 1812, the Army Surgeon General's Office had ordered hospital surgeons to make regular weather observations and to record climatological data.[14] The Army had camps all over the country, with personnel stationed at each one to allow for regular and consistent collection of weather data. Although the weather observations and recording of information was not yet sanctioned by Congress, the Surgeon General's Office used federal money to obtain equipment needed to make weather observations; for example, the estimate of expenses for the Surgeon General's Office in 1841 included $2,000 "for barometers, thermometers, and other meteorological instruments."[15] This initiative by the Surgeon General probably made the Army the first federally funded meteorological organization.

The Smithsonian Institution also had a system for collecting and reporting weather data in the mid-1800s. Beginning in 1849, Joseph Henry, Secretary of the Smithsonian Institution, gathered an organization of volunteer weather observers from around the country. He was able to make arrangements with the telegraph companies for timely delivery of weather reports to DC from the observers. By 1854, Henry was recording the current observational data on a synoptic[16] chart displayed daily at the Smithsonian.[17]

When the time came to designate an official entity to collect weather data, both the Smithsonian and the Army had infrastructures in place. They each had systems for recording data and available personnel throughout the United States. Congress debated the benefits of civilian versus military responsibility for a national weather service. The civilian group had developed the meteorological skills needed to make effective use of the data collected while some Congressional representatives argued that the military had the discipline to ensure consistent data collection. In 1870, Congress voted to delegate the responsibility to the War Department.

Despite, or perhaps because of, the expansions of the scope of the Signal Service's work to include the entire country and the addition of services such as the frost forecast and placement of cautionary signal flags at local Signal Service stations to warn the public of weather events, the Signal Service found itself in conflict with Congress and with the Army itself over the level of autonomy the Signal Service should enjoy. The Howgate scandal in 1881, in which the disbursing officer of the Signal Service was found guilty of embezzling up to $237,000 (over $5 million today), certainly did not help the Signal Service to gain additional support.[18]

A joint commission, known as the Allison Commission, was established by Congress in 1884 to review the duties of the Signal Service, the Geological Survey, the Coast and Geodetic Survey, and the Hydrographic Office of the Navy to determine how best to coordinate the activities of those agencies for "greater efficiency and economy." The commission did not recommend removal of the weather functions from the Army but did make clear that, if Congress did elect to transfer the functions, the transition should be done slowly and with no immediate release of the military personnel from service.[19] However, in 1890, 20 years after the first weather forecast and warning, Congress transferred the weather service for the United States from the Signal Service to the Department of Agriculture. Congress also provided for staffing of the new Weather Bureau by honorably discharging the entire enlisted force of the Signal Corps so they could be hired as civilian employees of the new bureau.[20]

After 50 years in the Department of Agriculture, the Weather Bureau was moved in 1940 to the Department of Commerce. This was done by President Roosevelt as recognition of the important role that weather plays in support of U.S. business interests. But this was not to be the Weather Bureau's last administrative change. In 1965, in Reorganization

Plan No. 2, President Johnson restructured and consolidated agencies within the Department of Commerce. The position of Chief of the Weather Bureau was abolished, along with the Director and Deputy Director of the Coast and Geodetic Survey, and the functions of the Weather Bureau and the Coast and Geodetic Survey were transferred to the Secretary of Commerce in a new agency, the Environmental Science Services Administration (ESSA).[21] The ESSA was to provide a "single national focus for our efforts to describe, understand, and predict the state of the oceans, the state of the lower and upper atmosphere, and the size and shape of the earth."[22] The ESSA was only in existence for 5 years but, during that time, it established four research institutes. In 1967, the institutes became the ESSA Research Laboratories.[23] These laboratories, such as National Severe Storms Laboratory, continue today. In 1970, the agency was placed under the Commerce Department's National Oceanic and Atmospheric Administration (NOAA) and the name was changed to the National Weather Service (NWS).[24]

By 1988, new technologies available for forecasting and warning systems allowed NOAA to move forward with plans for modernization of the NWS.[25] With the nationwide deployment in 1997 of the land-based Next Generation Doppler Radar (NEXRAD) to provide more precise measurement and better visualization of storms, along with the availability of sky-based GOES systems and the plans for enhanced computer processing capability of the Advanced Weather Interactive Processing System (AWIPS) in each NWS office, NOAA anticipated that the NWS could be made more efficient and cost-effective while providing more rapid warnings and longer-term forecasts. The implementation of NOAA's modernization plan for NWS operations has resulted in closure, consolidations, automation, or relocation of NWS field offices and reduction of the number of NWS employees.[26]

## FORECASTING THE WEATHER

While people are fascinated by the weather and love to record their observations of the weather as it occurs, they also want to predict weather events. *The Old Farmer's Almanac* is an example of an effort to forecast the weather dating back to 1792. *The Old Farmer's Almanac* was not the only almanac in publication in the late 1700s but it developed a very large and loyal following. The publishers' Web site claims that this following was the result of better forecasting[27] based on a secret formula[28] for forecasting the weather that is still in use and still locked away in Dublin, New Hampshire.[29]

The early official U.S. government weather forecasts, known originally as probabilities,[30] were limited in coverage and content. All forecasts were issued from Washington, DC, with local forecasts by the Signal Service offices forbidden until 1881, presumably to ensure accuracy and uniformity in reporting. The first official federal government weather forecast was on November 8, 1870, when the Signal Service issued a storm warning for the Great Lakes region. A sample forecast from 1872, the year in which the Signal Service's area of responsibility was extended from coverage of the Gulf and Atlantic coasts and the Great Lakes to coverage of the entire country, provided "probabilities" for regions but not for specific locales within those regions. The 7 P.M. report from May 4, 1872, which was printed in the *New York Times* on May 5th, included the following probability: "Clear weather will generally prevail on Sunday over the New-England, Middle and Southern States."[31]

The weather service began to move from simple reports of the previous day's weather into extended forecasting. By March 1910, forecasting included a regular weekly forecast for the United States.[32] Decades later, despite continuing research and the use of more powerful computers, forecasts still focus only 1 week into the future. Even with new technology such as Doppler radar and satellite systems that allow us to see storms and weather fronts more clearly, the unpredictable nature of weather prevents reliance on forecasts longer than 5 to 7 days for the general population.[33]

Those weekly forecasts have become much more accurate with new technology, however. Scientists and meteorological researchers continue to explore numerical modeling and new data collection methods using satellites to improve the accuracy of forecasts. Computer models in the early 1970s could predict highs, lows, and fronts better than human forecasters. By the mid-1980s, computer forecasts had reportedly increased the probability that the Weather Service would release a timely winter storm warning that was justifiable from 77 percent in 1985–1986 to 86 percent in 1986–1987. The false alarm rate also reportedly dropped from 34 percent to 17 percent over the same two winters.[34] The National Weather Service and the National Hurricane Center forecasts for Katrina demonstrated a remarkably accurate forecast. The Hurricane Center's warning stated that some levees could be overtopped. The NWS predicted that "most of the area would be uninhabitable for weeks ... perhaps longer."[35] While forecasters are generally not liable for inaccurate weather predictions under current law, as the technology improves and forecasts are more reliable, forecasters may find themselves defending against lawsuits for failure to provide an accurate forecast.

As new types of media have developed, the public availability of forecasts has increased. The telegraph was a prime force behind the creation of a national weather service. Joseph Henry from the Smithsonian and others recognized the value of being able to relay weather reports and forecasts widely and quickly using the telegraph system. Henry's negotiations with the telegraph companies led to priority status for weather reports, even higher status than death notices.[36] With the advent of the wireless telegraph, starting in 1902, weather reports could even be sent to and data received from ships at sea.[37]

But the ability to provide warnings and timely forecasts with the telegraph was limited to those in urban areas. Farmers and others in rural areas of the country did not have access to the daily forecasts that were becoming available. So, in the 1920s, the focus of attention for forecasters was on reaching those people who were out of timely range of telegraph, telephone, mails, newspapers, and signal devices. In evaluating possible avenues for communicating forecasts, the Weather Bureau found radio-phone broadcasting, the predecessor to cell phones, to be the most promising technology at the time; the only difficulty was getting the equipment to the people living in the less populated areas.[38]

The development of television and the prevalence of sets in most every American home by 1962 changed access to forecasts. The TV weather report, the Weather Channel on cable, and weather sites on the Internet have made access immediate for many people. No longer do you need to rely on the thermometer outside your window or the map in the newspaper for information about the coming weather events; you can turn to an electronic source for near-real-time data and forecasts.

Reliability of forecasts has also changed with the advent of new technology. Following World War II (WWII), the Weather Bureau received 25 surplus radars from the U.S. military, marking the ascendancy of the use of radar for weather surveillance. As computer technology began to develop rapidly after WWII and into the 1950s, forecasting moved into the age of mathematical or numerical weather models and forecasting, greatly increasing the accuracies of forecasts.[39] The move into the modern age of forecasting is happening with the addition of satellite systems such as GOES and advanced radar systems such as NEXRAD.

Basic weather reporting for the general public is not the only type of report offered by the federal weather service over the past century and a half. Special categories of forecasts were added over time. In November 1879, special frost indications were ordered to be forecasted and telegraphed from the DC office to New Orleans to aid the sugar interests in

Louisiana. The value of these forecasts to the sugar industry merited the Signal Service a resolution of appreciation from the New Orleans Chamber of Commerce.[40] The first fire weather forecast was issued in 1913.

Arctic region meteorological observation and recording stations were mandated by Congress in 1946 to improve the weather forecasting service within the United States and on the civil international air transport routes.[41] Later that same year, Congress further mandated Weather Bureau functions in relation to air navigation; the Congressional direction provided that the Weather Bureau was to work with people involved in air commerce to provide reports, forecasts, and warnings to facilitate safe air travel and to collect weather reports from aircraft in flight.[42] In keeping with that mission, today, the Federal Aviation Administration (FAA) flight service specialists provide weather briefings to airlines, whose dispatchers then brief the airlines' pilots on weather conditions. Air traffic controllers will also provide current weather information to pilots.

Other specialty forecasts aid with daily living. The State of Utah Department of Transportation hires avalanche forecasters to: monitor the snowpack and weather on a continual basis in order to maintain an understanding of conditions in the avalanche paths that threaten State Roads; determine when conditions exist that suggest snow avalanches may pose a threat to travel on State Roads; determine what measures are appropriate to mitigate the threat posed by snow avalanches to travel on State Roads; and participate in the mitigation of the avalanche hazard to State Roads.[43] Information about solar ultraviolet (UV) radiation is forecast to the public, just as it is in Europe.[44] And, forecasts that focus on specific natural phenonema such as water, heat, drought, and floods are provided by the federal government.

The current menu of services provided by NWS field offices includes: (1) public forecasts, statements, and warnings; (2) aviation forecasts, statements, and warnings; (3) marine forecasts, statements, and warnings; (4) hydrologic forecasts and warnings; (5) fire weather forecasts and warnings; and, (6) agricultural forecasts and advisories.[45] However, the NOAA has privatized or eliminated some of the specialty services. In 1995 and 1996, the NWS announced its plan to meet proposed federal budget reductions and to respond to the Clinton administration's "Reinventing Government" initiatives by transferring some specialized weather services to the private sector. For example, the NWS no longer provides the Agricultural Weather Forecast, the Fruit Frost Forecast, or the Haying Forecasts. The basic forecasts and frost and freeze warnings are still provided but the forecasts that were specifically tailored to agricultural users and broadcast over NOAA Weather Radio have been eliminated.[46]

In 2005, a U.S. senator from Pennsylvania attempted to modify the distribution of NWS data to the public. The bill, if it had passed, would have prohibited the Secretary of Commerce from competing with the private sector in providing any weather services. The Department of Commerce could not provide any product or service that is or could be provided by the private sector. In addition, no one associated with the NOAA, the NWS, or any other department or agency of the United States could release or comment on "weather data, information, guidance, forecast, or warning that might influence or affect the market value" of products, services, and businesses.[47] The bill might have been an extension of the government's elimination of specialty services implemented in 1995 and 1996 but news reports identified the senator's proposal as an effort to protect private weather services such as AccuWeather and WeatherBank.[48] While the bill did not become law, the NOAA did react by proposing its own revision to its information-sharing policy. The final adjusted language in NOAA's policy reads:

> NOAA recognizes cooperation, not competition, with private sector and academic and research entities best serves the public interest and best meets the varied needs of specific individuals, organizations, and economic entities. NOAA will take advantage of existing capabilities and services of commercial and academic sectors to support efficient performance of NOAA's mission and avoid duplication and competition in areas not related to the NOAA mission.[49]

Concerns about the public availability of weather forecasts sometimes offer surprising legal solutions. In 1909, Congress enacted a criminal measure that would penalize a person who knowingly issued or published counterfeit weather forecasts or warnings that were falsely represented as having been issued by the Weather Bureau, the U.S. Signal Service, or other branch of the government. If convicted, the person would be subject to a fine and/or imprisonment for not more than 90 days. While no instances of prosecution under this statute were located, the law has remained on the books through a 1948 and a 1994 review of the federal criminal statutes so, presumably, the law is still considered necessary.[50]

During WWII, the Office of Censorship issued the Censorship Code of Wartime Practices to provide guidelines for voluntary press censorship. The code set out the "specific information which newspapers, magazines and all other media of publication are asked not to publish except when such information is made available for publication by appropriate authority, or is specifically cleared by the Office of Censorship." One category of material specified in the code was "weather forecasts or maps, other than those officially released by the Weather Bureau."[51] In 1942, *The Old Farmer's Almanac* reportedly ran afoul of the Code when a German spy was found with a copy of the *Almanac* in his coat pocket. The government speculated that the Germans were using the book for weather forecasts, which meant that the *Almanac* was indirectly supplying information to the enemy. To avoid problems with the Office of Censorship, the publishers of *The Old Farmer's Almanac* stopped including forecasts and instead printed "weather indications" for the duration of the war.[52] Even the First Lady's newspaper column was subject to the censor; Eleanor Roosevelt received a "very stern letter" for telling readers about weather conditions in her daily column.[53] During the same period, pilots on commercial flights were directed by the Office of Censorship to broadcast weather information in a special code to prevent the enemy from obtaining data about visibility, cloud conditions, winds, and other weather elements critical to aviation safety.[54]

Failure to accurately report weather conditions may also lead to penalties. In 1990, an airman was found guilty at a special court-martial for negligent dereliction of duty for "his *willful* failure to *accurately* record and report weather conditions" [emphasis in original]. The accused had completed Air Weather Service Form 10, showing the same station pressure reading and the same altimeter reading for eight consecutive hours.[55] While no U.S. meteorologist has been charged with a crime for a bad forecast, a meteorologist in Beijing will face criminal penalties for "skipping over or wrongly reporting important weather information or warnings which leads to major losses."[56]

## WARNING SYSTEMS

Forecasting and recording data provide information about the weather but the warning function of the government's weather services can be the difference between life and death for many people. Warning systems over the years have included signal flags, lighthouses, signs, sirens, weather buoys, weather radio, the emergency alert (or emergency broadcast) system, and other communications such as telegraph, telephone, fax, ham radio, and international systems such as the Global Telecommunication System. Agencies have developed warning plans, often working interdependently to reduce duplication. The weather services have categorized weather to create a system of warning labels in an effort to make alerts more effective.

Visible signals have been in use longer than other types of warning systems. Lighthouses, along with the audio warning provided by shooting cannons during fog, and cautionary signal flags were in use for centuries before electronic devices were put in operation. The first lighthouse in the North American colonies was built near Boston in 1716. In 1789, the U.S. government assumed responsibility for administration of lighthouses if the lighthouses were ceded to the federal government by the states.[57] During the Second Congress, the federal government authorized the installation of floating beacons and buoys for the security of navigation at the entrance of the harbor in Charleston, South Carolina, with three additional floating beacons in Chesapeake Bay.[58] Management of lighthouses was first placed under the Treasury Department[59] and then moved to the U.S. Lighthouse Board, the Bureau of Lighthouses, and finally to the U.S. Coast Guard.

Throughout these changes in management, Congress kept close watch on lighthouse operations, as shown by the very specific instructions as to placement of lighthouses and floating beacons in legislative enactments. Congress appropriated funds for specific lighthouse construction and maintenance, monitored effectiveness of operations, and created lighthouse districts. When the management by the Treasury became the focus of a survey of ship's captains and a study of facilities in 1852, the recommendations of the investigatory panel led Congress to create the U.S. Lighthouse Board. At the same time, Congress established 12 lighthouse districts, each with an inspector to monitor operations in the district and an engineer to oversee lighthouse construction and maintenance.[60]

As new technologies such as new types of lenses and electricity were invented, the lighthouses became less labor-intensive to operate. New types of fog signals were developed such as the air fog whistle and reed horn and the mechanically rung fog bells. By 1900, when the transition to electric lights in the lamps of the lighthouses was underway despite the obstacles of lack of direct access to electric lines, the lighthouses were competing with other types of less costly and more effective warning systems.

After WWII, new technology reduced the need for the lighthouse keepers and, eventually, for the lighthouses themselves. Over the years, the need for lighthouse personnel was reduced as automated methods for changing lights and alarm systems that would alert off-site personnel if the lighthouse was not operating were developed. Eventually, navigation technology such as SHORAN (short-range navigation aids) and LORAN (long-range navigation aids) that could be installed on towers and large navigational buoys eliminated the need for lighthouses and lightships.[61]

Cautionary flags were another warning method that could be used at the local weather station level from the beginning of the Signal Service's weather reporting duties. Although local Signal Service stations were not allowed to release their own forecasts, they could put out warning flags once they had gotten the forecast from the Washington, D.C. headquarters. In the 1870s, Signal Service personnel in the field had two official flags they could fly to warn those within viewing distance of high winds and cold waves. The flags were 6 feet by 8 feet so they were visible for quite a distance. The high wind flag was plain red; the cold wave warning flag was white with a 2-foot square black center. After the weather services were transferred to the Department of Agriculture's Weather Bureau, more warning flags were added: a white flag for clear or fair weather; a blue flag for rain or snow; and, a white over blue flag for local rains. These flags were displayed at locations that had telegraphic communications, such as railroad stations.[62]

The warning flags were also used on coastal warning display towers. In 1898, President McKinley had ordered the Weather Bureau to implement a hurricane warning system for ships. The Weather Bureau's response was to build towers intended to be visible from the water and to display warning flags and lights. The flags had the following meanings: one red pennant—small craft warning; two red pennants—gale warning; two red square flags with a black square in the center—hurricane warning. Two red lights and one white light were used at night to warn about gales, storms, and hurricanes.[63]

The coastal warning display (CWD) system was deactivated by the NWS in 1989. The NWS decided to rely on the more flexible and more accessible options of frequently updated telephone recordings and the NOAA Weather Radio. The Service had determined that the displays were only useful to the small portion of mariners who were within sight of the towers, the flags and lights could not convey the specific information about the weather pattern that could be conveyed with electronic communications, and the time required to notify each tower individually was not a good use of staff time. If boaters relied on the flags and ignored the other more current and complete warnings, the CWDs were actually a disservice to the public.[64]

Broad public access to weather information is advancing with the development of technology and communications systems; however, for the information to be of value to the public, the information must be available in a convenient form and people must be aware that it exists. Consider the NOAA network which provides emergency weather warnings over the radio 24 hours a day. The format is a continuous loop of data, which means that a listener can just miss the forecast he needs and have to wait for the information to repeat, not always a convenient method for gaining information. Also, access may be an issue in some areas. In 1999, the NOAA Weather Radio network was available to approximately 80–90 percent of the U.S. population. Eight states—Hawaii, Idaho, Iowa, Montana, Nevada, South Dakota, Vermont, and Wyoming—were below that estimate for coverage, with less than 75 percent of their populations able to receive the radio signal.[65] And, most importantly, it is unclear that most people are even aware that NOAA Weather Radio exists.

However, widespread access to weather information because of the presence of televisions, radios, or computers in most homes and vehicles has made an all-hazard warning network feasible. The goal of an all-hazard warning system is to draw all possible methods of communication into the process to ensure that each individual has some form of warning tool available. Warning messages could go through televisions, landline telephones, cell phones, pagers, computers, and all manner of personal communication devices. With such options available, the person with a hearing disability can select a device that does not require sound to alert of danger, the person who does not speak English will be able to select a method that will translate information to her language, and the person who does not generally have broadcast equipment operating at all hours can select a method that will power itself on and sound an alarm. Without these various options, the nation is not addressing the security needs of all of its citizens.

The NOAA Weather Radio is part of the larger Emergency Alert System (EAS). The EAS replaced the Emergency Broadcast System in 1994, but you can still count on the test of the emergency system during the middle of your favorite television program. The EAS is composed of all types of media, including analog radio broadcast stations, digital audio broadcast stations, analog and digital television broadcast stations, and cable systems. The system allows the President of the United States to have immediate communication with the general public during national emergencies.[66]

U.S. participation in international warning systems dates back at least to the late 1800s and continues today. In 1891, the United States participated in the International Marine Conference. The delegates to the conference returned with the recommendation that the United States provide funding to aid in the development of an international system of storm warnings, including practical day and night warning signals with good visibility, convenience, and usability.[67] The current international structure is under the auspices of the World Meteorological Organization (WMO). The Global Telecommunications System connects all of the national meteorological and hydrological services to ensure that each country has access to information that will allow it to provide effective warnings.

The NWS has established phrases to use to alert the public to possible weather dangers: an advisory, a watch, and a warning. An advisory is used when a weather event "may cause significant inconvenience, and if caution is not exercised, . . . could lead to situations that may threaten life and/or property." A watch is issued "when the risk of a hazardous weather or hydrologic event has increased significantly, but its occurrence, location, and/or timing is still uncertain. [The watch] is intended to provide enough lead time so that those who need to set their plans in motion can do so." And, a warning, the highest level alert of the three, is issued "when a hazardous weather or hydrologic event is occurring, is imminent, or has a very high probability of occurring. A warning is used for conditions posing a threat to life or property."[68]

Some devices used in weather observation have been in existence for a century or two and can be used to describe a weather event. For example, the Beaufort Scale, which was created in 1806 and is still used by sailors, provides an empirical measure of the force of the wind. By identifying the expected intensity of the wind using the Beaufort Scale, the sailor will have a better idea of whether to expect a breeze, a gale, or a hurricane force wind. The Fujita Scale classifies tornadoes, the Saffir-Simpson Scale categorizes hurricanes, and now the Northeast Snowfall Impact Scale (NESIS) characterizes and ranks high-impact Northeast snowstorms that cover large areas with accumulations of 10 inches or more of snow.[69]

However, the warning systems are not always effective. Problems such as delays in releasing warnings or inaccuracy in warnings are matters of competence that need to be addressed but are individual issues. The more troubling aspects of warning systems are the problems that arise from people who do not receive the warnings, or who do not listen, believe, or understand them. To have an effective warning system, the government must avoid false alarms or alarms that are released beyond those directly affected by the disaster; this type of error in issuing a warning reduces the impact and credibility of future warnings. The government must also reach those people at risk who are not in the mainstream communication pathways. To reach these people, the government must be creative in communication tools, content, and phrasing used.[70]

## CONCLUSION

The NWS has evolved from a data collection unit in the Army Signal Service to a high-tech organization focused on collecting and collating weather and environmental data, using the data to predict weather patterns and major events, and issuing warnings of danger to the populace of the United States. As technology has advanced, the NWS has adopted that technology to improve the speed and accuracy of forecasts. While more citizens have access to weather forecasts and warnings than they did a century ago, difficulties still remain in providing an all-hazard warning system to all persons in the United States.

# CHAPTER 2

# "Taming the Weather" through Science and Technology

*The world read about the devastation in Rapid City, South Dakota on the front page of the New York Times on June 11, 1972. "More than 155 persons were reported dead today and 5,000 were homeless in a flash flood that swept through this city and several smaller towns on the eastern edge of the Black Hills last night. More than 500 residents were believed missing, and property damage was estimated at between $80-million and $120-million. There was no word on the fate of 4,000 tourists believed to be camping in the Black Hills that weekend."*[1]

*A few days before the flood, cloud-seeding experiments were being performed in the area. Cloud-seeding was not new to South Dakota; the Interior Department had declared an experiment in 1963 an "unqualified success."*[2] *But this time, it seemed that disaster followed the seeding and the families and representatives of those who died in the flooding sought remedies from the federal government.*[3]

If you were asked to think about technology and weather, you might think of forecasting or of how you keep warm in cold weather. Possibly you would think about your outdoor thermometer or accessing a weather report on your cell phone and how you decide what to wear each day. Perhaps you would think in terms of technology that allows us to change the weather.

Human beings have tried to adjust to the weather, predict the weather, alter the weather, and use the weather for centuries, probably since the beginning of the species. Technological developments and modifications range from the early inventions of thermometer and barometer to our latest satellite-based forecasting systems.

In the United States, law and weather technologies are connected through the incentive programs offered by the government to encourage creation of new devices and technologies and through the governmental regulation of our use of technologies to affect the weather or to use the weather. Patent law, governmental grants, and other research funding programs have offered incentives for individuals and corporations to explore ways to protect us from the elements. Governmental agencies have been directed to develop new methods for forecasting and warning about weather events. To limit losses and to protect Americans from harm, government agencies have set up special programs such as flood control and have used zoning and building codes to prevent or reduce damage from storms. Governmental entities have also established methods to monitor the impact of human activities on weather events and have established regulations for businesses that make their profits from the weather. Federal, state, and local governments all play roles in the development and use of technologies that help us to protect ourselves from the weather, utilize the weather for society's benefits, and prevent harm to the atmosphere from human activities.

## INCENTIVES TO DEVELOP NEW TECHNOLOGY

### Patent Law[4]

Patent law is one of the governmental protections intended to reward inventors and provide incentives for new creations. To simplify a complex topic, think of patent law as the balance between our interest in being able to learn about and use new inventions with the inventor's interest in recovering costs of development and making profits from her work. If the invention is a method or a system or a product that is novel (meaning no one has developed this idea before), functional (it is useful and performs a task), and is not obvious (meaning that the creation or modification is not one that would immediately come to mind), the invention can be patented.

An invention and its production process must be made public as part of the patent approval process but the monopoly right that the inventor receives is an incentive to share the invention. With a patent, the inventor can prevent others from using the invention for a certain period of time, currently 20 years, unless the author grants authorization for its use. By creating this monopoly for the inventor, patent law offers incentives for people to create new tools or methods for forecasting, for protection from the elements, for weather modification, for renewable energy, and for other functions.

Through patent law, the U.S. government provides incentives for companies to research and develop improvements to their products and provides the information necessary to build upon the work of earlier inventors. By offering the monopoly right to the inventor for disclosing her invention, the patent system encourages progress and development of new technologies and new methods. Specifically, an inventor can develop new approaches to old problems by studying the details of prior inventions, improving upon the earlier devices or processes, and then benefit through a monopoly over her modifications and improvements, however slight.

Patents have been issued on all kinds of products that relate to weather. There are inventions for weather forecasting programs and devices, for protective gear for facing weather hazards or ordinary weather events, for methods for modifying the weather, and for use of the weather for energy.[5]

The earliest weather-related inventions were used to record data about the atmosphere around us. The thermometer,[6] the barometer,[7] the weather vane,[8] and the rain gauge[9] were in use long before the United States achieved independence. The thermometer measures the temperature, the barometer gives the atmospheric pressure, the weather vane indicates wind direction, and the rain gauge measures the level of precipitation. These instruments were critical in allowing scientists to study weather patterns and to forge the science of meteorology.

These early devices are in the public domain and are not patentable in their basic forms but people have continued to make improvements to these devices and have received patents for their additions and modifications. Companies look for the modifications, however slight, that will give them a commercial advantage over a competitor.

For example, if you were looking for an anemometer, a device that will allow you to measure wind speed, you would find many options with slightly different features or designs, just as you would expect in any competitive market. Hand-held anemometers are manufactured by several companies. One company, Nielsen-Kellerman, manufactures the Kestrel® Pocket Weather™ Tracker. The device, about the size of a TV remote, can be used to measure wind speed, wind chill, temperature, relative humidity, barometric pressure, and heat stress index, depending upon the model. The company markets this item to sports training camps and the military as a way to ensure safety and prevent heat stroke. One press release discussed the use of the pocket weather meter by the military to increase the effectiveness of explosives-sniffing dogs in Afghanistan and to ensure that the dogs were not subject to extremely hot weather.[10]

Nielsen-Kellerman holds multiple patents on its inventions for modifications that were needed to create a handheld instrument capable of measuring various weather elements. One of the patents refers to another manufacturer's device.[11] The reference illustrates the interdependence of creative thought and the value of publicly documenting and sharing inventions. Without patent law to ensure public disclosure of inventions in exchange for monopoly protection over the invention, companies would not have the information readily available to further develop a product based on an existing design.

Inventors have created devices that will not only measure temperature, air pressure, and precipitation levels, but will also provide personal warnings of impending danger. Some recent inventions offer means of ensuring personal safety or, at least, mitigating possible harm by measuring very local conditions (e.g., within your house) and providing a warning alarm, similar to a smoke detector.

Within the past 10 years, several inventions have been patented that focus on warning individuals of their specific risk from tornados. Three inventions that are closely related illustrate how patent disclosures provide the opportunity for inventors to learn from other inventors to the benefit of the public: the tornado alarm system from 1999, the tornado warning system from 2000, and the personal severe weather warning microchip and pressure sensor from 2004. The tornado alarm system, which was invented by Henry Frank and Michael Frank Johnnie, itself built upon earlier tornado alarms. The patent document for Frank's tornado alarm system includes a description of the prior art, the previous inventions that are related to the invention being patented. Frank's patent description notes that:

Tornadoes are some of the most devastating of all weather phenomena. Part of the significance of their power is that they are relatively unpredictable. Although forecasters can monitor conditions for a wide area, there is no simple way to pinpoint where a tornado may hit. Once on the ground, a tornado is easy to monitor, but by then, it is often too late for victims in its path. If a tornado hits during waking hours, it is much more likely that people's lives may be saved. Warnings can be broadcast over the affected area and people will most likely hear them. It is at night, when people are sleeping that there is the most danger.

To help in these efforts, tornado alarms have been invented. Although these devices may prove useful, they are not as effective as they could be. Many devices monitor a single parameter associated with tornadoes. For example, [here the inventor has listed four patents that all use barometric pressure as the sole monitored element]. It is well known that a sudden drop in barometric pressure occurs just before a tornado strike. Unfortunately, the drop occurs at the time of inception of the tornado. In other words, the tornado is already there. Thus, these devices do not give enough time for an adequate warning. Moreover, by focusing only on the barometric pressure, there are likely to be times when the alarm does not really indicate a tornado. Such false alarms reduce the usefulness of these devices.[12]

The summary describes Frank's invention as eliminating the limitations and problems of these previous inventions by using an electronic monitor to measure not only barometric pressure but also humidity and static charge in the air. To minimize false alarms, the alarm on Frank's device is not activated until the level of static electricity increases to a certain amount and humidity level is at 100 percent.

Because the patent application process requires that the applicant cross-reference prior art and set out the details of her current invention, the process ensures that future inventors can learn from the inventions that have come before and can potentially build upon or modify and improve the earlier invention. For example, in 2004, inventors Ron Moore and Michael Collins developed the concept for a portable severe storm alarm,[13] now marketed as StormTell™. The device samples the air every minute and measures barometric pressure. Since low barometric pressure indicates a storm, if the StormTell™ identifies a drop in barometric pressure, the buzzer will sound.

The government and private weather forecasters also rely on technology to predict weather events. These forecasting methods, programs, and devices are generally patented. For example, in the 1990s, the U.S. government obtained a license to use a patented system for predicting lightning strikes. The system collected weather data and information on lightning strikes in a particular area with a set of data sensors. Then a processor would make the connections between the data about the weather and the occurrences of lightning that had been collected and use those connections to determine the probability of lightning in that area in the future.[14]

21

Inventions for weather protection gear and equipment have a large consumer market. To provide protection from the elements, inventors have created products to keep bodies warm or cool. Furnaces, air conditioning, fans, umbrellas, sun block, raincoats, and house insulation are all examples of ways humans have sought to protect themselves from the weather. Special types of patented devices intended to protect us from cold and damp weather include a disposable foot warmer small enough to attach to your socks and fit inside your shoes without hurting your feet,[15] plastic disposable rainwear shaped like a tent that can be dispensed from a roll,[16] and a microwave-heated stadium seat cushion that will retain an average temperature of about 90°F for up to 8 hours.[17]

Inventors also have patented means to ensure human safety from weather-related dangers. For example, concerns about children and animals dying while trapped or left in hot vehicles have led to the creation of sensors and alarms for infant carriers, car trunks, and vehicle seating areas. While the law has attempted to deal with deaths of infants and small children from heatstroke or hyperthermia by charging the caregiver with crimes ranging from neglect to murder or by instituting fines for leaving children unattended in cars,[18] inventors have taken a preventative approach. In 1997, a high school junior in Kentucky invented an alarm system to detect a person or an animal like a companion dog or cat locked in a parked vehicle in extremely hot or cold temperatures. The system included a motion detector, a temperature detector with a pre-set range of tolerable low and high temperatures, and a method to activate the car's horn if the system found both motion and an extreme temperature outside the acceptable range.[19]

A string of patents for infant and child car seats followed to address the problem of the child who will not be moving around and who might inadvertently be left inside the vehicle. First was the year 2000 patent for a warning system that had a sensor in the car seat to detect when the child was put in the seat; when the ignition was switched off, an alarm would sound reminding the driver to "PLEASE REMOVE CHILD FROM SEAT."[20] Patents issued for car seat alarms include one issued in 2005 for a system with an activation switch that could be affixed to any manufacturer's car seat and hooked into the car's fuse box; the alarm would sound when the ignition was turned off and the weight sensor still indicated that the baby was in the seat.[21] Another system that received a patent in 2006 ties a driver seat sensor to a switch on an infant seat buckle; if the driver leaves the car with the baby still buckled into the car seat, an alarm sounds.[22]

In an effort to reduce the problems of false alarms, that people stop paying attention and miss the situation that the alarm is meant to prevent, an inventor created a motion sensor system that is activated only when the temperature in the car goes above a set high temperature AND all the doors are shut. If the sensor detects no motion within an hour, even the limited motion of a sleeping infant, the system shuts itself off to conserve the car's battery power. But, if an occupant is detected in the car when the inside temperature is dangerously high, an audible alarm is activated.[23]

## Mandated Use of Technology

Federal and state legislative and executive branches can require that manufacturers incorporate certain technologies into their products. Basic safety equipment such as windshield wipers, which are standard on motor vehicles, are required by law; for example, driving in South Dakota without operational windshield wipers on any vehicle other than a tractor or a motorcycle is an offense under the state's statutes.[24]

As inventors create products to address safety issues, governments may draw upon the availability of the new devices and systems to require adoption of new protective or preventative measures. For example, in 2001, the National Highway Traffic Safety Administration adopted a new Federal motor vehicle safety standard that required all passenger cars with trunks be equipped with a release latch in the trunk. The release mechanism had to make it possible for a person to escape from inside the trunk compartment if she became trapped. A motivating factor for the rule that was identified in the rule's published background information was the deaths of 11 children who had locked themselves into trunks of cars in July and August of 1998.[25] At least one patent for an interior trunk release had been issued before these regulations were created; a patent for an emergency latch was issued in 1995.[26]

Legislators can mandate measures that are then implemented by executive agencies. Attempts to enact child safety measures to prevent deaths from hyperthermia were made in Congress in 2003 and 2005. Legislation was introduced but not passed by Congress in the 108th (2003–2004) and 109th (2005–2006) Congresses directing the Secretary of Transportation to issue regulations requiring all light passenger vehicles to be equipped with a system that would remind drivers that passengers are in the rear seat. This driver notification system would be initiated when the vehicle is turned off. The legislation would also have required that the Secretary undertake information programs to address ways that parents can mitigate dangers of hyperthermia in closed vehicles.[27] This legislation and subsequent agency regulation would mandate use of technologies such as those encouraged through the availability of patent protections.

## Governmental Financial Incentives

Federal agencies use their funding to develop or sponsor development of new products and methods for forecasting, modeling disasters, and ensuring safety. Current funding trends show that private industry provides more research and development funds overall than do government sources. However, the government still plays a significant role in encouraging research through funding. While the bulk of research funding (60–70 percent of total research and development funds available in the United States from 1996–2002) comes from industry, the government continues to contribute approximately 30 percent of research funding for a range of issues.[28]

Research funding by executive agencies and by Congress is not a new phenomenon. Federal agency and departmental appropriations have been used throughout U.S. history to fund experimentation and to create devices and systems to aid in weather activities. In fact, the first official weather observations and data recording were undertaken by the Surgeon General of the Army shortly after the War of 1812 and grew into a recording system that included 97 Army camps by 1853, each with equipment purchased from federal appropriations for the Army.[29] And, in 1891, Congress appropriated $9,000 (approximately $200,000 today) for the Secretary of Agriculture to use to fund experiments in rainmaking. This series of experiments in Texas used kites to send half-pound sticks of dynamite into the air, building upon previous attempts to make rain by setting off explosives from balloons.[30]

Activities such as forecasting have moved from the basics of recording data to sophisticated computer modeling and electronic data sensors and collectors because of the availability of research funding. In his testimony before a Senate committee hearing in March 1962, Deputy Attorney General Byron R. White, who less than three weeks later began service as a Justice of the U.S. Supreme Court, noted that, "Government programs in meteorology and weather modification finance a full range of theoretical studies, laboratory research, field experimentation work, and evaluation studies. From these come inventions advancing further research and offering opportunities for industrial enterprise."[31]

Government has been important in the development of technology to alleviate and prevent weather disasters and in the assessment and implementation of methods and policies to address safety and operational concerns in industries such as aviation, shipping, and agriculture—industries that are heavily affected by the weather. For example, government agencies from the federal to county level have experimented with assistance to agriculture through forecasts for planting times, evaluation of drought resistant plants, cloud seeding to produce rain, or weather modification to prevent hail. Following on the heels of the aviation forecasting and other weather research that developed out of the necessities of World War II (WWII),[32] continuing to the start of the space program and the launch of the world's first weather satellite known as Tiros I in 1960, through to today's research in the National Space Weather Program (NSWP) and in NASA's Earth Observation System (EOS),[33] the U.S. government has continued to be a force in research related to weather phenomena.

But, in addition to performing its own research, the U.S. government has also offered direct financial incentives to individuals and companies who work with weather technologies. Federal grants have funded many weather-related projects over the past decades. Following WWII, the Weather Bureau distributed some of its funds through research contracts to universities and other research institutions, beginning the transfer of research activities from the government agencies.[34] By 1980, industry was the dominant source of research and development funding and of research performance. By 2006, government entities were directly performing less than 10 percent of all research and development. For example, although the U.S. government supports the interagency NSWP and establishes the policies intended to hurry progress in space weather services, the research is largely done through federal grants to external researchers. Current funding for NSWP projects includes National Science Foundation (NSF) expenditures for research and development; for 2007, $1.5 million is expected to be available from NSF to support funded research proposals.[35]

Governmental financial support of research and development of new technologies through direct funding or through agency creation of market demand by procurement[36] of new technologies has enabled progress toward faster and more frequent collection of data, faster and more accurate manipulation of that data for forecasts, and improved warning systems.

## ATTEMPTS TO IGNORE THE WEATHER'S EFFECTS

People seem determined to build their homes, construct their businesses, and travel in areas with dangerous weather patterns or with a propensity for major weather disasters such as flooding, mudslides, forest fires, and erosion. Governments have attempted to minimize the impact of this human tendency by implementing zoning regulations and building codes regarding placement of homes and businesses in floodplains or other dangerous areas, by constructing protective devices such as levees, and by providing or regulating insurance offerings to reduce the impact of weather events on those in harm's way or to discourage continued rebuilding in danger areas.

On June 9 and 10, 1972, after several days of scattered showers had saturated the ground, the Black Hills of South Dakota received nearly 15 inches of rain in 6 hours. Rapid Creek, which runs through Rapid City, South Dakota, and other streams in the area overflowed their banks. Rapid Creek rose more than 13 feet in 5 hours during the flood. Two hundred thirty-eight people were killed and 3,057 were injured. Property damage was estimated at more than $160 million (over $746 million in 2005 dollars) with 1,335 homes and 5,000 cars destroyed.

Rapid City responded to the 1972 flood by approving a floodplain management program, limiting development in the identified floodway. Participation in the federal floodplain management program made residents of the city eligible for the Federal Emergency Management Agency's (FEMA) National Flood Insurance Program (NFIP). To determine floodplains, the government surveys and studies the characteristics of the land and identifies areas that are likely to suffer severe flooding. The local community must then implement land-use regulations to ensure safe building practices in the flood hazard areas. The area that flooded in Rapid City was in the 500-year floodplain,[37] which means that the area has a 0.2 percent chance of a disastrous flood every year. To prevent future losses of life and property, the city developed a "greenway" that removed all housing, including motels, from the floodway. The area was converted into parks and recreational areas where no permanent structures are allowed.[38]

Before 1968, disaster relief for flood victims, as well as victims of other types of natural disasters had been provided by the federal government with special appropriations. For example, in 1921, the U.S. House and U.S. Senate both approved a claim for damages submitted by the town of Hatch, New Mexico (population 50). The townspeople lost their adobe buildings and their belongings when natural rain run-off flowing through the nearby arroyos was stopped by a new concrete culvert crossing installed as part of a federal reclamation project. Rather than cut down one side of the canal immediately upon being notified of the flooding, the government employee waited. Because of the delay, the water was in contact with the buildings long enough to cause the adobe on the buildings in the small town to soften, allowing the walls and roofs to collapse.[39] A few decades later, the President was granted authority to provide relief for a major disaster such as a flood, drought, fire, hurricane, earthquake, or storm in any part of the United States where the governor certified the need for aid.[40] And, under the Pacific Northwest Disaster Relief Act of 1968, the President was specifically authorized by Congress to provide emergency assistance to Oregon, Washington, California, Nevada, and Idaho for reconstruction of areas damaged by floods and high water.[41]

The NFIP was created in 1968 to reduce the losses from flooding by requiring local governments to put zoning and other regulations in place for the areas at risk of flooding and to shift the burden for costs of flood losses from the general revenue funds to the people who live in the flood-prone areas.[42] To qualify for participation in the flood insurance program, the local communities were requried to take steps to ensure the safe use of land. If the community did not elect to implement regulations or did not meet the federal conditions, residents could not qualify for the insurance and were also no longer able to receive the relief that was available to victims of other types of disasters. In 1973, an amendment to the NFIP made federal flood insurance coverage mandatory for any property owners or developers who financed the property through a bank or savings and loan institution that was regulated by the federal government.[43]

But, these changes did not fulfill the goals of placing the costs and responsibility on the homeowners and their communities to the extent some Congressional representatives had hoped. Property would be flooded over and over, only to be repaired or rebuilt with federal insurance proceeds each time. To try to address the issue of "severe repetitive loss properties," Congress passed the Bunning-Bereuter-Blumenauer Flood Insurance Reform Act of 2004. This act provides a pilot program to encourage states and individual communities to take mitigating actions such as relocation, demolition, elevation, and floodproofing for property that has had four or more separate claims payments totaling over $20,000 or two claims that totaled more than the value of the property.[44]

Following Hurricane Katrina in August 2005, Congress focused again on the financial drain of the flood insurance program. Discussions about

H.R. 4973, the Flood Insurance Reform and Modernization Act of 2006, have included consideration of the subsidized premiums for property owners who held their property before the establishment of the Flood Insurance Rate Map (FIRM) and the depletion of the NFIP funds, not only for building repairs but for lengthy stays in alternative housing following flooding disasters.[45] Concerns about the solvency of the NFIP strengthened over the months following Hurricane Katrina as billions of dollars of borrowing had to be approved for the NFIP to meet the claims submitted.

For coastal properties, Congress moved a step beyond the limitations placed on the NFIP. The Coastal Barrier Resources Act (CBRA),[46] passed in 1982, clearly stated that the coastal barriers and the adjacent wetlands, marshes, estuaries, inlets, and nearshore waters provide habitats for wildlife, recreational and natural resources, and a natural protective buffer against storms.[47] When first created, the Coastal Barrier Resources System (CBRS) covered the shoreline from Maine to Texas; with an amendment to the act in 1990, the CBRS expanded to include the Virgin Islands, Puerto Rico, and the Great Lakes.

The coastal barriers are the islands and similar natural landforms that consist largely of sand and gravel, highly unstable areas on which to build.[48] By allowing development in these areas, the federal government had caused a "loss of barrier resources, threats to human life, health, and property, and the expenditure of millions of tax dollars each year." Congress acted to remedy the situation by prohibiting federal financial assistance that would encourage development in the coastal barrier areas and prohibiting disaster relief, including participation in the NFIP. While not preventing private owners from developing with their own funds but also not providing any federal resources including flood insurance or participation in other federal programs, Congress sought to reduce development and the impact on the barrier system. In a study by the U.S. Fish and Wildlife Service in 2002 following the reauthorization of the CBRA, the report noted that the prohibition on flood insurance was the "most important deterrent to development" in the coastal barrier system.[49]

The modifications to the NFIP that have been made since 1968, particularly those in 2004 and those proposed in 2006, reflect a concern that the government is enabling people to settle and develop in areas that are subject to repeated natural disasters, similar to the concerns that led to the CBRA. The irony is that, although governments now create regulations and have methods for enforcing zoning and building codes through inspections and denial of relief in case of future disasters, the government actually encouraged people to build and develop in areas that are subject to natural disasters. In 1850, the U.S. Congress enacted the "Swamp Lands Act" to allow the State of Arkansas and any other states that had "swamp and overflowed lands" to build levees and drains to reclaim the wetlands.[50] Unfortunately, these lands were river floodplains. Once the land was developed and the water held back with a levee, the land no longer provided the shield against massive flooding that it had been when the land was open and ready to absorb millions of gallons of water.

Over time, the United States has eliminated 120 million acres of floodplains, leaving only half of the amount that existed 200 years ago.[51] In efforts to control flooding as mandated by Congress in the various Flood Control Acts passed in the early to mid-1900s, the federal government undertook the construction of levees and dams. In the report issued following the 1993 floods in the Midwest, the National Oceanic and Atmospheric Administration (NOAA) noted that the more than 1,500 levees throughout the Mississippi and Missouri River basins had prevented floodplain storage of the huge volume of water. Without a floodplain into which the water could seep, when the water escaped the levees by overflowing or breaching the levee, both the velocity of the water and the depth of the channel created were much greater than they would have been had the natural floodplain been available.[52]

Not only does the government erect protective structures such as dams and levees, sometimes it must also destroy those that are in disrepair to prevent greater damage. In addition to the intense rainfall that caused flash flooding in Rapid City in June 1972, the dam upstream of the city failed, adding to the flood waters inundating the city. The failure of the Canyon Lake Dam influenced the decision of the Army Engineer to prevent a similar collapse of the Ft. Meade Dam in Sturgis, South Dakota, by deliberately demolishing the dam. The Ft. Meade Dam had withstood the storm but had been overtopped and was heavily eroded on the downstream side. Only a thin concrete slab had held back the gallons of water in the reservoir.[53] The town of Sturgis established an evacuation plan and preemptively moved hospital patients and the elderly to higher ground.[54] The Army Corps of Engineers ultimately blew up the Ft. Meade Dam with 3,000 pounds of explosives.[55]

Not only do humans build in unsafe areas but they also make changes to the landscape that can have a disastrous impact on the level of harm that results from a severe weather event and that can have unintentional long-term effects on weather, climate, and the land in the area. While some researchers dispute the level of the impact of these human actions on the world around us, stories of disasters seem to justify the concerns about the impact of humans on our own environmental safety. Removal of flood-plains by erecting levees is but one way that human activity can turn nor-mal weather events into disasters or make those disasters more powerful and life-threatening. We pave over land for roads and parking lots, caus-ing flooding from water run-off when rainwater and melting snow can not soak into the ground. We build homes on cliffs or on coastal land within 500 feet of the shoreline, which subjects the property to damage from erosion as much as from flooding.[56] We build underground spaces such as tunnels that can serve as conduit for storm run-off, which may threaten the structural integrity of the buildings above. We cut down forests, depleting the soil of nutrients and loosening top soil or subjecting the land to erosion and potentially causing desertification from overuse of the land. We carefully prevent forest fires that would have killed underbrush only to lose forests, homes, personal property, and possibly lives when lightning strikes a forest filled with quickly burning and dense kindling.

For example, when Hurricane Katrina struck in 2005, New Orleans faced many of the problems caused by human activity, problems that made the disaster more devastating. New Orleans, on average 6 feet below sea level, consisted largely of paved land, as do many other large urban ar-eas. The paved areas reduce the ability of the land to absorb storm runoff and other sources of water. In addition to the problems of large paved ar-eas, as we know now, New Orleans faced the problem of levees that were in need of repair to ensure structural integrity. When the levees were first built in 1718, much of the natural floodplain remained. Nearly 300 years later, that situation had changed dramatically. Since the Mississippi had not been allowed to flood, the silt and sediment that in the absence of the levees would have replenished the land on either side of the river instead poured into the Gulf of Mexico, affecting the viability of the surrounding wetlands. The efficacy of the wetlands had also been reduced by decades of oil exploration, shipping, and land development.

## ATTEMPTS TO CHANGE THE WEATHER

Despite the statement attributed to Mark Twain that "Everybody talks about the weather, but nobody does anything about it," people have been trying to modify the weather for centuries. While some human actions inadvertently affect the weather, weather modification programs are in-tentional efforts to make rain, suppress hail, and dissipate hurricanes. Weather modification was the subject of lawsuits and was a popular topic for legal commentary in the 1970s but had fallen out of the mainstream discussion in recent years. With the development of space weather programs, international interest in weather modification, and continued creation of new technologies for changing the weather, interest in weather modification is again under discussion.

The federal and state governments have been involved in weather modification experimentation for over 150 years. In the early years, efforts were made to increase the particulate in the clouds using cannon barrages or large fires. The frequency of rainstorms following large battles led experimenters to believe that the smoke from the cannons caused the rain.[57] The experiments were based on the concept that a rain drop forms around a speck of dust or other small particle that serves as the nuclei of the rain drop.[58] A "method of precipitating rain-falls" using balloons carrying torpedoes and cartridges charged with explosives to be detonated by magnetoelectric or mechanical force was patented in 1880; the invention was described as precipitating rainfall "by concussion or vibration of the atmosphere."[59]

Patents have continued to be issued for weather modification methods throughout the years. Methods for cloud seeding have been quite common. These cloud seeding patents include the use of urea instead of the widely used but expensive silver iodide as the seeding agent, the addition of solids such as hexachlorobenzene to the silver iodate cloud seeding compound to create a greater number of the ice freezing nuclei that form rain drops at higher temperatures than is usually possible (note that hexachlorobenzene, which was used as a pesticide on grain seeds until 1965, is known to cause liver disease and can remain in the environment for a long time),[60] and a high-speed cartridge dispenser that automatically ignites and dispenses the explosive weather modification rounds from an aircraft at rates up to one per second.[61]

Other patented inventions have created ways to interfere with an existing weather pattern or event. Temperature inversion, where warm air acts as a lid preventing air from rising and circulating, can trap pollutants at the earth's surface. One inventor developed a method to break apart the stationary cloud cover of a temperature inversion by sending balloons above the cloud cover to radiate heat, causing an updraft that will change the cloud formation.[62] A relatively recent invention, known commercially as Dyn-o-Gel, is intended for cloud seeding but not to cause rain. Dispersal of this superabsorbent polymer into a hurricane is intended to absorb large quantities of water from the cloud to reduce the storm's velocity.[63] Experimental numerical modeling based on the

31

Dyn-o-Gel product was performed by the Hurricane Research Division of NOAA's Atlantic Oceanographic and Meteorological Laboratory. The lab reportedly found that the effect of the polymer on a storm would be small. The Division also noted that it would require 37,000 tons of Dyn-o-Gel about every hour-and-a-half to have an impact on a hurricane.[64]

The U.S. government has itself tried to reduce the power of hurricanes by undertaking cloud seeding. Project Cirrus was an attempt to use dry ice to reduce the precipitation and wind speed of storms while they were still over the ocean. The goal was to lower the temperature inside a storm so that the clouds would produce rain or snow, dissipating the storm before it hit land. In 1947, a hurricane off the coast of Florida was seeded with dry ice but the only obvious effect was a shift in course from northeast to southwest. No further attempts were made under Project Cirrus until 1958 when several canisters of silver iodide crystals were flown into Hurricane Daisy.[65] The next step by the federal government was Project Stormfury, which continued the government's intermittent experimentation with cloud seeding. Hurricane Ginger in 1971 was the last test case for the government's seeding program. Results from the government's experimentations over the years were inconclusive, leading to the end of the project in 1983. The project ended on a controversial note, with accusations from Mexico's foreign minister that the drought that was plaguing northern Mexico had been caused by U.S. experimentation with rainfall.[66]

Private entities have also engaged in weather modification activities. Rainmakers in the late 1800s traveled the country, and sometimes the world, to provide their services to agricultural communities suffering through drought. A collective of rainmaking companies sent their agents into Kansas, Colorado, and Nebraska in April 1893 to get contracts with farmers. The rainmaker received $10 per day plus $1000 "when rain or even moisture descends, for he is not above accepting the dampness of a heavy fog." To ensure that neighboring counties and farms did not reap the benefit of rainmaking being done for other paying companies, the rainmakers went to surrounding counties and formed "rain districts" with them. The members of each rain district paid a smaller amount than the original contracting farmer in consideration for the "overlapping rains."[67]

Weather modification and cloud seeding is making a come-back, particularly in the western states. In a 2005 letter to the U.S. Secretary of the Interior, seven western states (Arizona, California, Colorado, Nevada, New Mexico, Utah, and Wyoming) informed the federal government that cloud seeding was a key component for handling future water shortage. The Wyoming legislature, for example, allocated $8.8 million for its 5-year cloud seeding project.[68] Only a handful of states have retained the weather modification laws that a majority had enacted in the 1970s but that handful includes Kansas, Oklahoma, and Texas,[69] states that had utilized rainmaker services in the early part of the last century and that continue to look at weather modification as a way to counteract drought conditions. The weather modification laws are intended to make clear that use of weather modification activities is a state or municipal function, not one that individuals can undertake without regulation and permits. Exemptions from the license and permit requirements are generally in the areas of research and experimentation; however, Oklahoma has made an exception for "religious ceremonies, rites or acts and American Indian or other cultural ceremonies which do not utilize chemical or mechanical means to alter weather phenomena and which are not performed for profit."[70]

The application of cloud seeding to the water shortage problem is not without controversy. At the request of the NOAA, the National Academies convened a workshop in 2000 to review the status of weather modification. The National Academies' Committee on the Status and Future Directions in U.S. Weather Modification Research and Operations concluded that scientific proof of the effectiveness of cloud seeding is still lacking and recommended a coordinated national research program, just as the National Academies had noted in all of its previous reports on weather modification since 1964. The 2003 report goes on to say that the lack of federal funding for any of the projects applying the technology as well as the drop in federal research on weather modification from $20 million per year in the late 1970s to less than one-half million dollars in 2001 illustrates the lack of commitment to the use of cloud seeding.[71] However, state governments continue to fund weather modification projects in an effort to increase their annual rain or snow fall.

Even if Congress is not currently funding research on weather modification at a very significant level, Congress is interested in studying weather modification. In the 109th Congress, the Senate considered legislation to establish the Weather Modification Operations and Research Board.[72] The act would have established a weather modification subcommittee within the Office of Science and Technology Policy (OSTP) to coordinate a national research program on weather modification and to report to Congress on research goals and priorities for the next 10 years. The legislation would also have created a Weather Modification Research Advisory Board made up of non-governmental weather experts to advise the subcommittee. The bill did not move beyond the Senate; on December 13, 2005, a letter from the Director of the OSTP within the Executive

Office of the President requested that the Senate defer consideration of the bill until the OSTP had had the opportunity to discuss issues of liability, foreign policy, and national security with the appropriate executive departments.[73]

The bill introduced in the 109th Congress is not the first that Congress has considered for creation of an advisory group to evaluate weather control; in 1953, Congress created the Advisory Committee on Weather Control, which studied and evaluated "public and private experiments in weather control for the purpose of determining the extent to which the United States should experiment with, engage in, or regulate activities designed to control weather conditions."[74] In 1958, the NSF was given responsibility for study, research, and evaluation of weather modification.[75] After 10 years, the responsibility was removed from NSF in favor of the Departments of Commerce and Interior, which could look beyond the scientific issues to the other ramifications of weather modification.[76]

In addition to mandating the research and study of weather modification, legislators have regulated the use of weather modification. At the federal level, the regulation is in the form of required reporting of weather modification activities. Any weather modification activity, meaning "any activity performed with the intention of producing artificial changes in the composition, behavior, or dynamics of the atmosphere," must be reported to the Secretary of Commerce.[77] The NOAA within the Department of Commerce has further defined weather modification activities. Actions that must be reported include:

1. seeding or dispersing any substance into clouds or fog;
2. using fires or heat sources to evaporate fog;
3. modifying solar radiation exchange of earth or clouds through release of gases, dusts, liquids, or aerosols into the atmosphere;
4. modifying the characteristics of land or water surfaces by dusting or treating with powders, liquid sprays, dyes, or other materials;
5. releasing electrically charged or radioactive particles into the atmosphere;
6. applying shock waves, sonic energy sources, or other explosive or acoustic sources to the atmosphere;
7. using aircraft propeller downwash, jet wash, or other sources of artificial wind generation; or,
8. using lasers or other sources of electromagnetic radiation.[78]

The regulation does make clear that reporting does not apply to activities that are purely local and that can reasonably be expected not to modify the weather outside of the area of operation.[79]

As the federal regulation notes, impact of weather modification activities may be felt beyond the immediate area. Concerns have been raised about the effect of rainmaking on surrounding areas, either in terms of loss of rainfall for other locations or in terms of flooding caused by heavy rainfall in an unintended area. The long-standing principle that a property owner has rights to the air space above her property or has rights to the water "on" her property has implications for cloud seeding and the potential for cloud seeding to remove moisture from clouds over one person's land to create rainfall for another property owner. There also might be liability for negligence in the way in which the weather modification method is applied.

In Rapid City, South Dakota, in June 1972, heavy rains caused flooding. In the midst of the deluge, the dam above the city failed, causing more water to rush into the city. The flooding left 238 dead and caused millions of dollars worth of property damage. It was known that the South Dakota School of Mines and Technology was conducting experimental cloud seeding under the auspices of the U.S. Department of the Interior's Bureau of Reclamation.

In the suit filed against the United States for damages for the loss of life and property that resulted from the flooding, the representatives of those harmed in the storm claimed that the government had a duty to supervise an inherently dangerous program.[80] Under the theory of liability argued in the case, the claim was made that experimental cloud seeding was inherently dangerous. In this situation, conducting the cloud seeding at a time when the weather was already threatening rain was a failure of the government to fulfill its duty to supervise.

While the ultimate outcome of the case was not a reported decision, it is likely that the government was not held liable for any harm. Before sending the case back to the trial court for more action, the appellate court discussed the immunity enjoyed by the federal government. As a sovereign entity, the government can not be sued unless it agrees to be sued. The focus of the court's analysis was the government's immunity from suit under the Flood Control Act of 1928. Under that act, "no liability of any kind shall attach to or rest upon the United States for any damage from or by floods or flood waters at any place[.]"[81] The situation in Rapid City was clearly flooding so the only question was whether the act really meant flooding in such a broad sense or whether the act was only intended to shield the government from liability for damage that arises from a federal flood control program. It would seem that deliberately causing rain at a time when rain was already likely would not show an effort to "control" a flood.

However, it is unclear if the cloud seeding actually caused the disaster. Causation of the harm is an essential part of the proof in a claim for damages such as this, but causation is very difficult to prove in weather modification cases. Since the weather varies naturally, it is impossible to predict the exact course a weather system would have had without the weather modification. It is not possible to prove that the cloud seeding, rather than simply the uncertainty of nature, caused the flooding. While it could be shown that there were two on-going weather modification projects in Rapid City in the weeks preceding the flood,[82] it could not be proven that without the cloud seeding the flooding would not have happened. In fact, a study undertaken by a board of inquiry appointed by the Governor of South Dakota exonerated everyone involved in the weather modification activities, stating unequivocally that "[t]he June 9 flood was caused by meteorological conditions beyond the control of man" and that "[w]eather modification activities . . . did not contribute materially to the flood."[83]

Other lawsuits that have been raised in the context of weather modification have tended to focus not on harm that has resulted from cloud seeding or other weather modification activity, but on efforts to prevent the weather modification activity from happening. To get an injunction to stop or prevent certain action, the person must prove injury from the activity he is trying to get the court to prohibit. There must be "clear and convincing evidence of an intended or threatened injury, which must be actually threatened and not merely anticipated, and must be practically certain and not merely probable."[84]

Cloud seeding cases have raised issues of ownership of the clouds and the moisture in the clouds that affected the right of the rainmaker to operate in certain places. If the property owner had property rights in the clouds that were located over his property, the owner would be able to prevent others from performing weather modification activities in those clouds. In 1950, New York City was experiencing a serious water shortage. The city had proposed experimenting with artificial rainmaking to address the water shortage. A vacation resort in Ulster County wanted to prevent New York City from using weather modification to replenish its water supply, claiming that the rainmaking experiments would produce inundations, make the streams in the Catskills swell inordinately, and cause considerable damage to riparian owners along such streams.

The resort also claimed that the actual or threatened rainfall on the resort would have a harmful effect on resort business since the success of a resort depends on a moderate and desirable climate. In evaluating the claims, the court noted that the resort owners had "no vested property rights in the clouds or the moisture therein." Ultimately, the court's decision against the resort focused on the balance between the positive public advantage to New York City of having a supply of water for its residents and the possible private injury the resort owner might suffer. In deciding in favor of the city, the court held that the resort owner's concern that rain would hurt his business was unfounded speculation.[85]

But who owns the clouds and the moisture in the clouds? Even though the court decision against the resort owner in New York noted a lack of property rights in the clouds, the case result did not rest on the principle of property right. Some later cases related to cloud seeding discussed the basic concept of property law that landowners have a recognized right to enjoy the use of the land in its natural condition without interference from neighbors.[86] According to both a Pennsylvania court and a Texas court, the natural condition of land includes the land's weather with all forms of natural precipitation. In both states, the cloud seeding at issue was being done to suppress hail as a way to protect crops.

In the Texas cases, ranchers claimed that the cloud seeding destroyed potential rain clouds over their property. Witnesses in the two Texas cases, experienced ranchers familiar with the appearance of clouds that would produce rain, related that they had been observing rain clouds over their property only to see the potential rain cloud or thunderhead destroyed 10 to 20 minutes after the cloud seeding planes began spraying in the sky over their land. The court upheld the injunctions prohibiting cloud seeding over the ranchers' lands. The court was careful to explain that the decision did not give the landowner the right to prevent or control weather modification over other people's land.[87]

A few years later, a Pennsylvania court applied the reasoning from the Texas cases in an action by a landowner who was seeking an injunction to stop the implementation of a hail mitigation program intended to protect orchards. The court clearly stated that every landowner has a property right in the clouds and the water in them and that no one has the right to meet his own needs for water by using artificial means that are detrimental to his neighbors. The court likened the cloud seeding and its potential impact on the landowner's right to the clouds to people who contaminate the air and cause injury or harm to people "down-wind"; both can be held responsible for their actions under the law. However, in this case, the court determined that the landowners had not proven that they were injured by the cloud seeding and had only provided evidence of "possible" harm.[88]

Given the ways in which weather patterns travel, the limitation of an injunction to the specific clouds overhead on your own land does not ensure that the landowner will receive all the natural precipitation she might normally receive. When cloud seeding intended to suppress rain or snow or unintentional overseeding that can have the same suppression effect is done on someone else's land, that activity can affect a landowner without violating the injunction. The rain that might have been on its way toward the landowner's property through the natural progression of storms could be stopped by cloud seeding on neighboring land. The landowner would still be without the benefit of the rain he would have gotten naturally once the clouds entered his air space but, under the existing case law, would have no recourse to prevent the effect.

## CONCLUSION

Human efforts to lessen the impact of the weather on daily activities have taken many forms. Sometimes we try to control the weather and sometimes we try to ignore the impact of the weather. Either approach may invite government intervention. The government can provide patent protection for inventions, can regulate interference with other people's property rights, and can allocate risk and costs to implement policy decisions. In these ways, government can regulate human efforts to tame the weather through science and technology.

# CHAPTER 3

# Governmental Liability for Injury to Individuals

*It was early morning on January 11, 1948, sixteen days after the "Big Snow" in New York City. The young man was walking along Broadway, past Baker Field in upper Manhattan. The sidewalk was still covered with the ice and snow from the record-setting snowstorm of December 26-27, 1947—25.8 inches of snow and 2.67 inches of other precipitation—along with the accumulation of other snowfall and flurries from the past two weeks. The young man fell and his life changed forever.*[1]

Governments—federal, state, and local—have assumed a range of responsibilities for the safety and protection of their citizens. The weather-related functions include: providing forecasting and warning systems; maintaining roads and sidewalks in usable condition; removing citizens from harms' way by directing traffic or offering shelter; and, seeking to mitigate harm to property and persons by instituting programs to protect society from weather disasters and harm. When the government puts systems in place to protect society as a whole, individual citizens may be harmed unintentionally, perhaps as the byproduct of the government program or policy, as an oversight, or as the result of limited governmental resources that make it impossible to address every individual's needs.

Individuals harmed by weather events often look to the law for relief or compensation, but, when the party at fault is the government, liability may be limited. For the person harmed because of failure of a government weather warning system or device or for a bad forecast, the government may claim that the function is discretionary and not subject to claims for liability. For the person who is injured in a traffic accident resulting from faulty road or highway maintenance,[2] government defenses of "natural accumulation" or "open and obvious danger" may prevent recovery. The person harmed when left out in the weather without shelter, such as the homeless or the intoxicated, may claim that the government has a duty to protect her from the elements while the homeless person with mental illness who does not want protection but wants only to be left alone may seek redress for his involuntary commitment by the government.

The federal and state governments, as sovereign entities, can not be sued for negligence or other wrongful acts unless the government consents to the suit. The doctrine of sovereign immunity[3] prevents individuals who have been harmed by government action or inaction from recovering damages from the government for their losses. However, the federal government has consented to suit under certain conditions as spelled out by statute in either the Tucker Act[4] for non-tort claims such as breach of contract or the Federal Tort Claims Act (FTCA)[5] for tort actions against the federal government or its employees. Under their own individual state tort claims acts, state governments have also waived their immunity from lawsuits for wrongful action (or wrongful failure to act, also known as nonfeasance), with certain limitations on the waiver of liability.

The characterization of a particular governmental function as ministerial or discretionary affects the application of immunity from liability. Generally, ministerial acts will be subject to claims for negligence and breach while discretionary acts of state and federal governments are immune from lawsuits. Ministerial functions are those that are mandated with clear directions on the way a policy is to be implemented while discretionary functions are those that leave the implementation and policy decisions to the judgment and discretion of the agency and its employees. The government will not be held responsible for harm resulting from discretionary functions unless there is malice, oppression in office (abuse of the office), or willful misconduct. Another exception actually moves out of tort law into contract law: A government official can incur liability for government action or lack of action (nonfeasance) if there is an express agreement between the government official and the person harmed to take a particular action, such as warning of bad weather.[6]

Local governments such as cities or counties, while not sovereign entities like the federal and state governments, do have immunity for governmental acts. However, local governmental immunity from suit does not apply to proprietary functions performed by the local government. A proprietary function is one that relates "to special corporate benefit or profit as in the operation of utilities to supply water, light, and public markets." But, when the local government is performing functions for the common good such as providing police and fire services, the local government can not be sued for harm resulting from those governmental functions.

If the government has waived immunity, it can still assert other defenses that private defendants use such as assumption of risk, natural accumulation, and open and obvious dangers. Or, the government can declare that it does not owe a duty of care toward a particular individual. Since the "duty to preserve the peace and protect the public welfare is owed to the public at large and not to particular individuals,"[7] the government does not have a duty to warn specific persons of severe weather.

## FAULTY FORECASTS OR FAILURE TO WARN

Governments have developed programs and services that provide forecasts and reports of the weather and warnings of severe weather dangers. The federal government has assumed responsibility for forecasting the weather and providing warnings to various people and entities through the National Weather Service (NWS), the Federal Aviation Administration (FAA), the Coast Guard, and other agencies. State and local governments have procedures in place to alert law enforcement and other agencies of dangers so they can provide warning services to citizens.

Various federal agencies and state and local governments have been sued for inadequate forecasts or inadequate warnings regarding the weather. The suits against governmental entities are generally not successful because the activity is a discretionary function and fits within an exception to the FTCA or the state tort claims act. Courts have almost uniformly held that forecasting and warnings require that the government employee use her own judgment and discretion in preparing the weather prediction based on the available data and deciding if the prediction warrants a weather alert under the general policies and guidelines.

To prove a negligence claim against the government, the plaintiff must prove that a duty of care exists between the government and the specific plaintiff. Generally, the government's duty to society does not equal a special duty to each individual citizen. For example, when a Kansas police chief heard a NWS tornado warning for his city, he ordered the tornado siren to be sounded. When the siren did not work, he ordered police officers to drive through the city sounding their sirens. Soon after one of the police cars passed within the plaintiff's neighborhood, she was injured when the tornado struck her mobile home park. She sued the city and county governments for failing to adequately warn her of the approaching storm. In denying her claim, the court emphasized that the city and county governments had no duty to warn a particular person of a danger, that the duty was to the public at large and not to this woman individually.[8]

To recover damages, the plaintiff must also overcome the defense of governmental immunity from negligence claims. The first, second, and third graders at East Coldenham Elementary School in Orange County, New York, were at lunch in the cafeteria when a hurricane-force gust of wind blew in the wall.[9] Seven children were killed and others injured, four critically.[10] A little before 10:00 that morning, the County had received a NWS tornado watch weather statement through the New York State Police Information Network. The Orange County Emergency Manager relayed the statement to the County Public Information Officer at 11:50 A.M. for distribution to the Emergency Broadcast System radio stations in the County. The statement was not released to the stations before the tornado hit at 12:30 P.M., collapsing the wall at the elementary school.[11]

In a suit against the County for failing to fulfill its duty to warn the school directly, the County was held to be immune from liability under the discretionary function principle. The County's emergency preparedness plan provided that the schools were to be notified "as conditions warrant." This discretionary language did not create a duty to warn the school directly; instead, the plan left the decision to warn to the discretion or judgment of the County officials and made the County immune from liability. The failure to complete the dissemination of the warning to the radio stations was likewise determined to be discretionary.[12]

However, in several aviation cases, the courts have found that FAA personnel such as air traffic controllers have a particular duty to provide accurate and complete weather information to pilots. Two elements lead to a duty of care owed by air traffic controllers to pilots: (1) reliance by pilots on the information that is provided by air traffic controllers and that the pilots cannot get for themselves and (2) obligation of the pilot to follow the air traffic controller's direction. The FTCA provides that the federal government may be liable if it negligently provides services the public has come to rely on. By providing a weather alert service, the government is in effect reducing the pilot and air carrier incentives to provide their own weather support. Reliance on the government for weather information makes it essential that the government properly perform the weather advisory services it has elected to provide.[13]

The government's duty of due care toward airplane pilots can also be based on the procedures manuals from the FAA that set out the functions of air traffic controllers. For example, in 1963, the Federal Aviation Agency Manual, ATP 7110.1A, was at issue in a suit against the government for negligent delivery of flight weather information to the pilot of Cessna in Texas. The manual section that set out the air traffic controllers' "bad weather function" included the duty to provide information about storm areas to pilots when the controller considered it advisable and to either comply with the pilot's request or volunteer to provide vectoring service to help the pilot avoid the storm areas.

The pilot in this case was flying from Texarkana Airport to San Antonio. His rating was for Visual Flight Rules only so he needed visibility to operate the aircraft legally.[14] He had learned of turbulent weather on his route before he left Texarkana but did not receive information about severe thunderstorms. During the flight, the pilot contacted air traffic personnel in Waco for weather information on his planned flight course. When the Waco operator contacted Austin for a weather update, he was told that there was severe weather and that the pilot should land in Waco and wait for the storm to clear. Unfortunately, the information was not relayed fully and with the same urgency to the pilot of the Cessna, who continued on toward Austin. The plane crashed near College Station, killing the pilot and his two passengers.

In reviewing the government's duty toward the pilot, the court looked at the interplay of the government's duty to warn and the pilot's duty to fly his aircraft safely. The government has a superior duty to warn because the air traffic controller is in a better physical position to observe the dangers. Also, once the government offered the weather reporting and alert service, it also had a duty to relay weather information accurately and completely. The pilot needed and asked for localized and current weather information about an area he had not yet reached, an area he could only learn about through the air traffic controller. This pilot instead received an incomplete report on the weather conditions, with both the severity and location of the bad weather misdescribed by Waco's controller, leading the pilot directly into dangerous weather. In a situation such as this, where the government breached its duty to warn this pilot by providing incomplete information, the government could be held liable for the losses suffered.[15]

The government has immunity from liability for false statements and misrepresentations under an exception to the FTCA. Erroneous weather information given as a forecast has been covered by this exception. Several business owners, concerned about flooding along the Kansas River in Missouri in July 1951, sought assurances from the federal government about the course and action of the flood waters. Agencies such as the Weather Bureau River Forecasters Division, the Geological Survey Section, and the Army Corps of Engineers had studied the river, yet the information they disseminated was incorrect. The businesses alleged that they were misinformed about the flood stage of the river and about the likelihood of the water overflowing the dikes and levees along the river, particularly in Kansas City. All of the businesses claimed that, if they had been given correct information, they would have been able to move their merchandise and other property and prevented the losses they suffered. The businesses were not claiming that the government was at fault for the actual flooding, only for the negligent assurances they were given that the river would not overflow and for the negligent dissemination of incorrect information and the failure to give notice and warning so they could take action to preserve their property. The claims were denied under the FTCA misrepresentation exception and the 1928 Flood Control Act's absolute prohibition on liability for the government for any damage resulting from floods.

Sometimes warning devices, such as lighthouse lights, do not work. The U.S. Supreme Court found that a lighthouse warning system was an operational (or ministerial) function of government and not a discretionary function. (Apparently, operation of a lighthouse does not require exercise of judgment; it simply requires keeping the light on.) The negligence claim in the case was made by a towing company whose tug was towing a barge loaded with cargo. The barge ran aground on Chandeleur Island, Louisiana. The cargo was ruined by sea water. The light on the lighthouse that stood on the Island[16] had failed. The Coast Guard personnel responsible for the lighthouse were alleged to have failed to check the battery and sun relay system and to have failed to properly examine the connections for the light that were out in the weather. The Supreme Court held that the federal government was not immune from liability under the FTCA since the function was not discretionary. The Court also stated that "one who undertakes to warn the public of danger and thereby induces reliance must perform his 'good Samaritan' task in a careful manner." Even though the Coast Guard was not required to provide lighthouse services, once it chose to do so, it was obligated to use due care to make sure the light was working and, if it was not, to repair the light or warn the public that it was not working.[17]

Forecasts and warnings do not only cover specific weather events. Water supply implicated by seasonal weather predications is also the subject of federal government calculations and alerts. Under a consent decree that established the rights of the water districts in the Yakima River Valley of South Central Washington State, the U.S. Bureau of Reclamation provides water supply forecasts for farmers and irrigation system users. The forecasts announce the amount of water to be distributed among the districts as calculated by the formulae set out in the consent decree.

In 1977, the Yakima River basin was experiencing a dry spell. In announcing its calculations for available water, the Bureau couched them in the context of the "worst possible scenario." The Bureau later revised its calculations three times, taking the estimate from its original estimate of 7 percent of normal flow of water up to its final estimate of 83 percent of normal flow. The 83 percent of normal flow of water in essence provided the farmers with 100 percent of the amount of water they historically used for irrigation.

However, the low early predictions of available water led the farmers and irrigation system users to plan for drought conditions forecast by the Bureau. They changed crops, sold cattle, and invested in wells and additional irrigation equipment, incurring economic losses. In their suit against the government, the farmers argued that the Bureau was negligent in its calculations and that, under the FTCA, the government waived its immunity from claims for damages. The court, however, held that "regardless of alleged negligence on the part of Bureau officials and undisputed losses,... the conduct of the Bureau falls within the discretionary functions exception" of the FTCA. Since discretionary functions are immune from liability as an exception to the FTCA, the farmers were not able to recover for the changes in farming practices they had made based on the Bureau of Reclamation's inaccurate forecasts of the year's water supply.[18]

Sovereign immunity and the modern equivalent in the exceptions to the FTCA and the individual state acts limit the ability of individuals to recover damages for injury. While governments may assume responsibility for forecasting the weather and providing warning of severe weather events, generally the government is effectively shielded from liability for dissemination of incomplete or incorrect information or for failure to warn individuals of impending danger. The only general exception to the exemption from liability arises in the context of pilots, where a special duty and special relationship is created by the superior knowledge and direct connection the government has with the individual.

## STREETS, HIGHWAYS, AND SIDEWALKS

> The tendency in modern times of the inhabitants of our country to congregate in our great cities has enormously increased the population of our different municipalities, and this, in conjunction with the severe and changeable winter weather in the State of New York, and the consequent slippery and snowy condition of our sidewalks during several months of the each year, has given rise to almost numberless litigations against our cities for injuries caused by falling on ice-coated and snow-covered sidewalks, . . .

Although this statement, with its talk of "numberless litigations," sounds as if it could have been written in the modern day, in fact, the statement is from an 1897 *Yale Law Journal* article.[19] Suits for falls on icy sidewalks that the city has not cleared, for auto accidents on icy bridges, and for failure to provide warnings about dangerous road conditions are no less common against the government than they are against homeowners or businesses. But, the government can claim immunity if the function is discretionary.[20] And, in some states, the statutes provide specific immunity from any claims related to snow-and-ice removal or the effect of weather conditions on use of the streets and highways.[21]

Despite the principles of sovereign immunity and limited liability for government entities, lawsuits have been filed in jurisdictions around the country over the past two centuries for governmental failure either to remove ice and snow or to mitigate dangerous road conditions by sanding and salting. Over time, various legal doctrines have been formulated by the courts concerning government liability toward individuals who are injured on public streets, highways, and sidewalks. The standard today requires that the city, county, or state must have notice of the dangerous conditions and a reasonable amount of time to correct the problem. Notice can be actual notice where someone calls the appropriate agency and alerts it to the location or it can be constructive notice. Constructive notice can be assessed simply by the fact that a significant amount of time has elapsed since a major storm without governmental action to clean up ice and snow.

During major storms, where entire cities or regions are affected and covered with snow or ice, the government can not be bound to a standard of "unreasonable, persistent and extraordinary diligence" to remove ice (or snow) formed from natural causes; the government is simply bound to keep sidewalks reasonably clean and safe.[22] The government is not expected to keep shovels at the ready and clean up the snow as it falls.

The "Big Snow" of December 1947 closed down New York City. Transportation virtually ceased: air traffic was shut down; the Long Island Rail Road suspended operations and other train lines ran more and more slowly; bus lines, both interstate and local, came to a standstill; ferries ran behind schedule; and, the subways experienced delays. Deliveries of coal and oil were reduced because of blocked streets. And, Broadway theaters canceled performances.[23]

The city workers scrambled to remove the snow to allow emergency vehicles to travel but, even with additional workers, the city could not clear all the streets and sidewalks as quickly as people wanted or expected.[24] Dozens of lawsuits were filed on behalf of people who slipped on the ice or fell in the snow. For most of these lawsuits, the courts denied liability. Frequently, liability was denied because, given the number of inches of snow that had fallen, the city had not yet had a reasonable amount of time to clear all of the streets.[25]

But, what of the young man described at the beginning of this chapter, who slipped and fell near Baker Field? When he fell on the snow, he fractured his leg. He was repeatedly hospitalized and had to leave college. During the early part of the recovery period, different methods were tried by his doctors. For 3 months, until mid-April, he wore a cast, sometimes from toe to hip. For part of that time, he wore an iron wedge beneath the cast and used crutches. After 3 months, the fracture had not healed and he was advised to wear a brace. As a result of the fall and failure of the fracture to heal, the young man walked with a limp for a year. Five years after the fall, the break in the bone still had not rejoined.

The young man suffered permanent loss of motion and function and related pain. His doctor stated that the young man had difficulty walking and had a deformity of the left foot. The young man had had to give up athletics and had had to postpone his return to college, eventually graduating in 1950 instead of 1949 as he had planned. Clearly, this young man's life would never be the same as it was before the fall.

Although other courts had denied recovery for persons who had slipped and fallen in the aftermath of the same storm, this court decided that the city was liable for not having removed the snow or required the adjoining property owner to remove the snow sooner than 16 days after the "Big Snow." The young man was awarded the maximum amount possible, $6,000.[26] Although the length of time between the snowfall and the injury is a bit longer than for the other persons injured in falls after the snowstorm, it seems likely that the sad story of this young man swayed the court more than the law of governmental liability or immunity.

The government can be held liable when it creates the hazardous road condition and the danger is not the result of natural accumulations. For example, a mound of snow that is formed by snow removal is not a natural accumulation of snow. In an Illinois case, as the driver edged out into the intersection to make a left turn, he was hit broadside and suffered major internal injuries. A mound of snow taller than a car and extending down the street for some 20 to 30 feet obstructed the driver's view of traffic crossing into an intersection. The snow bank displayed marks that showed that it had been pushed together by a snowplow and had not just drifted into place.

At the driver's trial against Cook County, the county was found liable for the injury to the driver for creating an unnatural hazard. County employees testified that they were instructed not to leave snow at intersections where it could create a hazard by blocking a driver's view. An expert witness stated that he believed that the county snowplow operators had violated normal safety standards by leaving the snow as they did. The County argued that the snow pile was a natural accumulation of snow; the County could not be held liable for injuries resulting from a natural accumulation, both under the state tort claims act and the natural accumulation rule. However, the court did not accept the County's argument and concluded instead that the "mound of snow created by the defendant county's snow-removal efforts is properly considered an unnatural accumulation and that liability can be imposed . . . "[27] Snow melting from a snow bank onto the sidewalk and refreezing or snow drifting into the road during a storm are natural accumulations; pushing snow into a large bank obstructing the view of an intersection is an unnatural accumulation.

Procedures for road and sidewalk maintenance establish the standard of care to be observed by government employees and agencies. Under the Illinois tort claims act, local public entities are required to exercise due care in maintenance of property. The Illinois court noted that, "if a local public entity undertakes snow-removal operations, it must exercise due care in doing so."[28] By piling the snow so high and obstructing the view of the intersection, the snowplow operators did not follow their own departmental policies and procedures regarding snow removal. The employees' failure to follow the established procedures with resulting harm to someone leaves the government liable for lack of reasonable care in performing road maintenance.

Many local and state governments have established procedures for snow removal. For example, the "Snow and Ice Control Operations Manual" for the Columbia, Missouri Public Works Department sets out procedures to be followed by the city's crews. The section of operating guidelines specifies when to plow and when to salt the roads.[29] The manual also describes the use of forecasting and weather tracking systems and identifies characteristics of critical areas to be given priority attention. If the city of Columbia employees were to fail to follow the procedures, the city could be held liable.

The state of Iowa was held liable when its employees failed to comply with established procedures for preventing icy conditions on bridges resulting in a one-car accident. The Iowa highway maintenance manual included a statement of policy and procedure concerning frost on bridge floors. Under the procedures, to prepare for potentially hazardous early morning driving conditions, highway department employees were to obtain Weather Bureau forecasts during the late afternoon. The employees were then to apply the rule[30] set out in the manual to determine if frost was to be expected on bridges so they could make their preparations for the next morning's salting and sanding. Determining when frost would form on bridges was a critical road maintenance task because bridges freeze before the road, creating a hazard for the driver who is driving on a clear, dry road and suddenly hits a bridge with frost on it. The change from dry road to ice is unexpected and results in accidents if preventative steps are not taken.

On the afternoon of November 8, 1971, the state of Iowa's employees did not take the steps required to adequately maintain the bridge; they did not follow the procedures from the operations manual. The next morning, when a driver who was unaware of the icy conditions on the bridge left the dry road surface and passed over onto the bridge, he lost control of his car and overturned. The 20-year-old driver received massive permanent injuries including paralysis in the lower part of his body. The state of Iowa was found liable and was ordered to pay the young man over $500,000.[31]

Just as a municipal government may be subject to negligence for failure to maintain roads, the government may also be subject to claims of negligence for failure to maintain an airport runway. A pilot was awarded $2.3 million for her injuries and her airline was awarded $836,000 for damage to the plane because of negligent maintenance of a runway.

Freezing rain pelted the runways at the Broome County Airport (BCA) in Binghamton, New York. Runway 28 was closed down at 6:50 A.M. because of absence of braking action on the surface of the runway. This left

Runway 16 as the only operational runway. Air traffic control did not want to shut Runway 16 to allow the airport operations specialist to evaluate that runway's braking action or the airport maintenance employee to finish sanding. Although both the operations specialist and the maintenance worker had the authority to suspend activities on the runway so they could complete their duties, they did not do so.

The pilot of an approaching plane, who could have landed at Albany if she had been warned of the icy runway at BCA, touched down in the freezing rain, the airplane rolled off the end of the runway and down a berm. In finding in favor of the pilot, the court commented upon the failure of the airport personnel to follow FAA advisories that recommended friction (or braking) testing every hour during bad weather and the use of urea as a de-icer during freezing rain. The failure of the airport employees to follow airport procedures and the FAA recommendations left the county subject to liability for the resulting harm.[32]

A similar claim of negligent runway maintenance was made against the city of Chicago for the 2005 crash of a Southwest Airlines flight. The airplane skidded off the end of the runway when landing at Midway Airport during a snowstorm, finally coming to rest on an automobile and killing a small boy.[33]

The established standard for government maintenance of highways, streets, and sidewalks limits liability to those cases in which the government had notice of a problem and had a reasonable time to correct the problem. Liability for failing to follow the government's own procedures resulting in harm fits within the established standard. The establishment of procedures indicates that the government not only is aware of a dangerous situation but has also established its own time frame for addressing the problem, one that the government presumably has determined is reasonable.

## SHELTER FROM THE STORM

Government policies are intended to serve the good of society. One element of governmental power is focused on removing people from harm or protecting people from harm in an effort to prevent losses. During storms, evacuation plans may be put into effect. Traffic may be stopped or rerouted around a dangerous situation on a road. Shelters may be established to protect the homeless from the elements. And, zoning or government programs may set standards for uses of property to ensure safety of the community.

But, the governmental action does not always have the intended result. People of limited means may not be able to leave at notice of evacuation, as was the case during Hurricane Katrina. Others may not want to leave because they do not want to leave their property, loved ones, or animals behind. Persons who are delayed or rerouted to avoid a travel danger may be harmed financially or even physically by the government action. The shelters created for the homeless may not be safe or hospitable environments. Homeless persons with mental illness may not want protection from the elements and resist government intrusion into their lives. And, government programs, including zoning, may limit the uses that people can make of their own property, harming their financial or personal interests.

**Impact of Disaster Relief and Protection Programs on Individuals**

Disparate distribution of relief funds or of resources to mitigate hazards is being litigated in the aftermath of Hurricane Katrina. While thousands of victims of the storm have received housing allowances and other assistance, class action lawsuits[34] are being certified and litigated questioning the way in which Federal Emergency Management Agency (FEMA) programs have been administered. One such action, with the lead plaintiff McWaters, claims that many applicants for assistance had not received either approval or denial of benefits from FEMA as of November 28, 2005, 3 months after the storm devastated Louisiana, and instead "have existed in a black-hole denominated as 'pending' for months."[35] The McWaters suit also claims that FEMA has given incorrect information about available benefits and procedures and has changed the rules in ways that have harmed applicants for benefits. For example, the complaint alleges that some evacuees were provided with rental assistance but were not told that the funds could only be used for rent; those who had no other resources and who used the money for essentials such as food and clothing now are being required to pay back the money they received or forego Continued Rental Assistance. The lawsuit claims that the impact is being felt most by those least able to afford delays in receiving benefits. Eva Paterson, the president of the Equal Justice Society, one of the groups providing assistance on the class action suit, is quoted as saying: "this disaster is less about rain and wind than it is about race and class."[36]

Concerns about disparate impact in the distribution of aid and access to rescue measures are not new to the victims of Hurricane Katrina. In April 1974, a tornado tore through Xenia, Ohio, cutting a "quarter-mile swath through the center of town, killing 34 people and causing $500 million in damage." The predominantly African-American areas of town were left without food and supplies for 3 days while the other affected parts of town received outside assistance almost immediately. Some claim that this delay was caused by downed communications systems that left the area of town isolated and the outside world with no knowledge that the tornado had had such widespread effect while others place the blame for the delay on disparate impact based on race. The delay in obtaining state funding to rebuild Central State University, Ohio's only public historically Black university,[37] was also seen as reflective of racial disparity in disaster relief. Rebuilding at the university was reportedly underway in 1978, four years after the tornado destroyed much of the campus, while it appears that, by 1978, homes, schools, office buildings, and a new library had already been built or rebuilt in other parts of the affected area with the use of federal, state, and local aid.[38]

The issues of race, class, gender, and age disparity in availability of resources for evacuation, for relief in the immediate aftermath of a weather disaster, and for funds for rebuilding and post-disaster restoration of lives to a sense of normalcy are critical to ways in which law deals with weather disasters. The ongoing class action litigation and the continuing discussions about the impact of disasters on vulnerable populations will help to frame the discussion and to shape the legal response.

### Harm to an Individual from a Weather-Related Traffic Detour or Delay

Storms can cause traffic jams, accidents that close roads, or road conditions that require detours or delays in travel. When an avalanche blocked one lane of a two-lane road near Alta, Utah, a local marshal stopped all traffic to allow a loader to clear the road of the snow and other debris. Many of the drivers got out of their cars to watch the clean up. Some of the vehicles were stopped under a known avalanche slide area. Just as the loader was picking up its last scoop, a second avalanche covered the area where the vehicles were stopped. Many people were caught in the avalanche, one of whom was seriously injured. That person sued both the town of Alta and the Utah Department of Transportation, alleging that their negligent management of the first avalanche resulted in his injuries. Both the town and the state were immune from liability under Utah's Governmental Immunity Act[39] because the injuries arose out of, were in connection with, or resulted from a natural condition on public lands or from the management of a natural disaster.[40]

## Government Protection from the Elements

Society has assumed a duty to protect people from exposure to inclement weather. Shelters for those without homes and involuntary civil commitment for those who are mentally ill are two ways government has tried to protect its citizens. But, sometimes help is not wanted or the help that is offered is worse to the person than being exposed to the elements.[41]

In most, if not all, states, the government has the authority to involuntarily commit a person with mental illness who is a danger to himself or to others. The threat of substantial harm to self or to others does not have to be an overt act such as a suicide attempt or an assault; your neglect or refusal to take care of yourself can be sufficient. However, the law requires that a judge determine if the person meets the medical standard of mental illness and if the person is at substantial risk of physical harm to himself or others.[42]

A 27-year-old woman who described herself as an anarchist and an activist in the nudist movement was found riding her bicycle in Eugene, Oregon, naked and in near-freezing weather. She was admitted to a psychiatric hospital and diagnosed as bipolar and having a manic episode. She challenged the involuntary civil commitment order that was based on a finding that she "suffers from a mental disorder that renders her a danger to herself or unable to provide for her basic needs." She denied that she was a danger to herself. The court agreed that, although "there certainly is a possibility of harm in riding around nude in the cold," the evidence presented in this case shows nothing more than a mere possibility. The court noted that, "[a]lthough the law does not require that a threat of harm be immediate, it does require that the threat be real and exist in the near future." The woman appeared to be able to take care of herself and in no immediate danger from her bike-riding in cold weather. Without more than a mere apprehension that the woman might suffer harm in the future, the commitment was not justified.[43]

Media coverage of deaths from exposure has led to use of involuntary commitment laws to protect homeless people and the intoxicated from exposure to extremely cold temperatures.[44] New York City was one of the first municipalities to use the mental hygiene laws widely to attempt to prevent deaths from exposure. When Rebecca Smith died in Manhattan of hypothermia in 1982, her refusal to leave her handmade hut of cardboard and newspapers and go to a shelter was reported in the news. New York City officials were trying to obtain a court order to forcibly remove her to a shelter or a hospital when she died.[45]

In the mid-1980s, Mayor Koch of New York City developed plans to remove homeless people from the streets, involuntarily if necessary, in extremely cold weather.[46] As Mayor Koch's plan for protecting the homeless was unveiled in 1985, the Smith case was noted as an illustration that "a person's presence on the street during periods of bitter cold created a presumption that he was unable to protect himself."[47] But, simply refusing offers of shelter and choosing to remain on the streets during extremely cold weather in imminent danger of freezing to death does not mean that a person is mentally ill. Not only are there not enough spaces at shelters for all of the people who are living on the streets, but the street can be the lesser of two evils without the violence, theft, and overcrowding the homeless experience in the shelters.[48]

Koch's plan was implemented through the Police Department. New York City Police Department Operations Order Number 111[49] from November 20, 1985 set out the procedures for the police to follow "to assist homeless in obtaining shelter during cold weather emergencies." On days when the temperature was 32°F or below,[50] the Department of Health would declare a "cold weather emergency." On those "cold weather emergency days," officers on patrol between 4:00 P.M. and 8:00 A.M. were to be alert for homeless persons. The officers were to determine if the homeless person had protection from the elements. If not and the person consented, the officer was to take the person to the nearest emergency shelter. If the person did not consent, the patrol supervisor was to assess the situation and determine if the person was at substantial risk of harm. If the person was at substantial risk of harm, the person would be transported to the nearest hospital for a psychiatric evaluation.

Two years later, Mayor Koch instituted another program to provide care for the homeless who are mentally ill but who refuse shelter and treatment. The Homeless Emergency Liaison Project (Project HELP) put a team comprised of psychiatrists, nurses, and social workers out into the streets to evaluate homeless persons and to have them removed from the street to a hospital if they were mentally ill, in need of hospital as opposed to outpatient care, and at risk of physical harm to themselves in the near future because they were neglecting basic needs such as shelter from the weather. The program also provided for legal representation for those who were admitted to the hospital and for evaluation by two more psychiatrists within 48 hours of admission. These steps were intended to expedite care in compliance with the state's mental hygiene law.[51]

The first person forcibly removed from the street and involuntarily hospitalized under Koch's HELP program was Joyce Brown, also known as Billie Boggs. Prior to being picked up by the HELP program, Brown lived on a sidewalk on the Upper East Side of Manhattan in front of a restaurant's hot air vent. The city psychiatrists who evaluated Brown diagnosed her with chronic schizophrenia and held her against her will at Bellevue Hospital. The psychiatrists retained by her attorneys concluded that Brown was not psychotic. Although she reportedly was abusive toward passers-by, defecated on the street, and was not dressed for the weather when she lived on the street, at the hearing on her petition to be released from involuntary confinement, the judge noted that Brown was rational, logical, and coherent. She testified that she has developed the skills to survive on the streets. She also was aware of the options open to her for shelter and other basic needs.

Based on the judge's own observations of Brown and the conflicting psychiatric testimony, the judge did not find the clear and convincing proof that she was mentally ill that is required as the first hurdle for involuntary commitment. But the judge noted that, even if the city did meet that first requirement, the city still must prove that her mental condition is likely to result in serious harm to her or to others. Looking at the facts as given, the court determined that Brown was not suicidal, she had no history of violent contact with others, and she could provide food and shelter for herself albeit not in the way society approves. The court pointed out that, since the question to be answered was whether Brown was mentally capable of providing for herself and not whether she was financially able to do so, the conclusion had to be in Brown's favor. The court granted her petition for release. The city immediately appealed the release order and requested permission to continue Brown's hospitalization during the appeal process. A month later, with Brown still institutionalized, the appellate court reversed the hearing court's decision, finding that Brown was mentally ill and a danger to herself or others. This ruling by the appellate court supported the action taken by the government. While Brown's appeal of the appellate court decision was pending, the city petitioned the court for permission to administer drugs against Brown's wishes. When the city's request to medicate Brown was denied, the hospital released Brown on its own, noting that institutionalization without medication would not be helpful to her.

Brown went on the talk show circuit and became a folk hero of sorts. Her fight to be released and to be allowed to live as she wanted raised awareness that harm to self may not be as obvious as exposure to the elements. She serves as an example of the impact on an individual of a governmental effort to provide protection from the weather to its citizens.

Sometimes, on the other hand, the citizen needs and has a right to expect governmental protection and concern for her personal safety but instead is subjected to a "state-created danger." A civil rights complaint filed against the city of Philadelphia and police officers alleged that city police officers increased a woman's risk of harm, which ultimately resulted in her severe injury. Shortly after midnight on January 24, 1993, a woman and her husband were stopped by a police officer about a third of a block from their apartment. The couple, who were walking home from a tavern after a night of drinking, were quarreling over the woman's request that he buy a six pack of beer to take home; the husband refused so the woman would not continue on her way home.

When the officer stopped the couple, the woman was unable to stand on her own and was leaning on the police car. The husband claimed that she was visibly intoxicated, smelling of urine, staggering when she walked, and unable to walk without assistance. The officer reported in his deposition that he smelled alcohol on the woman and that both the woman and her husband were intoxicated. The officer told the couple to "'either knock it off or go in the house or [he] was going to take him in for intoxication.'" The husband told the officer that he just wanted to get his wife into their apartment.

While the officer was talking with the couple, three other police officers arrived and watched from across the street. The husband left his wife with the first officer and crossed the street to talk with other officers on the scene. When he told those officers that he needed to get home to let the babysitter leave and asked if he could go home, one of the officers said, "Yeah, sure."

When the husband left to walk home, his wife was leaning on the front of a police car with several officers around. The husband testified that he thought the officers would either take her to a hospital or to the police station because she was drunk. He thought that she should not be left alone in her inebriated state but that the officers would take care of her, so he went home without her.

Instead of taking the woman to a hospital, to jail, or to her home, the officer sent her home alone. She never reached her apartment. A little before 2:00 A.M., the woman was found unconscious at the bottom of an embankment and taken to the hospital. Her exposure to the near-freezing temperatures caused hypothermia and anoxia, a decrease in the amount of oxygen to the brain. As a result, the woman suffered permanent brain damage and was functioning at a very low level—unable to swallow, fed by a tube, virtually blind, unable to walk or sit, unable to speak clearly, and incontinent—but with an average life expectancy.

The civil rights action claimed that the officers were aware that the woman was intoxicated and that she could get hurt as a result. By telling the husband—who was trying to get the woman home—that he could leave, the officers voluntarily assumed responsibility for the woman's safety. When they later abandoned her by sending her on her way alone, the officers created a danger and made the woman more vulnerable to harm than when her husband was with her. Based on these facts, the court determined that, because of this state-created danger, the husband could sustain the claim that the officers violated the woman's Constitutional interest in personal security.[52]

### Impact of Governmental Disaster Prevention and Mitigation Programs on Individuals

To preserve and protect the largest number of people and the greatest amount of property in a given area from harm related to weather events, the government may create programs for prevention or mitigation of harm. These programs may adversely affect some members of the community, either by immediate limitations on the uses they can make of their property or by potential future harm if the mitigation or prevention programs are not successful. For example, if the U.S. Army Corps of Engineers were to design and build a system of levees with the goal of preventing flooding but, over time, the structural integrity of the levees failed and, with the arrival of a major storm, the levees crumbled, flooding and destroying areas that would not have been so seriously damaged in the course of ordinary storm flooding, property owners would want relief for such losses and would turn to the law. When the property owner sued for damages, the government would likely raise the defense of immunity from suit. Not only might the FTCA's discretionary function exception be applicable, the Flood Control Act of 1928 would bar recovery. The Flood Control Act provides for complete immunity from liability for floodwater damage arising in connection with flood control works.[53]

A municipality may limit the types of uses that can be made of lands in high risk areas to reduce the amount of damage that results from a weather disaster. While the more likely scenario is for a local government to permit development in areas that are attractive but hazard-prone, the zoning authority and land use planning agencies have the authority to prevent building and exploitation of land where hurricanes, mudslides, forest fires, and other natural disasters are likely to occur. If you own property very close to the ocean along the Atlantic Coast, you might be limited by regulation as to the type of structure you build or if you can build at all. This regulation helps to ensure public safety and the public budget by preventing a need for rescues, evacuations, and clean up following a major storm. However, if the limitations are so strict that the value of property decreases significantly, the government regulation might constitute a "taking," which would require compensation to the property owner by the government.[54]

The government also has an interest in post-disaster removal of debris to preserve public health and safety and to allow effective rebuilding and recovery of the damaged area. However, the debris that is removed must go somewhere and that removal can affect other people. Following Hurricane Andrew in 1992, a private landowner entered a lease agreement to allow his land to be used temporarily to store building debris resulting from the storm. Some of the materials deposited on the land contained hazardous substances. The landowner claimed that the property was not properly treated to remove the hazardous materials as required by the lease and sued both the federal government and the company that had worked with the government on removing debris. The suit against the federal government was dismissed based on governmental immunity under the Disaster Relief and Emergency Assistance Act,[55] which has language similar to the FTCA. The court held that the removal of debris was a discretionary function so the government was immune from liability.[56] The landowner would still be able to pursue legal action against the private company for violating the lease provisions but, regardless of recovery of damages, the land will need to be cleaned up under federal environmental laws.

## CONCLUSION

The government's assumption of responsibility to provide protection for the public at large sometimes harms individuals. When an individual is harmed by government action or inaction, the government is generally immune from liability, leaving the person harmed with no recovery. Although statutory exceptions to governmental immunity from claims for damages, such as the FTCA, have ameliorated this result and allowed suit for certain types of action, generally, unless the government intentionally violates rights or causes harm or has an established duty to a particular person, the harm to an individual caused by a government program, a government employee's decision, or other government action will leave the injured without compensation.

# CHAPTER 4

# Civil Liabilities for Weather-Related Harm

*On a warm, muggy June morning, a father watched his son play in an amateur rugby match. As the teams waited to play, a thunderstorm passed through the area. Rain began to fall at the start of the match while lightning struck and thunder clapped nearby. The rain increased in intensity, the weather conditions deteriorated, the lightning flashed directly overhead, and yet the match continued.*

*When the match was finally stopped because of the weather, the father and son ran from the field to the row of trees where they had stashed their belongings. Just as they exited from under the trees to get to the safety of their car, each was struck by lightning.*[1]

**W**eather events have the potential to cause personal and financial losses. When loss occurs, people turn to the law for remedy. But not every loss has a legal remedy. The father and son who were struck by lightning were harmed but, in order for the law to provide a remedy, some person or group or institution or organization would have to be responsible for the harm.

## LAW AND CIVIL LIABILITY

A person who is harmed by someone else may file a civil lawsuit to recover damages. While the state may pursue criminal charges for conduct that causes harm, the person who is injured by the same conduct has the right to sue to recover damages for her losses. For example, a person who drives recklessly and causes a death can be charged by the state with a crime AND can be sued for wrongful death by the family of the person killed. Other acts that cause harm are not criminal but still represent the fault of one person in causing harm to another. Civil lawsuits are a way that an injured party can be compensated for his injuries. Americans have embraced this option enthusiastically with over 15 million civil cases filed in U.S. state courts in 2004.[2]

The law will only impose civil liability if the law recognizes a legal obligation, known as a duty, owed to the person harmed by the person who caused the harm. A duty can arise from a relationship such as a contract where all parties to the contract have agreed to perform according to specified contract terms. Because of the agreement, each party has a duty to the other parties to the contract. If one person does not fulfill her obligations under the contract terms, the other parties can sue for the losses suffered from the failure to perform as promised; these losses are called damages.

A duty may also arise under tort law. A tort is a wrongful act, meaning an act that does not conform to the legal standard of proper conduct. A tort can be intentional (the person meant to cause the harm) or negligent (the person who caused the harm was careless or possibly reckless). While the intent to cause the harm is enough to create liability for an act such as deliberately punching someone in the nose, negligence requires a relationship, a duty, between the person who causes the harm and person harmed.

Under negligence doctrine of tort law, the duty recognized by the law is an obligation that each person owes to every other person—to act with reasonable care by taking into account the potential harm that an action might foreseeably cause to other people.[3] We are each required to recognize when our actions could injure someone or damage someone else's property. We must then either modify our behavior to prevent the injury or be held accountable for the harm we cause. If we fail to take reasonable care not to injure another person or her property, we are liable for the harm. This does not mean that we have to take affirmative steps to protect someone from harm that we do not cause, even if we could reasonably be expected to know that the person is in need of help.

For example, if you own a business, you have a duty to take reasonable steps to maintain the property so that your customers are safe from injury but you do not have a duty to provide for the safety of your customers away from your business. You do not even have a duty to warn them of dangers that you are aware of that are off the business premises. A store in Kansas was sued for negligence by customers who were "shooed . . . out of the . . . store and, as it turned out, into the path of a tornado." While driving home, the customers were injured when the tornado "threw a truck into their car." Even though the business's employees knew that a tornado warning was in effect and that a tornado had been sighted in the area when they told the customers in the store to leave, the court ruled that the store had no duty to warn the customers of the danger outside the store.[4] Even if providing the warning and possibly offering shelter in a safe place seems like it was the reasonable and humane thing to do, the law does not impose liability for failure to warn of or provide shelter from a danger that is not on the property.[5]

Weather-related civil cases include "slip-and-fall" injuries; wrongful death actions or claims for injuries in sports or athletics against coaches, schools, and sports facilities; suits over the loss of animals or property by common carriers such as railroads, shipping lines, and airlines; breach of contract actions for failure to complete performance of a contract; and claims against the government for negligence in activities such as highway maintenance or weather forecasting and warnings.

Although people file civil lawsuits in tort and contract law expecting to be able to hold the person who has harmed them by failing to act with reasonable care or failing to fulfill contract obligations liable for the resulting losses, those who file lawsuits can be unsuccessful because of the weather. Once lawsuits are filed for injuries, deaths, and other losses, those being sued may assert defenses such as the natural accumulation rule, assumption of risk and contributory negligence,[6] waiver of liability, *force majeure* (an inability to complete one's part of a contract because of weather) or "act of God" (a natural event beyond control or prevention), sudden emergency, "open and obvious danger," storm in progress, and sovereign or qualified immunity (which protects governmental entities from suit by private parties). The results are quite fact specific so the outcome of a case is not guaranteed. However, under U.S. law as it has been applied in the past, the government and its employees will likely be able to assert an immunity defense successfully and non-governmental defendants will attempt to escape liability by blaming the weather.

These results coincide with the policies that underlie the law of tort. The law is based on the concept that the person who is best able to prevent a harm should have responsibility for the injuries and losses if the harm should occur. In situations where the injured person was best able to take care of himself and to take reasonable care to protect himself from obvious harm or where he voluntarily assumed a risk, the duty of care remains with him. No one else has responsibility for the harm that has befallen him. In other cases, a defendant may have a greater ability to prevent harm by removing a hazard such as ice on a path or by warning of danger on his property. In those situations, the courts will consider the foreseeability of the harm that the defendant caused and the level of control the defendant could have exerted to prevent the harm to determine if the defendant owed a duty of reasonable care to the person injured. Where there is a duty and the failure to fulfill that duty is the proximate cause of injury or loss, the person with the legal duty is liable for the harm. Each of these aspects of civil law comes into play with weather-related incidents.

Sports played outdoors provide a wide lens through which to view the intersection of weather and liability. Are there or should there be different assumptions on liability depending on the sport? In a thunder storm, is there a difference between an adult playing golf and a little league baseball game? What about skiing down icy ski slopes?

## THE RUGBY MATCH: THE RESULT

In the early morning of June 17, 2000, the Saturday of Father's Day weekend, a father went to watch his adult son play rugby in a tournament sanctioned by the national and regional rugby football unions. Possible thunderstorms were forecast for that day, which was already warm and muggy. When they arrived at the field, the father and son put their equipment and belongings under a row of trees.

The tournament was to be an all-day event, with over two dozen rugby teams competing. Sometime before the son's afternoon match started, a thunderstorm moved through the area surrounding the rugby fields. By the time the match started, the National Weather Service (NWS) had issued a thunderstorm warning for the municipal area.

As rain started to fall and lightning appeared in the proximity of the field, the volunteer referee for the son's match began the 20-minute game. The rugby match continued under the referee's direction as the intensity of the rain increased and lightning flashed overhead. Other matches ended while the son's match continued through the rain and lightning. The son continued to play and the father continued to watch until the match was stopped just before its normal conclusion.

The father and son ran to collect their belongings from under the trees. As they emerged from the trees, each was struck by lightning. The son was injured; he had to be hospitalized, but he recovered. The father was killed.

The man's widow, his parents, and his son and his daughter filed a civil lawsuit against the U.S.A. Rugby Football Union, the local rugby union, the local society for rugby football referees, the referee who directed the son's match, and the tournament coordinator. The lawsuit alleged that the named defendants were negligent in that they failed to develop and implement "proper policies and procedures to protect players and spectators at the tournament from lightning strikes."[7]

To prove that the defendants were liable for the wrongful death of the father and the injuries suffered by the son, the plaintiffs first had to prove that the defendants owed a duty to the player and spectator at the match. The plaintiffs claimed that the defendants had a duty to: have and implement policies to protect them from adverse weather conditions and to provide for safe evacuation of players and spectators from the fields in case of lightning; terminate the rugby match and tournament when lightning is present; monitor for dangerous conditions during matches; and, train, supervise, monitor, and control the actions of the match officials.

The court ruled that the families had not established that a duty was owed to the father or the son by any of the defendants. In reviewing the factors to consider in establishing a legal duty, the court focused on the requirement that there be a "special relationship" between the parties. The court assessed the family's argument regarding the "special relationship" between the father and son who were struck by lightning and the organizers, volunteers, and sponsors of the tournament. The special relationship in this case would have to be established by evidence of dependence and ceding of control by the injured persons to the tournament staff and entities.

So, who was responsible for the safety of the father and the son? The court found no evidence that the father and son had relinquished control over their own safety or were dependent on the defendants to protect them from the lightning. The father and son were "free to leave the voluntary, amateur tournament[8] at any time and their ability to do so was not restricted in any meaningful manner by the tournament organizers." Presumably, the two men were able to see the deterioration of the weather around them and could have sought shelter at any time. While seeking shelter would have required the son to desert his teammates on the field and the father to stop watching his son's athletic match, technically, they both had the opportunity and the ability to leave the field to get to shelter. It was their choice to stay. The court compared the rugby match on an open field to a round of golf. Most adults are aware of the risks associated with playing golf in a lightning storm and take the appropriate precautions without being warned or evacuated by those who are in charge of the golf course.[9] As a result, because the plaintiffs could protect themselves from harm, the defendants had no duty to the father-spectator and the son-player.

In a similar situation from 1984, a 19-year-old who was playing for a summer league baseball team was struck and killed by lightning. In the mother's wrongful death suit against the defendant athletic association and the umpires for the death of her son, the mother claimed that the defendants were negligent for not stopping the game when the weather became threatening. The court, however, placed the responsibility on the young player, noting that he "assumed the risks inherent in continued play." He elected to continue to play in weather conditions where lightning was visible. He was not compelled to continue to play by an order of an employer or other person he needed to follow, by an economic necessity to remain on the field, or by some other circumstance. Since there did not appear to be any "inherent compulsion" for him to continue to play in the midst of a thunderstorm, the young man voluntarily assumed the risk of continued exposure to the weather. The liability for the injuries and death remained with the deceased.[10]

## LIABILITY OF COACHES FOR ATHLETE DEATHS

While the lack of duty to adult spectators and players who have the ability and opportunity to seek shelter from a lightning storm is understandable, surely coaches of high school and college athletes and of professional sports teams have a special relationship and a duty that creates liability for death and other harm to their players. But, that is not the case. These coaches, school districts, and professional team owners can generally turn to defenses such as assumption of risk, sovereign or qualified immunity, waivers of liability signed by players and/or parents, volunteer statutes that relieve volunteer coaches of liability, and workers' compensation statutes that preempt separate tort claims to evade liability. However, even without legal liability and recovery of damages, the publicity surrounding weather-related harm and resulting, albeit unsuccessful, lawsuits can, and has, resulted in changes in practice policies, such as requiring frequent rest and water breaks to prevent heatstroke, and in closer adherence to regulations and association rules.[11]

In the summer of 2001, hyperthermia (heatstroke) caused three deaths on football practice fields.[12] Summer practices are the norm for both professional and amateur football teams. High school and college programs are governed by the policies of education departments and the National Collegiate Athletic Association (NCAA) regarding timing and length of the summer training camps and sometimes the specifics of the daily practice program; for example, one set of regulations limits the first two days to no-contact drills and mandates that summer training is not to require full uniforms. But, even with these regulations, players still succumb to the heat.

The most publicized heat-related death in 2001 was probably that of professional football player Korey Stringer of the Minnesota Vikings, who died of complications of heatstroke[13] following a preseason practice. Stringer became ill during the first day of preseason training but continued with the practice and returned for the second day of training. Stringer collapsed during the second day of practice and died the following morning.

The professional athlete will generally be covered by workers' compensation as an employee of the team and will be foreclosed by state laws from pursuing any private action for harm resulting from lack of care. Since Stringer was an employee of the Vikings, his estate would be limited to recovery under Minnesota's workers' compensation statutes unless the family could prove that the defendants had a special duty to Stringer beyond their duties as employees of the Vikings and that they acted with conscious or deliberate intent to injure Stringer.[14]

In the lawsuit filed by his widow, the Vikings and various coaches and trainers were accused of grossly negligent behavior for lack of treatment of Stringer for heat exhaustion and for making no accommodations for his heat illness.[15] The complaint filed against the team owners and the coaches and trainers alleged that:

> Despite the extremely hot and humid conditions and the lack of shade that existed at the Vikings' Mankato practice facility in late July 2001, the individual defendants [who included the head coach, the offensive line coach/assistant head coach, the coordinator of medical services, and the head trainer] did not take necessary steps to acclimatize Korey and did not change, recommend changing, or make the slightest effort to change the planned times or duration of practice for Korey on the first day of training camp . . .
>
> As a result of participating in mandatory practice that day under those conditions, Korey vomited numerous times on the practice field and became severely dehydrated and ill from the heat, forcing him to leave the July 30 afternoon practice early.
>
> At one point, after observing Korey vomiting, [the assistant head coach] derided him, calling him a "big baby."

. . .

On the morning of July 31, 2001, instead of defendants assessing, . . . caring for, or monitoring Korey's heat illness from the previous day, [assistant head coach] actually taunted, mocked, and humiliated him for it in the presence of his teammates, displaying a newspaper photograph depicting Korey while he was doubled-over, vomiting, and gasping for breath.

. . .

Stringer collapsed on the practice field in plain view of Vikings coaches (including [Stringer's coach]), players, trainers, and officials, as well as observers. A short distance away, [Stringer's coach] was casually leaning against a pole, watching the other offensive linemen hit a blocking dummy . . .

As Korey lay there for several minutes writhing and moaning and growing more desperately ill from his developing heatstroke with each passing second, [Stringer's coach] ignored his suffering and continued watching the other offensive linemen . . . Other responsible Vikings personnel, including defendants, simply attended to other matters.

Defendants left Korey Stringer desperately ill, unattended, and without proper care or aid during the crucial period that he lay helpless on the field at the end of the July 31 morning practice. It was left to Korey to get himself up off the ground.

. . .

As critical minutes of inattention passed inside the [first aid] trailer, Korey's heatstroke progressively attacked his brain and other vital organs, causing him to hyperventilate violently and to lapse into unconsciousness.[16]

The result in the Stringer lawsuit makes clear that professional athletes will find it difficult to pursue civil actions against the coaches and trainers who have responsibility for their welfare during practices and training sessions. The trial court dismissed the intentional harm claim against the Vikings very early in the process, saying that "[the Vikings] were operating squarely within the master-servant relationship with the intent to field a winning football team, not with the intent to injure Stringer."[17] Later the appellate court held that the actions of the coaches and trainers were the direct result of their employment by the Vikings and of their duties to provide a safe workplace for the Vikings players. With no special duty owed to Stringer by the defendant coaches and trainers beyond those of their jobs with the team, the defendants were immune from tort claims for their actions. The court dismissed the lawsuit against the defendants, leaving Stringer's widow and estate with the remedies available under the Minnesota workers' compensation law.[18]

While the coaches and trainers of professional athletes will likely be immune from liability under the workers' compensation laws, high school and college students are not employees. Therefore, coaches at the high school and college levels do not have that protection from liability. However, the law generally has held that coaches are not liable for care or lack of care they take with their student athletes under other defense theories, including assumption of risk and inherent danger, express waiver of liability, and qualified immunity.

The defense of assumption of risk and inherent danger holds the athlete liable for injuries from specific dangers that she knows and understands and that are a normal part of the particular sports activity. One example of a sport where risk is assumed by the participants is boxing, where each boxer is voluntarily entering the ring to have another person punch him, understanding that physical injuries that are likely to result are an inherent element of the sport. Another sport with inherent risks is snow skiing. Over half the states have laws that protect ski area operators from liability by identifying the inherent risks of skiing and denying liability for injuries resulting from those risks. The risks include: "changing weather conditions; existing and changing snow conditions; [and] surface or subsurface conditions."[19]

In addition to its specific statutory limitation on liability for injuries suffered by skiers, Vermont has enacted a general inherent risk statute that provides that any person who participates in any sport accepts the inherent dangers in the sport as long as the dangers are obvious and necessary.[20] In 1993, this statute barred an expert skier from recovery for injuries sustained when she collided with a tree after she hit ice on a marked "double black diamond trail."[21] In holding that the ski operator was not liable for the injuries, the court stated that "no reasonable mind could fail to immediately conclude that ice is a necessary and obvious danger of skiing in Vermont."[22]

Most weather-related risks do not tend to be inherent to a sport because weather can usually be countered in some way. A game can be called because of the weather. Athletes can protect themselves from frostbite and other physical effects of exposure to elements by dressing to fit the weather as well as the sporting event.

Football is unusual, however, and may be one of the few sports in which the weather is considered a factor in the game (ask any Green Bay Packers or Chicago Bears fan) *and* an inherent danger and a risk assumed by each player. The countermeasures for bad weather that occur in other sports do not occur in football. Football games are not called off because of any kind of weather; the games are played despite heat or cold, blizzard or rain. And, players must wear their helmets and their shoulder pads, if not their full uniforms, to protect themselves from other serious injuries during practice and play. As a result, a football player likely knows and understands that he is expected to participate in football games in heat and cold in full uniform and that he is expected to begin season practice during the heat of the summer to get acclimated for the early season games. With the application of the assumption of risk defense, coaches are not liable for injuries resulting from those risks.

The coach cannot, however, increase the risks beyond those inherent to the sport and still escape liability. If a coach requires the players to practice in 102°F heat and refuses to let them stop because he cannot be certain if they simply need to be pushed further or if they are really in danger, the coach may be moving out of the realm of inherent dangers and assumed risk. Or, the court may simply conclude that the coach is challenging the players to improve and condition themselves for better performance.[23]

Another type of defense relied upon by schools and coaches is the express waiver of liability, usually a release form provided by the school. Parents and students are asked to sign these forms before students are allowed to participate in school athletic programs. This contract relieves the school and the athletic personnel from liability for injuries and harm that befalls the student athlete during practice and during games. The form serves as another means of ensuring that the student is fully aware of the risks involved in the particular sport.

In a case that involved both assumption of risk and waiver of liability, the Indiana Court of Appeals ruled on October 26, 2006 that the case should be returned to the trial court for a new trial.[24] On the same day that Minnesota Viking Korey Stringer died, a high school junior in Indiana died after collapsing on the second day of preseason football practice. Both days of practice were hot and humid but no heat advisories had been issued by the NWS. The coach had checked weather reports before starting practice each day and had posted notices and talked with players about the dangers of heat-related illnesses. He had incorporated rest periods and water breaks into the practice schedule and also instructed the players to leave practice to get water any time they felt they needed it. After the boy had gotten ill during the morning of the second day of practice, the coaches had made a point of checking on him and confirming that he felt well enough to continue to practice. About 10 to 15 minutes before practice was to end for the day, the boy approached his head coach to tell him that he did not feel well but could not tell the coach exactly what was wrong. When he spoke with the boy, the coach did not see any signs that the boy was ill or suffering from heat-related problems. Shortly after speaking with the coach, the boy collapsed, was taken to the locker room for a cool shower and ice packs, and then was taken by ambulance to the hospital. The boy, who had lost consciousness in the locker room, never awoke and died early the next morning.

In the parents' lawsuit against the school, the court addressed both the parents' claim that the school was negligent for conducting the football practice in the heat and for a longer time than allowed by the Indiana High School Athletic Association (IHSAA) rules[25] and the school's defenses that the boy was contributorily negligent or that he had incurred the risk of playing football. Contributory negligence doctrine considers the plaintiff's conduct to determine if the plaintiff has acted in a way that an ordinary person would in similar circumstances in order to provide for his own protection and safety. In this situation, the court needed to determine if the boy contributed to his own heatstroke and death by not using the opportunities and warnings he was given to take care of himself by taking breaks, drinking sufficient water to stay hydrated, and informing his coaches if he did not feel well. The other defense, incurred risk (or assumption of risk), requires that the plaintiff know and appreciate the specific risks involved in the activity he is undertaking and, that knowing and understanding those specific risks, he voluntarily participates in the activity. In this case, for the incurred risk defense to apply, the boy would have to have had actual knowledge that heatstroke was an inherent danger of playing football.

While the final outcome of this case is still uncertain, the Court of Appeals decision does offer some insights that help to further explain the legal issues related to this case involving heat risk, high school football, and negligence. The court made clear that a waiver of liability signed by the player and the parents is enforceable and that, under Indiana law, the parties could agree that one party does not have a duty of care toward the other party and will not be liable for consequences that would otherwise be considered negligent. However, to absolve the school from liability, the release form had to specifically make reference to release of the school from liability for negligence. The release form signed by the boy and his mother did not contain any specific reference to the negligence of the school or the IHSAA; it simply stated that the mother and son "acknowledged that there was a risk of serious injury and even death from athletic participation and showed that they [not the school] accepted all responsibility for the boy's safety."[26] This language did not meet the requirements for release from liability for negligent conduct by the school. The jury for the new trial could find that the waiver did not serve to release the school or the coach from liability for holding practice in the heat and holding practice for a longer period than the IHSAA rules allowed.

As for the issue of incurred risk, a question still remains as to whether the boy had actual knowledge that heat stroke was a specific risk of playing football. If the boy did not have knowledge of this specific risk, he could not voluntarily assume that risk as required for the incurred risk/assumption of risk defense. In this case, the boy received information about heat stroke and the need to drink fluids in the heat from both his parents and his coaches. His parents also warned him not to overdo the exercise in the heat after the boy told them about other players who had gotten sick on the first day of practice. Whether these warnings from his parents and coaches will qualify as actual knowledge of the risk of heat stroke will need to be determined at the new trial.

Sovereign immunity, the exemption from lawsuit, is a defense that is available to government agencies. Each state has a tort claims act that has granted citizens the right to sue the government despite sovereign immunity. A tort claims act provides that a governmental agency, such as a public school, and those acting on the agency's behalf can be sued for negligent or wrongful conduct to the same extent as private parties can be held liable. However, the right to sue the government under the tort claims acts is itself limited. Under the discretionary conduct exception to a tort claims act, the government can not be held liable for injuries resulting from negligence or wrongful conduct if the activity involved is a discretionary governmental function.[27] A discretionary governmental function is one that requires that the governmental employee use his own judgment or discretion to implement government policy.

So, if a school athletic program is a discretionary governmental function, the schools and the coaches are immune from liability for harm resulting from student participation in athletics. When a Mississippi high school football player sued his school district for his coaches' negligence, the coaches were protected from liability by the immunity that applies to discretionary functions. The player complained that the coaches did not properly monitor his health and condition and did not provide necessary fluids, resulting in his suffering heat stroke in football practice in late August of 1991. The court determined the coaches were immune from liability because their coaching activities required them to make daily coaching decisions about players, using their own judgment and discretion. The only exception to the discretionary governmental function immunity occurs if the conduct of the government employee is outrageous. In this case, the court found no evidence that the two coaches in any way showed disregard for the player's health or performed any other outrageous acts that would have removed them from immunity from liability.[28]

Lawsuits against coaches, trainers, and school districts may have an impact on the availability of sports programs in schools. According to a sports equipment manufacturer reporting on its own decision not to continue the manufacture of football helmets, the fear of costly litigation has caused schools to eliminate football programs because of the impact on funds available for other budget items.[29] With lawsuits filed in response to deaths and injuries resulting from play during storms and practice on hot and humid days, the intersection of the weather and the law might have a similar impact on athletic programs.

## LIABILITY FOR FAULTY FORECASTS

Weather forecasts are predictions, not guarantees. Even as the world watched Internet and televised images of Hurricane Katrina move toward New Orleans, the predicted path and point of landfall was not certain. When tornados are expected, forecasters can tell the general area for a tornado watch but they do not know the exact location at which a tornado will touch down.

Despite advancements in the weather data collection and forecasting technologies and computer processing capability, we are still not able to forecast weather with precision. Until the late 1960s, a wide-spread belief was that weather forecasting inaccuracies were simply a matter of limitations in computing power. Then, two researchers, P.D. Thompson and E.N. Lorenz, concluded that, even with high-resolution models and improvements in computational processes, the basic problem was "the atmosphere was not indefinitely predictable."[30] While we can collect data very effectively, the forecasts based on available data and the use of modeling software and formulae are still educated guesses. The tiniest changes in the initial data used to predict the weather can alter the outcome in ways no computer model can yet accurately predict.[31]

Under the tort law concepts discussed above, liability for negligence should only attach when one person has a duty to another and is better able to prevent harm than the other person. Neither public nor private forecasters are held liable for negligence in their forecasting—public/governmental forecasters because of tort claim immunity and private forecasters both because they have no duty to the people listening to their forecasts and because they have no better ability to prevent harm than those listening due to the uncertainty of forecasting.

A 1999 lawsuit against the Weather Channel was dismissed by the trial court because the broadcaster had no duty to the viewer, imposition of liability would have a detrimental effect on the First Amendment rights of the broadcaster, and weather forecasts are predictions. The plaintiff, representing a passenger on a fishing boat who drowned when he was thrown off the boat in bad weather, filed a wrongful death claim against the Weather Channel. The drowning victim had monitored the Weather Channel from his home in the morning before going out on his friend's boat. The lawsuit alleged that the Weather Channel had failed to issue a small craft warning and had not forecast bad weather on the morning of the drowning. The suit further claimed that the weather data and current weather forecasts showing the change in the weather from the report the victim viewed were available to the broadcaster in real time, presumably from the NWS, but the Weather Channel failed to release the information in time for the victim to be warned of the dangers on the water that day.

In dismissing the case, the court discussed the issues of tort law raised by the suit. The court held that the Weather Channel, as a mass media broadcaster, owed no "general duty to viewers who watch a forecast and take action in reliance on that forecast." To do so, said the court, would make broadcasters liable "to farmers who plant their crops based on a forecast of no rain, construction workers who pour concrete or lay foundation based on the forecast of dry weather, or families who go to the beach for a weekend based on a forecast of sunny weather." The court noted that to impose such a liability on a broadcaster would have a chilling effect on the broadcaster's First Amendment rights, discouraging it from publishing information and reporting events for fear of liability to the general public. Finally, the court stated that the lack of certainty surrounding weather forecasts makes imposition of negligence liability for allegedly incorrect weather forecasts contrary to public policy. The court declined "to create a heretofore nonexistent 'forecaster's duty.'"[32]

A further point might also have been made about the lack of relationship between the viewer and the Weather Channel; the purpose underlying negligence is to place the responsibility for prevention of harm on the party with the best ability to foresee and avoid injury. As noted in another maritime case, "[o]bserving the conditions first-hand provide[s] a reasonable—and *arguably more accurate* [emphasis added]—method of determining whether sea conditions were prohibitive for navigation."[33] The victim in this case had other resources to turn to for information about the prudence of sailing that morning; the Weather Channel was not the only source of information about the weather. He could have listened to the NWS's marine forecasts on weather radio or he could have observed the change in the weather about which, according to the lawsuit, the Weather Channel had information.

Obviously, the most frequently utilized forecasting service is the NWS but non-governmental entities are entering the weather forecasting business. Municipal snow removal departments are making use of private weather forecasting services to get more detailed and more localized information than is available from media and Internet forecasts. In 2006, the reported cost to communities near Boston was about $1,000 per season for snow and ice forecasts.[34]

While the government can rely on sovereign immunity principles to foreclose recovery by persons relying on its forecasts, private forecasters may find that the law may recognize a duty and potential liability in the relationship between a private forecaster and a customer. These private forecasters will generally have a contract to provide specific services for a set fee. A contract establishes a special relationship unlike the situation between a broadcaster like the Weather Channel and a member of the viewing public. That special relationship creates a duty and may make the forecasting company liable for inaccurate forecasts. Some forecasters will include waiver provisions in the contracts to avoid liability.[35] Other private forecasters have taken the opposite tack and are actually offering weather guarantees with "credit or additional services to compensate clients who aren't satisfied with the accuracy of their forecasts."[36]

While forecasts are still currently considered to be less than certain predictions of the likely weather, liability might attach for private forecasts if the science of weather forecasting becomes more definite. As the technology advances and the computing algorithms improve, liability for negligent forecasts might be in the weather reporter's future if a relationship of duty can be established between the forecaster and the public who relies on the forecasts for various ventures.

## LIABILITY FOR FAILURE TO WARN OF DANGEROUS WEATHER

Liability for failure to warn others of dangerous weather or weather-related conditions can arise under either tort or contract law. A claim of negligence under tort law will, of course, require the establishment of a relationship that leads to a duty of care toward the injured person before liability will attach. Duty of care is the legal requirement that a person exercise a reasonable standard of care to protect others from harm. Under contract law, the relationship is established by the agreement between the parties.

A 7-year-old girl left the movies with her parents on an August evening in 1985. While the family had been inside the darkened theater watching the movie, a severe thunderstorm came through Cheyenne.[37] The NWS, civil defense authorities, and local law enforcement officials issued severe thunderstorm, flash flood, and tornado warnings. Local officials told people to stay indoors and off the streets to avoid being injured or killed. While the staff of the theater was aware of the serious storm and the various warnings, the family was not. When the family left the theater along with the other moviegoers, the theater staff did not warn them of the severe weather facing them on their drive home. As the family drove, their vehicle was struck by flood waters. When the family attempted to escape the vehicle, the little girl drowned.

In the lawsuit against the movie theater and the owners of the mall where the theater rents its building, the family claimed that both defendants were negligent and reckless in not warning them about the storm. Tort law provides that businesses owe a duty of care to their business visitor-invitees, their customers. The duty requires that a business protect and warn its customers of dangers that might be anticipated. The court explained that a duty was owed to the family by the theater which had invited them in as customers but that the mall owners did not owe such a duty. The mall's status as landlord for the theater did not place it in close enough relationship to the family to justify imposing a duty to warn.

Normally, the duty of a business to its customers is limited to the business premises but the court in this case determined that the movie theater had a duty to warn of dangers off the premises as well. The court applied eight factors in determining that the theater had a duty to warn its customers, including the facts that the theater personnel were aware of the storm and of the official warnings, that the injury occurred very close to the premises—in fact only minutes away from the theater, that the theater was morally to blame for the tragedy because its personnel knew of the dangers yet did nothing to warn its customers, and that the future costs to the community and the business of imposing a duty to warn would be minor compared to consequences of not holding the theater responsible for warning customers in a similar situation in the future.[38]

The Wyoming case is unusual in its finding of tort liability for failing to warn customers of weather dangers, especially dangers that are off the business premises.[39] More commonly, the courts find that the business or property owner does not owe a duty to warn because storms are not predictable and the customer or other member of the public is better suited to observe and protect himself from the weather than the defendant is suited to provide warnings of impending storms or dangerous weather events.

The limitations on a duty to warn are illustrated by a relatively recent case relating to a storm that suddenly struck a public festival. The attendees of the 1992 "Let the Good Times Roll" Festival on the riverfront in Shreveport, Louisiana, were enjoying a hot, sunny, dry June day full of activities. At about 5:30 P.M., the local station of the NWS issued a weather advisory and severe thunderstorm watch for the areas north and east of Shreveport, primarily in central Arkansas and western Mississippi.

The sunny and warm weather at the festival continued until 8:00 P.M. when it appeared that a typical June rainstorm was beginning. But, at 8:13 P.M., a severe thunderstorm warning was issued for the Shreveport area by the NWS. The local NWS station relayed the warning over the public weather radio band and on the weather wire to all news media subscribers and also phoned the City of Shreveport's police and fire dispatcher to pass on the essence of the weather warning.

Just after 8:30 P.M., the performance of blues singer and entertainer Irma Thomas began under a large tent on the riverfront before a capacity crowd of 1,000 people. Fifteen minutes after the start of the performance, the off-duty police officers who were providing security and public safety services for the festival received a tone on the police radio frequency, alerting them that a severe weather warning had been issued for the Shreveport area. Before the police officers could respond to the alert, the riverfront was hit by one or more microbursts, sudden and violent wind gusts of up to 75 miles per hour with twisting force near the ground. The wind lifted the main tent from its anchors, twisting and breaking poles, breaking the chains securing the tent stakes, and pulling the tent stakes out of the ground, collapsing the tent. People under the tent were injured by the tent poles, chains, and other debris.

The injured filed suit against the City of Shreveport and the cosponsors of the festival, claiming that the defendants were "negligent in failing to warn of the impending severe weather." The court focused its attention on the microbursts that caused the damage and the issue of a duty to warn the attendees of the festival of that extremely rare and unforeseeable weather event. Although the court granted that the sponsors had a general duty to use reasonable care to provide a safe environment for the people attending this public festival, the court concluded that the sponsors did not have a duty "to protect the public from all possible risks of injury, especially when the injury stems from an extraordinary, rare and reasonably unexpected weather occurrence or circumstance." While the NWS warned of winds in excess of 60 mph with the storm, the microbursts were of much greater velocity than the forecast winds and were unusual events in a Shreveport thunderstorm. The sponsors of the event could not be expected to protect attendees from unforeseeable harms or to serve as guarantors of the public's safety.

In a statement regarding responsibility for individual safety in bad weather, the Louisiana court likened the situation in Shreveport to two other cases in which the courts had held that the defendants did not have a duty to warn participants or attendees at outdoor events of the dangers of approaching storms. In a Michigan case, a spectator at a public outdoor basketball tournament was paralyzed when he was struck by a falling tree limb in a thunderstorm with 40 mph winds.[40] The Michigan court noted that no jurisdiction has imposed a duty to warn of an approaching thunderstorm, reasoning that, since a reasonably prudent person would notice a thunderstorm approaching, each person is responsible for protecting himself from the weather. The second case, from Tennessee, held that, while a golf course has a general duty of reasonable care to its patrons, it does not have a specific duty to warn golfers of the obvious danger of lightning when a severe thunderstorm is approaching.[41] As the Louisiana court stated, "[m]ost animals, especially we who are in the higher order, do not have to be told or warned about the vagaries of the weather, that wind and clouds may produce a rainstorm; that a rainstorm and wind and rain may suddenly escalate to become more severe and dangerous to lives and property." Clearly, the courts are saying that we should know enough to come in out of the rain and should not expect the law to hold others responsible from protecting us from the elements.

Unlike tort law where a duty must be established before liability will be considered by the courts, in contract law, the duty between the parties is expressed in the agreement itself. The parties to the contract have agreed to fulfill the terms of the contract, whatever those terms may be. The terms of a contract can impose limits on liability or can create liabilities that would not be available under tort law.

Contracts between private weather companies and their customers provide the terms for the forecasting and notification (or warning/alert) services that are to be provided. One such contract between the City of Wilmington, Delaware, and a private weather company provided that the forecasting company would: (1) furnish forecasts of severe winds, specified as winds over 35 mph, and (2) would notify the customer of thunderstorms, hail, and lightning that entered the area. During a storm "with violent wind, lightning and heavy rain," the customer, the City of Wilmington, suffered over $90,000 worth of wind damage to cranes used in the Port of Wilmington. The City sued the forecasting company for failure to fulfill its contractual obligations to warn of the heavy winds.

At trial, testimony by a certified meteorologist and the forecasting company's own employee indicated that the weather met the contractual terms and that the City should have been warned of the impending severe weather. The forecasting company argued that it was the City's negligence in securing the cranes that was the cause of the damage; however, the court determined, if the City had been warned of the severe weather approaching, it would have had time to secure the cranes and avoid the damage. Therefore, the court ruled that the company had not met its contractual obligation to provide warnings to its customer and was liable for the damages to the cranes.[42]

## PREMISES LIABILITY

Today, if you are a property or business owner, you very likely have insurance to protect you in case someone slips and falls on your property. You want this protection because of the possibility of being held financially liable for harm that occurs to people who come onto your land; this type of liability is known as premises liability.

As a property owner or occupier, you owe a duty of reasonable care to persons who come onto your land, whether they are invited or not. The duty does not obligate you to guarantee the safety of everyone who enters your property, but you do need to maintain the premises as safe for the person who "exercises such minimum care as the circumstances reasonably indicate."[43] If you do not keep the area to this level of safety from physical injury and someone is injured, you may be held responsible for damages.

While the law of some states tends to focus on the reasonableness of the preventative actions taken by the property owner and the foreseeability of injury to the person who comes on the property, historically, case law has made a distinction among the duties you owed to those you invited onto your property, those who had license to enter your property but that you did not specifically invite, and those who trespassed on your property. People whom you invited onto your property could expect you to protect them from dangerous conditions you knew about and those you would discover upon inspection of your property. Those people with a right to enter your property but whom you did not specifically invite, such as meter readers and telephone company repair people, could expect you to remove known dangers. And, even though you did not have a duty to keep your property safe just in case a trespasser happened to enter, you could still be held liable to a trespasser if you did not act reasonably once you knew the trespasser was on your property.[44]

The person who enters your property also has responsibility under the law to avoid hazards. He cannot simply walk around, tripping and falling, without paying attention to obstructions and dangers around him. A person of average intelligence is presumed to be aware of his surroundings and to be capable of taking basic steps to protect himself from obvious dangers. In other words, he is expected to "watch where he is going."

Dangerous situations can develop from weather events or from equipment and other materials you leave lying around that can turn into a danger when combined with a weather event. The most common weather-related lawsuits against property owners are for injuries resulting from falls on ice or snow patches or on floors that have become slippery from rain or melted snow. But, property owners have also been sued for harm caused when wind has blown glass out onto the street[45] or has blown ladders down onto passers-by or has caught a door, knocking the person holding the door to the ground. In most of these situations, the defendant property owner has not been held liable.

For the business owner, slip and fall cases can be a high cost of doing business. These property owners/occupiers owe a duty to the customers who enter their premises, whether the building or the parking lot. They are not required to *guarantee* the safety of those who come onto the property but they are required to take reasonable precautions against harm such as keeping floors clear of water from rain or melted snow and parking lots clear of ice and snow. Liability for failure to take reasonable precautions is especially likely if the property owner/occupier had notice, either actual notice or constructive notice, of a potential slip and fall hazard.[46]

So, for weather-related dangers, such as wet floors or icy sidewalks or parking lots, the property owner can be held liable for the harm that results from someone slipping and falling because she has a duty to the invited customers to try to prevent the harmful situation. Although the owner does have a continuing duty to take reasonable steps to keep the property safe for others (clearing and salting the sidewalks once in the early morning and ignoring the sidewalks the rest of the day will not meet that continuing duty), the owner does not have to have someone on continuous watch to clean up wet spots or to shovel snow. There must be notice of the hazard, either actual notice such as being told by a customer or constructive notice such as from a general awareness that it has been snowing for the past hour or so.

As a general principle, the law is going to allocate risk of injury to the party best able to control the situation and to prevent the harm. In an area that gets lots of snow, everyone can anticipate that snow and ice will be on the ground during the winter months. You should expect to be held responsible for taking proper precautions to protect yourself and not be able to hold a property owner liable for injuries that you could have avoided.

In suits for premises liability, the defendant property owner will raise defenses to place the risk of injury back on the person who was injured, thus eliminating any duty to the injured person. Without a duty of reasonable care established, the negligence action will be dismissed. One defense that may be raised in a premises liability case is the doctrine of "open and obvious danger." Under this doctrine, the property owner is still subject to liability if he should be able to foresee that the person coming onto the property will encounter the dangerous condition even if the danger is open and obvious. This situation might arise when the decision to risk contact with the danger is reasonable, such as when the only access route to enter or exit is over an icy sidewalk.[47]

But, as the person entering the property, you should not forget your common sense and sense of self-protection. If you see an icy patch on a sidewalk, you should step around it if you can. If you see a puddle on the floor of a store or a restaurant, you should avoid it by going down a different aisle or stepping over it. The "open and obvious danger" doctrine recognizes that we have the ability to prevent harm to ourselves by avoiding dangers. If you fail to sidestep a danger that is in plain view, the "open and obvious danger" doctrine may hold you responsible for your harm and will relieve the property owner of liability.

In two cases involving the "open and obvious danger" defense, one plaintiff was denied recovery while the other was awarded $40,000 in damages by the judge. The plaintiff who was denied recovery had slipped on the ice outside of her apartment. The other plaintiff was visiting someone else's apartment and was injured when an unattended ladder blew over in the wind.

These two cases illustrate the purpose and the application of the open and obvious danger doctrine. The first case of non-recovery appears to stand for the principle that, if you are familiar with the terrain and the possible dangers and do not take steps to avoid them, you will be held responsible for your own injury. In affirming the denial of recovery for the woman who slipped on the ice and broke her ankle, the Michigan court noted that "[i]t is reasonable to expect that an average person with ordinary intelligence would have anticipated that the sidewalk would be slippery between 5:00 A.M. and 5:15 A.M. the morning after a night of freezing rain fell. An average person of ordinary intelligence would have discovered the slippery walk upon casual inspection."

The court also rejected the woman's argument that, even if the icy sidewalk was an open and obvious danger, there were special aspects to the situation that made it unreasonably dangerous. The court stated that there were not special aspects to the situation and that the woman could have walked around the sidewalk avoiding the ice altogether or could have been more careful stepping down onto the sidewalk. In its decision, the court seemed to focus on several key facts: the woman had lived in Michigan her entire life so she had experience with Michigan weather and icy sidewalks and the night before she had watched a broadcast that called for freezing rain during the night, both of which gave the woman knowledge of the potential danger. Even though the weather was dry when she left her apartment that morning and even though she stated that she did not notice the ice until she slipped and fell, the court ruled that the defendant property owner was not liable because the icy sidewalk was an open and obvious danger to the woman.[48]

The Ohio trial court reached the opposite conclusion on open and obvious danger in the case of a 76-year-old woman who was injured when a ladder that was left leaning unattended against the apartment building she was visiting fell over in the wind. Although this case was more about negligence than open and obvious danger defense, the defendant did argue that it had no duty to warn of an open and obvious danger. It would seem that a ladder leaning against a building would be an obvious danger, which point is reinforced by the woman's efforts to walk around the ladder upon entering and exiting the building. In fact, she reported that, when she came out of the building, she walked away from the ladder at a distance of 15 feet. If the wind had not blown the ladder into her, she would not have been injured. The negligence action and recovery was based upon the ladder being left unattended by the building superintendent on a windy day when the ladder had a warning label[49] about use of the ladder during windy conditions.[50] Under the circumstances, it does not appear that the woman could have done more to try to avoid the injury. The unavailability of the open and obvious danger defense in this case placed the duty on the property owner to make reasonable efforts to prevent the foreseeable harm.

Another potential defense for the property owner/occupier is the natural accumulation rule. The traditional statement of the rule based on a nineteenth-century Massachusetts case is that the property owner will not be liable for the harm to someone on his property if the injury is the result of a natural accumulation of ice or snow. In some cases, the natural accumulation defense has included accumulation of water or wind. This rule is needed for the climates where frequent snowstorms, thaws, and refreezes make conditions dangerous but virtually impossible to correct by the property owner as they are happening without stationing someone to do nothing but shovel or salt all day long. The potential plaintiffs are much better equipped to prevent injuries to themselves from ice or snow because they can see the immediate conditions and the ways they can avoid dangers.

To hold a property owner liable for harm when this defense is asserted: (1) the accumulation would have to be "unnatural"; (2) the property owner would have to have been negligent in his attempts to remove the hazard; or, (3) the property owner would have to have assumed a contractual duty to remove the natural accumulation and did not do so. An unnatural accumulation is an accumulation of snow or ice or other naturally occurring condition that was made worse by the actions of the property owner (i.e., the property owner either created or aggravated the condition through some action such as allowing water to run onto a sidewalk where it would freeze), that the property owner knew about or should have known about, and where the condition was made substantially more dangerous than it would have been in its natural state.[51] The apartment complex has placed its dumpster in a specially designated area that included a slope away from the parking spots and toward a drainage gutter. The lids opened to the rear of the dumpster so trash could be tossed in from the sides or the front. As a separate precaution, the manager plowed and applied Ice Melt to the areas around the dumpster unless there was a car parked next to the dumpster.

On a clear day in November, a tenant loaded her car with garbage and drove to the dumpster. There had not been snow for a week and the weather was dry so the manager had not plowed or put on Ice Melt for several days. Most of the parking lot area was clear since the ice and snow that had accumulated during the last storm was melting where the sun hit directly. But the sun could not get to one area between the dumpster and a parked car; the shadows from the two objects effectively kept the ice from melting from that spot. As a result, a patch of black ice had formed between the car and the dumpster, just where the woman stepped to toss her garbage into the container. As she lifted the bag, she slipped on the ice and fractured her leg. The case required a determination on whether the location of the dumpster in relation to the parking lot was a condition that caused ice to accumulate unnaturally, in a way that was different than the accumulation of ice that would occur naturally. While the court did not reach an answer, sending the case back to the trial court for further consideration, it seems that a natural accumulation defense might be effective. However, the open and obvious defense might also come into play in this situation since the woman would have seen the ice and would have been able to avoid the situation by either not tossing her trash at that time or using one of the other sides to deposit her garbage in the dumpster.[52]

Wind may seem an unusual type of weather condition to discuss under the natural accumulation doctrine but, in Wyoming, the court noted that "[a]nyone who has ever lived anywhere in Wyoming knows that the wind and its potential severity are just as natural as the accumulation of ice and snow." The sign on the restaurant door said, "Please Hold Door Tight Due to Wind." When a 75-year-old woman opened the front door of the restaurant, she held onto the door as the sign instructed. Just as she opened the door, the wind caught the door. She fell to the ground and broke her hip. The court concluded that, in Wyoming, the possibility of a sudden gust of wind is an obvious danger foreseeable to anyone. Since the woman was in a superior position to the property owner to be able to protect herself from hazards caused by the wind at the moment those hazards occurred, arguably she and not the property owner would be responsible for her injury.[53]

Assumption of risk, the defense that was discussed above in relation to athletes who assume the inherent risks of the sports they play, has also been raised as a defense in slip and fall cases. Assumption of risk requires that the defendant prove that the plaintiff (the injured party) "has knowledge of the facts constituting the dangerous condition, knew [sic] that the condition was dangerous; appreciated the nature and extent of the danger; and, voluntarily exposed herself to the danger."[54] For this to apply in a slip and fall injury case, one court required actual knowledge of the wet floor; however, the court equated actual knowledge with common knowledge that floors get wet during rainstorms and that the store owner had no better knowledge than the injured woman about the wet floor.[55]

Two cases with similar facts, one from Kentucky and one from New Jersey, reach opposite conclusions on liability for slip and fall incidents that happened at the entrance to two different banks. In the Kentucky case, the customer entered the bank on a rainy morning and slipped and fell on the marble floor inside the bank's entrance. At trial, the customer testified that she has stepped carefully because she had seen the water on the floor. The court determined that this testimony illustrated that she had the requisite knowledge of the facts of the situation and understanding of the dangers, resulting in no liability for the bank because the customer had assumed the risk of entering the bank despite dangerous conditions.[56]

A few years earlier in New Jersey, the state court had reached the opposite conclusion on similar facts. A customer entering the bank slipped on a tile floor that was wet from snow and slush that had been tracked in by customer traffic. Here the customer was farther into the bank, beyond the entryway. There was no evidence presented that the injured customer had noticed that the floor was wet so there could be no argument made that she had assumed the risk of walking on a wet tile floor.[57]

The concept of comparative negligence has changed recovery for injuries somewhat. In the past, under contributory negligence doctrine, if the person who fell was at all at fault, if he had contributed to the harm, he would not be able to recover anything for damages such as medical bills or lost wages or pain and suffering. With comparative negligence, rather than having a choice between zero recovery for the plaintiff if there was any liability on the plaintiff's part and full recovery if there was no liability, a jury can now allocate the amount of negligence between the parties, offering the plaintiff some, if not full, recovery of damages.[58]

## MOTOR VEHICLE ACCIDENTS AND THE WEATHER

In tort law, the law related to wrongful acts that are civil as opposed to criminal, the defendant (the person being sued) can avoid liability by asserting a legal excuse. One such legal excuse that the defendant can claim is the sudden emergency defense. The sudden emergency defense provides that, if you find yourself in imminent peril without time to consider all the circumstances and without time to determine the best means for avoiding the impending danger, you are not negligent if you fail to choose the approach to avoid the danger that in hindsight might have been the better method. As long as you acted in a reasonably prudent manner and the emergency was not the result of your own negligence, the sudden emergency will excuse the act or conduct.

If you live in an area with frequent snowstorms and icy road conditions, you can probably relate to the situation in which you lose control of your car. You step on the brakes and, instead of feeling your tires grip the road, you find yourself sliding sideways or headlong into another car. The time between hitting the brakes and losing control of the car on an icy road can be as little as few seconds. The courts might view this as a sudden emergency, where you do not have the luxury of reviewing all of your available courses of action and choosing the best one.

Courts have found that unexpected weather conditions can trigger the sudden emergency defense. The defense was upheld in an Iowa case in which two nurses, who were carpooling to their jobs in Minnesota, went into a ditch, rolled three times, and landed on the passenger side. The driver, who was traveling through blowing snow at about 50 miles per hour at 9:30 P.M., asserted the sudden emergency defense. The passenger claimed that the sudden emergency defense should not be available because the driver created the situation herself by tapping the brakes and causing the van to slide into the ditch. The driver's defense was successful because, as reported by the drivers of the two other vehicles that had gone into the ditch in that area of County Road A23 that evening, that area of the road had an unexpected patch of black ice. The court said that the jury could reasonably find that the black ice created a sudden emergency for the driver and excuse the driver from liability for injuries.[59]

Similarly, courts have found that winds that were unusual and unsuspected[60] and a car that turns unexpectedly in front of the driver ahead of you, resulting in your car skidding on wet pavement into the vehicle ahead of you,[61] are appropriate cases for the sudden emergency defense. Normally, in a rear-end collision the doctrine of assured clear distance comes into play. This doctrine, frequently set out in a statute, places liability on the driver who had a view in front of him and should have ensured that he had adequate space to stop to avoid the collision. But, the courts also look at other factors, such as a stopped car suddenly pulling in front of the car you are following or a child running into the street, forcing the car in front of you to slam on its brakes. Where there is another factor other than failure to leave enough stopping room, the courts have often allowed the driver to escape liability under the sudden emergency defense.

But, consider the poor medical student in Michigan who was on the way to a racquet club in January 1997 and was driving behind the doctor supervising his internship rotation. It was snowy and icy but traffic was moving along at about 35–45 miles per hour. Suddenly, the driver in front of the supervising doctor lost control of his car. The doctor put on the brakes and was able to avoid hitting the car in front of him. The medical student saw the doctor's car slow down and applied his brakes but, instead of stopping, he slid on the icy road. Even though he tried to pull off onto the shoulder, he hit the doctor's car from behind.

While the jury found that the medical student was excused because he used ordinary care, the appellate court (which reviews trial court decisions for error) held that the ice and snow did not excuse the collision. The medical student was liable for the damage to the doctor's car because state law required that he drive for the road conditions and not drive at a speed greater than would allow him to stop with an "assured, clear distance ahead." The court noted that it is "well-established that ice and snow cannot qualify as a sudden emergency exception to the assured clear distance statute, which requires that a driver take such road conditions into account."[62] In this case, the implication was that the medical student should have anticipated that a car, even one a car away, going in the same direction as his car could lose control on the ice and snow, requiring him to stop suddenly. The fact that you have a clear view of what is happening ahead of you and should drive for the road and weather conditions and the traffic ahead of you outweighs the sudden emergency defense unless there is a completely unexpected occurrence.

## WEATHER AS EXCUSE IN CONTRACTS

The weather is often used as an excuse for human behavior and actions. In common occurrences such as motor vehicle accidents, the driver somehow seems less culpable if the weather is to blame. Employees who are unable to get to work because of the weather hope that their employers will accept the weather as an excuse and not dock their pay or fire them for missing work or being late.

In civil actions, such as contract law or tort claims, weather can be a complete defense or a mitigating factor. In a contract action, *force majeure* (also known as *vis major*) or impossibility of performance protects the parties from being held responsible if they cannot perform part of the contract. The defense requires that there be some event that was outside their control and that could not be avoided by exercise of due care.

This doctrine is sometimes equated with the "act of God" doctrine but "act of God" is a subset of *force majeure*. An "act of God" is a force of nature that could not have been foreseen and the effects of which could not be avoided by reasonable means while *force majeure* encompasses acts of God and other events such as labor strikes and suppliers going out of business.

An "act of God" (also known as an "act of providence") has historically prevented recovery for injuries and damages resulting from weather events. "Act of God" is defined as "a misadventure or casualty . . . [which occurs] by the direct, immediate, and exclusive operation of the forces of nature, uncontrolled and uninfluenced by the power of man, and without human intervention, and is of such a character that it could not have been prevented or escaped from by any amount of foresight or prudence, or by any reasonable degree of care or diligence, or by the aid of any appliances which the situation of the party might reasonably require him to use."[63]

Frequently, cases with a *force majeure* or "act of God" defense involve carriers who were unable to deliver goods due to weather conditions. In 1982, Mohammed Jahanger was trying to get documents related to his claim against the Iranian government to The Hague. His lawyer contracted with Purolator Sky Courier to ship the legal documents from New Jersey. The case ultimately turned upon the contract terms and the inapplicability of the verbal statements of the courier's employees as to time for delivery. However, the court noted that, given the inevitable hazards of air navigation (which in this case were affected by fog and diversion of the plane to another airport), delivery of the package in 5 days instead of Purolator's normal 4-day timetable for delivery to The Netherlands could not be considered a delay.[64]

In *Southern Pacific v. Loden*, the carrier also tried to use the "act of God" defense. The court did not accept this defense in the breach of contract action against Southern Pacific, focusing on the railroad's failure to prove that the heavy rainfall that washed away part of its tracks and caused bridges to fall in the water was unforeseeable or of greater intensity than the usual rainfall in the area. The railroad had been hired to transport perishable produce, cucumbers, from Nogales, Arizona, to Los Angeles. The delivery was delayed for 3 days in Yuma, Arizona, because two railroad bridges on the way from Yuma to LA had fallen into the water. The railroad tried to blame the week-long rain in California for the delay but the court found that the damage to the tracks and delay in transportation was foreseeable and there had been no evidence of precautions taken by the railroad to avoid the possible consequences of the rain.[65]

In another carrier case, the "act of God" defense was countered by the negligence of the railroad. A railroad passenger bought a ticket for travel between Cincinnati and New York City. His train was an express that was to arrive two hours before the regular train. While the passenger arrived safely in New York City, his trunk did not. Instead of being transferred in Pittsburgh to the faster train, the baggage stayed on the regular train. Under normal circumstances, this 2-hour delay would not have been problematic. However, on May 31, 1889, the regular train was caught by the rising waters at Johnstown, Pennsylvania. The baggage car with the passenger's trunk aboard was swept away in the Johnstown flood. While the court agreed that the flood itself was an "act of God" that could remove the railroad's liability for the loss of the trunk, the negligence in the transfer of the trunk from the regular train to the express train and the resulting 2-hour schedule delay which put the trunk in the midst of the huge flood subjected the railroad to liability for the passenger's loss.[66]

Increased prices will generally not serve as a *force majeure* excuse for a party to a contract. Clearly, large storms can have an impact on companies that provide supplies. Say that a logging company and construction companies enter into contracts for lumber at a low price. A lightning strike starts a forest fire that destroys the timber that was to be used to fulfill the logging outfit's contracts. The logging company can rely on *force majeure* to nullify the contracts with the construction companies since their supplies are gone. However, even though the construction companies are left without the low-cost source for the lumber, they still need to fulfill their contracts. The construction companies can not rely on *force majeure* to excuse their non-performance; they will need to locate other sources for their supplies, even if the price is higher and they will lose money.

This situation will likely be visited in reviewing cases from the Gulf Coast in the wake of Hurricanes Katrina and Rita. Contractors and suppliers in Louisiana whose construction contracts and projects were disrupted by the storms will be excused from performance. But, those suppliers elsewhere in the country who are faced with rising prices for supplies because of increased demand will have to suffer the "economic disruptions and price fluctuations caused by *force majeure* events."[67]

## CONCLUSION

In a civil case, the weather can be the factor that prevents liability. People may seek relief under the law for wrongful death, damage to property, or losses caused by delays in delivery only to find that the law recognizes the weather as the cause. Concepts such as "act of God" provide defenses against claims where no person was to blame; it was simply the weather.

# CHAPTER 5

# Crime and Weather

*In May 1970, the Las Vegas Police Department received a report of a suspicious automobile in the parking lot of an apartment complex. The officer who responded noticed the very strong odor of a decomposing human body coming from the car. After forcing open a window to unlock the car door, the officer found the dead body of a one-year-old girl under two suitcases on the right front floorboard. The Clark County Medical Examiner determined that the little girl had died from heat prostration and dehydration at least six days before she was found.*

*At the grand jury hearing, the father of the little girl and other witnesses testified that the mother had threatened her daughter's life. A resident of the apartment complex where the car was found testified that she had offered to let the mother leave the car in the lot a week before the little girl was found because the mother said the car's brakes were not working right.*

*The little girl's mother was indicted for murder.[1]*

**W**e blame the weather for all sorts of human acts or omissions. Accidents, lost time from work, episodes of mental illness, and deaths have all been attributed to the weather. The fields of psychology, medicine, forensics, and criminal justice have all contributed to the literature and the consideration of weather as a cause of behavior or as an excuse or defense for human action or inaction that resulted in harm to self or others.

The courts have been filled with cases in which weather conditions were a factor. Weather has played a role in murder cases, moving an assault to a murder charge because of the effect of the weather on the victim. In some cases, the weather has been the instrument of the crime while, in others, the weather has been the impetus for the crime. And, criminals have used the weather as a defense, not always successfully.

## CRIMES FOLLOWING A WEATHER DISASTER

While looting is the crime that comes to mind when considering weather disasters, there are other crimes that regularly occur in the aftermath of a weather disaster. People may be arrested for crimes ranging from violating curfew to fraud.

### Looting

The images in the news in the aftermath of Hurricane Katrina of people wading through waist-deep water clutching milk and bread[2] provide a counterpoint to the description of a Wal-Mart being emptied of everything but country-western CDs before the storm had passed.[3] Business owners returned to find their stores had been looted and vandalized; one store owner was quoted as saying, "What they didn't steal they trashed. They got what they could and ruined what they left."[4]

To be found guilty under the statutory definition of looting, the accused person would have to enter a home or business without authorization and get or exert control over or injure or remove the owner's property during a period when "normal security of property is not present" because of an event such as a hurricane, flood, fire, other act of God, or human agencies such as a riot or a mob.[5] Commentators on criminal statutes defining looting have focused attention on the way in which the term "looting" passes beyond the basic crimes of theft, burglary, and trespass into "evidence of human depravity"[6] or the way the term expresses the revulsion we feel toward a "form of burglary or larceny that is dependent on the unique vulnerability of its victims."[7] People who themselves are victims of weather disasters and are simply trying to survive do not fit this category and perhaps should be excused from criminal charges because of necessity, which is a defense discussed below. But, those who are using the opportunity to take people's personal possessions and not seeking means of personal survival should not be excused and should be labeled as "looters" with all of the negative connotations attached to that term.

In June 2005, Louisiana had amended its looting statute to increase the penalties if the looting occurred during a declared state of emergency; the amendment provided a mandatory sentence for looting of a prison term of no less than 3 years and no more than 15 years.[8] Any people convicted of looting during a state of emergency would have to be sentenced to at least 3 years in prison. For those convicted of looting, the new Louisiana law is not offering leniency. In the case of three people convicted of looting for taking 27 bottles of liquor and wine, 6 cases of beer, and 1 case of wine coolers from a grocery store, the judge sent a message that looting would not be tolerated by giving each the maximum sentence of 15 years in prison.[9]

Looting is, of course, not a new phenomenon. During the riots in 1967, where a tie between heat and aggression was noted, the majority of arrests were for looting;[10] for example, in Detroit, 6,253 people were arrested during the July 1967 event[11] with 89.3 percent of those arrests for looting.[12] Then, in July 1977, lightning struck two high-voltage power lines just north of New York City in July 1977, plunging the city into darkness. When it became apparent that the electricity was not going to return soon, law-abiding citizens quickly joined in the widespread looting.[13]

Unlike these looting events in the 1960s and 1970s where the theft or burglary did not reflect necessity but instead seemed more the result of mob mentality, the food rioting in the 1930s had an element of desperation based on survival needs. When a disaster such as Hurricane Katrina hits a city or a region, the devastation is immediate and very visible. Persons are placed in immediate harm and may not have any choice but to commit a crime to stay alive. But, with a disaster such as the drought in the Midwest that extends over several years, the impact is less immediate and the necessity defense less viable. When farmers, who were suffering from the extensive drought in the "Dust Bowl" and the nationwide economic depression, needed food for themselves and their families, they turned to the Red Cross. When the Red Cross ran out of vouchers that would allow the farmers to collect food from the local stores, the farmers in England, Arkansas, demanded food directly from the shopkeepers in town. According to news reports at the time, 500 farmers and their wives, about half of them carrying guns, "stormed the business section . . . demanding food and threatening to forcibly seize it in the event it was not forthcoming." The riot was settled peacefully by storekeepers providing the food needed for the farmers and their families, even though the storekeepers were also in difficult financial circumstances because of the drought.[14]

Two other incidents of the same period, both based on demands for food and relief, did not end so peaceably. In January 1931, just a few weeks after the farmers' raid in England, Arkansas, a similar event occurred in

Oklahoma City. During that incident, 26 men were arrested for raiding a grocery store. The crowd of hungry and jobless, who had demanded relief from the City Manager, stripped the shelves in the store. The five hundred people in the crowd were dispersed with tear gas.[15] Then, in September 1932, a crowd in Anacortes, Washington, made a demand to the Red Cross for a greater allowance of flour. When the demand was not met, 40 to 75 people went to the local store. They helped themselves to groceries and left without paying. Three men who were arrested and convicted for grand larceny and riot tried to use the conditions of poverty and want as a defense. In upholding their convictions, the appellate court stated that "[e]conomic necessity has never been accepted as a defense to a criminal charge,"[16] making clear that the imminent physical harm requirement of the necessity defense is not met by economic conditions.

The demands for food made by the somewhat organized groups from the 1930s represent an unusual type of robbery. More commonly, theft or burglary defendable as necessity occurs in the aftermath of a disaster when resources are not available to those in need. Unlike the food riots of the 1930s, the type of activity commonly seen in the aftermath of a disaster, such as a tornado or hurricane, disasters which leave an immediate and devastating mark on a locale, is the result of lack of food, water, and shelter for large numbers of people. Resources might be unavailable because owners of stores or other supplying companies have closed their businesses and evacuated or because supplies can not get into the area because the weather event cut off access through flooding, treacherous roads, or governmental barricades. Individuals trying to survive seek out food and water and shelter wherever they can find them and may claim the defense of necessity to their actions of theft, larceny, burglary, and trespass.[17]

But what about those people who simply take advantage of the disastrous situation to take other people's possessions? Those people fit within the statutory crime of "looting" found in states that have decided not to rely on larceny, robbery, burglary, or trespass statutes, but instead to define a specific offense of looting.[18] A common theme in many of these laws is the element that unlawful entry to someone's property or the theft of property occurs when the "usual security of property is not effective" because of an event or the aftermath of an event such as a hurricane, a storm, a fire, a flood, or other act of God in addition to events caused by humans. A second element to the crime of looting is the exertion of control or obtaining "control over or damaging or removing property of the owner." Some states have specified that looting occurs when a crime such as theft is committed "during and within an affected county in a 'state of emergency' or a 'local emergency'" resulting from a natural or manmade disaster. The penalties for looting include fines, mandatory community service, and jail time. However, these very specific elements make the crime of looting difficult to prove so prosecutors prefer to charge offenders with burglary and larceny rather than looting.[19]

Looting is the most noted crime during times of weather disasters,[20] probably because it takes the conventional crimes of larceny, theft, and burglary and gives them a new name and stronger penalties. Sometimes, crimes that might be classed as looting are charged as regular old burglary or theft. In the aftermath of Katrina, one of a FEMA subcontractor's employees who was supposed to be installing a trailer on a storm victim's property, allegedly decided instead to go into the house and come out with some of the owner's personal belongings. The owner happened to be in the yard and called the police. The employee was charged with burglary, not looting. Possibly the fact that the homeowner was in control of his property or because it happened in January 2006, several months after the hurricane, had an impact on the decision not to charge the accused with looting.[21]

To prevent looting, theories of deterrence or rational choice suggest increased law enforcement.[22] During natural disasters such as Hurricane Katrina, we see increased shows of force such as National Guard and other military presence to prevent looting. In 1983, when Hurricane Alicia struck south Texas, the police chief of Jamaica Beach on Galveston Island noted looting was the number one problem, with looters arriving "by boat, car and by foot." With the increase of patrols by police, state troopers, and the National Guard and the imposition of a dusk to dawn curfew, the level of looting drastically declined.[23]

The use of National Guard forces and military troops to assist civilian forces during times of natural disaster do not place the locality under martial law.[24] The Constitution of the United States carefully separates responsibility for maintaining civil order and protecting citizens' lives and property between the federal and state governments. The state government has primary responsibility for civil order and safety within its borders and may call out the militia to handle "domestic violence." However, the state government may also call upon the federal government to provide that protection if circumstances prevent the state from being able to deal with the situation.[25] Under the Posse Comitatus Act (PCA),[26] using "any part of the Army or Air Force as a posse comitatus is a federal crime unless an act of Congress has authorized use of the military for law enforcement. "Posse comitatus" is the posse you remember from old Westerns; the posse is the group of people called together by the sheriff to preserve the peace in an emergency. So, the PCA establishes that the Army and the Air Force can not step in to preserve the peace inside the United States but other acts can allow the use of the military. For example, the Insurrection Act[27] allows the President to use the military to suppress insurrection and domestic violence that hinders the execution of the laws of a state or of the United States if the proper procedures required by the act are followed. In 1989, when wide-spread looting was reported in St. Croix, Virgin Islands, during Hurricane Hugo, the President first issued a proclamation ordering those violating the public peace to disperse.[28] When they did not disperse, he issued an executive order stating that the U.S. Armed Forces were to be used to "suppress the violence . . . and to restore law and order in and about the Virgin Islands."[29]

The ability of both state and federal government to take action to prevent looting[30] and to ensure safety during times of natural disasters addresses the law enforcement concerns but does not deal with the underlying problems which caused the looting. When Mayor Nagin reportedly ordered 1,500 police officers to focus on stopping looters, he took them away from search-and-rescue.[31] People in such disasters have need of food, water, shelter, and medical care. By treating looting as a separate aggravated property crime and by focusing on the increased show of law enforcement to deter looting, government is not providing the resources needed by those who must resort to looting. Even if they are able to assert the necessity defense against a charge of looting to ensure that they will not go to jail for locating bread and milk, if food is not available without crime, crime will be committed.

**Curfew Violations**

During the aftermath of disasters, the authorities will often institute a curfew to reduce looting and to heighten personal safety for those left in the area. On September 28, 2005, Mayor Nagin of New Orleans announced to those people returning to the city that a curfew was in effect for the hours of 8 P.M. to 6 A.M. every day, forbidding anyone from being outside during those hours whether in a vehicle or on foot.[32] As of October 14, 2006, New Orleans's curfew was still in effect from midnight to 6 A.M. in certain parts of the City.[33] Curfews were also in place in aftermath of other recent weather disasters including Hurricane Hugo in 1989, Hurricane Andrew in 1992, and Hurricane Frances in 2004.

Despite the governmental interest in maintaining security, people object to the curfews. Objections have been based on grounds that the law was unconstitutionally vague and overbroad and that the law was selectively enforced. A statute is unconstitutionally vague when a person of ordinary intelligence can not identify the conduct that will subject him to arrest. It is overbroad when it criminalizes legal as well as illegal activity.

Courts have tended to uphold the curfews enacted during emergencies. During the period when a 6 P.M. to 6 A.M. nocturnal curfew was in effect in St. Croix, Virgin Islands, in 1989, an attorney was arrested while traveling to visit clients during prohibited hours. In dismissing the attorney's argument that the Governor had no authority to enact and enforce a curfew, the court held that: the Virgin Islands Territorial Emergency Management Act gives the Governor the authority to restrict movement, the curfew was not overly restrictive so the Governor did not exceed his authority, and the "trivial inconvenience to plaintiff in this time of a major disaster does not outweigh the compelling interest of the government and the public in maintaining safety for all citizens."[34]

In reviewing a challenge of unconstitutional vagueness to a curfew established in Dade County, Florida, following Hurricane Hugo in 1992, the court found that the language[35] was not unconstitutionally vague or overbroad even though it did not contain any exceptions for necessary activity. The court noted the unusual circumstances of a hurricane and stated that, in emergency situations, "fundamental rights such as the right of travel and free speech may be temporarily limited or suspended."[36]

The constitutional challenges of the governmental right to enact and enforce a curfew in time of weather emergencies have been dismissed in favor of the greater public good. However, the issue of selective enforcement may take a different turn. While no cases have yet been decided related to selective enforcement of curfews during weather emergencies, claims are being made following recent weather disasters that those arrested for curfew violations are people of color.[37] Claims such as this may lead to consideration of unconstitutional enforcement of the crime in violation of the due process rights of those arrested.

## Fraud

Scams and fraud are common in any type of emergency. The Hurricane Katrina Fraud Task Force, which is coordinating efforts of multiple federal, state, and local relief and law enforcement agencies to prevent and prosecute fraud related to Hurricanes Katrina, Rita, and Wilma, identified three cycles of fraud following a major disaster: (1) charity-fraud schemes that start as soon as the disaster strikes and last for four to six weeks; (2) emergency-assistance schemes that start when the public is informed that assistance is being made available to disaster victims and last for several months or longer; and, (3) procurement and insurance fraud that starts as soon as the public is informed that recovery and reconstruction funds are available.[38]

Just as looting seems particularly egregious because of the circumstances of the victims, scams and fraud that prey on victims of disasters who are already suffering loss seem particularly appalling. The frauds include people calling or coming to the door claiming to be offering services such as negotiation with the government for larger payouts, to be collecting fees for a governmental agency, to be collecting data, or to be inspecting for damage. The Federal Emergency Management Agency (FEMA) has regularly issued warnings to alert the public. A recent press release from FEMA outlined the precautions to take. For example, FEMA employees will always be able to prove their legitimacy by identifying the two FEMA identifying numbers that go along with each person's case file. And, governmental agencies such as FEMA and the U.S. Small Business Administration do not ask for money for their services.[39]

In the 109th Congress, representatives considered legislation[40] to create a "new criminal penalty specifically targeted at fraud in connection with major disaster or emergency benefits" and to increase criminal penalties for wire and mail fraud when committed in connection with a major disaster or emergency. The House of Representatives Committee report on the Emergency and Disaster Assistance Fraud Penalty Enhancement Act of 2005[41] noted that the incidences of benefit-related fraud that arose after Katrina and which led to the creation of the Hurricane Katrina Fraud Task Force were the impetus for the newly defined crime and the increased penalties for fraud. The goal of the legislation was to set levels of consequences that would deter fraudulent activities that attempt to illegally obtain money intended for disaster relief. To increase the deterrent factors, the sentences for violations of the new act would have included fines up to $250,000 for individuals and prison terms up to 30 years. The other option to prevent fraud would be to increase auditing and to slow down the process for those desperate for assistance while the agencies and bureaucracies validated claims. As noted by Representative Scott in his comments to the committee, deterrence through penalties for those who are trying to take advantage of the government's and charitable organizations' efforts to provide speedy assistance is a more appropriate method than slowing down the process for those in need.[42]

Fraud and scams are not new to disaster victims. From the late 1800s through the 1930s, farmers, desperate for rain during times of drought, sought the assistance of "pluviculturists" such as "Dr." George Ambrosius Immanuel Morrison Sykes.[43] The term "pluviculture," a "never-failing drought crop," was coined in 1925 to describe the "growing and marketing of rainmaking schemes."[44] While the federal government was also involved in experiments at rainmaking, and continues to study weather modification today,[45] the rainmakers who advertised their services to desperate farming communities and other areas suffering from droughts were largely considered to be quacks at best and frauds at worst.[46] While few, if any, were prosecuted, the U.S. Weather Bureau did initiate an investigation of Sykes in 1931, asking the U.S. Post Office Department to ascertain if Sykes was taking money under false pretenses. The Post Office replied that, because Sykes did not use the mail for his operation, there was not enough evidence to prosecute.[47]

More recent schemes for defrauding victims of weather-related disasters tend to focus on separating victims from insurance proceeds or governmental benefits. The flooding in Louisiana associated with Tropical Storm Isidore and Hurricane Lili in 2002 led FEMA and the Louisiana Attorney General's Office to warn the public about con artists posing as insurance adjustment experts or claims attorneys who would offer to bargain with the insurer to get higher payouts in exchange for a percentage of the flood claim proceeds. The problem with the offer to negotiate for the victims, of course, was that the National Flood Insurance Program (NFIP) only pays set amounts for damage claims with no opportunity for bargaining;[48] people would be giving up a share of their claims for no services.[49]

People also try to defraud the government or organizations such as the Red Cross by filing false claims for disaster funds or to defraud insurance companies by filing false claims. From September 6, 2005 through September 6, 2006, more than 400 people in 16 states were charged with federal crimes for hurricane-related fraud.[50] The unlawful conduct included: filing false claims with FEMA by using false addresses in New Orleans even though the accused lived in another state and was not affected by the hurricanes; filing claims for housing and then subletting the rooms; submitting false claims through the American Red Cross call center; filing claims using someone else's identity; creating and submitting false claims for services performed such as debris removal that was never done; stealing and using Red Cross debit cards to buy cars and jewelry; bribing a government employee to allow false claims for payment; and, committing wire and mail fraud to file claims.[51]

In addition, criminals prey upon the altruistic people who want to assist those who have been affected by weather disasters. In the recent events of Katrina, the Internet has added a whole new dimension to fraud, with individuals and companies creating Web sites that look like legitimate charity fundraising or that appear connected to well-known charities such as the American Red Cross. They also are able to craft emails inviting donations while using techniques that mask their true identities. Federal law imposes criminal penalties for use of the U.S. mail,[52] interstate telephone or wire communications,[53] or credit cards[54] for fraudulent schemes. A Florida man recently pled guilty to wire fraud for his efforts to profit from the Katrina disaster. He created a website with the URL www.AirKatrina.com. Via the Web site and Internet communications, he claimed that he was providing relief flights between Florida and Louisiana and described the horrific sights he had seen such as "dogs wrapped in electrical lines still alive and sparks flying from their bodies being electrocuted."[55] His solicitation of funds for his fictitious relief efforts resulted in almost $40,000 in donations in 2 days. Following his plea of guilty to the charge of wire fraud, he was sentenced to 21 months in prison.[56] In an interesting twist on the Internet scam, two men in California were indicted for wire fraud and identity fraud for holding "bogus auctions on eBay, Yahoo! Auctions, and Autotrader.com," claiming that the sales of over $150,000 were to benefit Hurricane Katrina relief organizations.[57]

Victims of disasters are also subject to fraud by contractors who take money but do not complete repairs they agreed to perform. Some states have enacted criminal laws specifically directed at contractors. Louisiana, for example, has both civil and criminal penalties for contractors who misapply payments.[58] A Mississippi contractor who only completed a portion of the work he was paid to do and some of whose work had to be redone was arrested in February 2006 under Louisiana's criminal statute prohibiting contractor misapplication of payments.[59] According to the Kenner (Louisiana) Police Department news release, four residents paid the contractor a total of $23,546 between October 22, 2005 and December 26, 2005 to buy materials and make repairs on their hurricane-damaged homes.[60] The criminal penalties for misapplying payments of more than one thousand dollars are: a fine of between 100 and 500 dollars, imprisonment with or without hard labor for between 90 days and 6 months, or both for *each* one thousand dollars in misapplied funds. The prison term on aggregate can not exceed 5 years. The contractor also must repay the amount misapplied, legal costs, and court fees.[61]

## Price Gouging

In the aftermath of a weather disaster, resources are often scarce. The temptation to try to profit from that scarcity may lead some business owners to increase prices directly or through anticompetitive means. While generally this conduct is treated as a non-criminal violation of state or federal unfair trade practice laws,[62] businesses can be held criminally liable for price gouging and for anticompetitive conduct. The Virgin Islands has a specific statute that, during a state of emergency, gives the governor the authority to impose limits on sales of alcoholic beverages, guns, and explosives and to freeze and maintain costs of goods and services at the pre-disaster level.[63] Violators of the price limitations imposed by the governor are subject to fines and imprisonment.[64]

The U.S. Department of Justice investigates claims of anticompetitive conduct, also known as antitrust violations, for bid rigging, price fixing, and market allocation. Bid rigging is the agreement by two or more companies to bid in a way that ensures that a particular company will win the contract for the work to be done. Price fixing is the agreement by two or more companies about their prices including agreement that they will not sell their goods below a certain price or that they will increase prices in tandem. And, market allocation is the agreement to divide customer bases, such as by territories, to reduce competition.[65] These anticompetitive measures violate the Sherman Antitrust Act and are punishable by fines and imprisonment.[66]

## WEATHER AS AN INSTRUMENT OF CRIME

Although a person may not intend a criminal result, the weather may compound the effect of an action or inaction to cause death or other serious harm. The harm caused may fit within the categories of criminal fault. For example, leaving an infant or a dog in a hot car for even a short period of time can result in the child's or the animal's death.[67] Until recently, these deaths of infants and children and of companion animals in hot cars have been called tragic accidents, rather than the result of human inattention or poor behavior. Now, criminal charges may attach.[68] Abandoning an unwanted new-born baby outside, in a dumpster, or exposed to the elements can result in criminal abandonment charges.[69] Under federal statute, the captain, engineer, pilot, or other person employed on a boat will be liable for murder or manslaughter if her misconduct, negligence, or inattention to her duties on the boat results in the loss of life of any person and can be fined and imprisoned or both.[70]

Generally, a person who has a legal duty to supply clothing and shelter for a dependent such as a child or a spouse but does not provide the clothing or shelter, whether intentionally or with culpable negligence, can be charged with and convicted of murder or manslaughter.[71] Even if the person with the duty does not have the resources personally to provide the protection from exposure to the elements and to prevent harm, the person still has a duty to seek public aid if it is available.[72] A duty arises in different situations such as: (1) a statute creates a duty to take care of someone, (2) there is a certain status relationship such as parent or spouse, (3) a contract creates the duty, or (4) the person voluntarily assumes responsibility for the care of another person precluding other people from providing assistance and care.[73]

A tugboat captain has a duty under federal statute to protect crew members. In 1993, the captain of a tugboat entered a contract to tow two early twentieth-century wooden barges across Lake Ontario and through the New York State Canal System to Onondaga Lake. As part of the negotiation, a marine surveyor hired by the barges' owner warned the captain about the delicate and fragile construction of the two barges. The captain was also warned that the trip would need to be made slowly and under weather conditions of wind of less than ten knots and seas less than 2 feet. After a false start on the morning of November 25, 1993 due to heavy weather off the Port of Oswego, the captain arrived at Point Pleasant where he was to pick up the barges. The captain decided to move only the smaller of the two barges for the first run, with two crew members running the bilge pumps on the barge. Instead of inspecting the barges for seaworthiness and for safety equipment, the captain stayed aboard his tugboat during the preparations for towing. The forecasts, to which the captain did not listen either before starting out from port or once underway, called for severe weather for Lake Ontario. After about 4.5 hours, the tug and the towed barge were on Lake Ontario in increasingly deteriorating weather conditions. The captain could see waves going over the sides and bow of the barge.

At about 2 A.M., with waves of 6 to 8 feet and wind at 30 knots, the barge began to break apart and sink. One crew member on the barge was seen going into the water. The captain radioed a "Mayday" signal, reporting that the barge with men aboard had sunk. When help arrived, they were able to recover the body of one crew member but the other was not found.

The federal statutory duty of a tugboat captain to care for his crew members subjected the captain to charges of involuntary manslaughter for not demonstrating the standard of care that a reasonable captain would exercise, including following the weather forecasts, adhering to the marine surveyor's limitations on weather condition suitable for towing the barge, and ensuring the safety of the crew by inspecting the barge and providing proper safety gear and communications devices. The tugboat captain was sentenced to 12 months plus 2 years of supervised release and was fined $10,000.[74]

Parents, of course, have an obligation to provide shelter against the weather for their children. In Wharton's treatise on homicide, the author offers an example of a woman leaving her young infant at a place where it could be found or taken care of. If the child died under these conditions, the woman would be guilty of manslaughter. But, if the woman left the child in a remote location where it was not likely to be found and the child died, the woman would be guilty of murder.[75]

A small basket covered by a shawl and containing the body of a tiny baby was found by a Louisville police officer early in the morning of November 12, 1897. The 2-month-old baby girl had been deposited in the yard of the residence by her unmarried mother. The coroner determined that the baby probably died from starvation or exposure. The mother claimed that the baby had died in the morning on the 11th and that she hid that fact until she could remove the body from the house and place it someplace where it would be found and buried. Other witnesses testified, however, that they had seen the baby alive and well during the day on the 11th. Witnesses also testified that the mother was "anxious to be relieved of the burden of its support." The court stated that the "law imposed upon defendant the duty of protecting and caring for her offspring to the best of her ability; and when she willfully abandoned it on a cold, raw night, and left it to die from exposure, she was guilty of a felony [voluntary manslaughter], whatever may have been her purpose in leaving it."[76]

The parental duty of care does not apply only to adult parents. A 15-year-old girl, known only in the court as "B.L.M.", gave birth to a premature baby at home in the cold early morning of December 10, 1994. According to B.L.M., the baby showed no signs of life so she wrapped the baby in a towel, put it in a trash bag, and set the bag on the porch with the garbage. B.L.M.'s mother heard whimpering coming from the trash bag and discovered the baby girl covered with household trash. The baby died at the hospital on December 14, 1994.

The autopsy revealed that the baby had health problems that gave her only a one in one hundred chance of surviving; however, in determining the cause of death, the pathologist could not separate the prematurity from the exposure to the elements as the cause of death, leaving an issue of proximate cause[77] of the baby's death. Was the baby's death the result of the health issues that arose because of the prematurity or was the death caused by B.L.M.'s actions in placing the baby in the garbage bag and leaving her on the porch with the garbage?

Under Georgia statute, reckless abandonment by a parent of a child under 1 year of age is a criminal offense.[78] Even though B.L.M. claimed that no evidence proved that she caused the baby's death and that the pathologist's testimony did not give exposure as the sole proximate cause of death, under Georgia law on homicide, B.L.M's actions could be considered the cause of the baby's death if they materially contributed to the death or if they accelerated the baby's death. The Georgia appellate court held that the trial court was "authorized to find that exposure materially contributed to or accelerated the cause of death" and that the court was "authorized to find that [B.L.M.'s] actions legally resulted in the child's death" as required under the Georgia reckless abandonment statute. As a minor, B.L.M. was found delinquent for the acts she committed that would have been charged as reckless abandonment if committed by an adult.[79]

The nature of responsibility for deaths of children changes as the children mature. For the parent to be held liable for the death from exposure, the child must be dependent on the parents for protection from the elements. In a case from the 1930s, the court found that a 13-year-old boy who had the strength and intelligence to go rabbit hunting and to ask neighbors for food when he was hungry and who generally was able to take care of himself did not have the same level of dependence on his parents as infants and toddlers have. The boy's stepfather and mother were indicted for "unlawfully, willfully, and feloniously" killing and murdering the 13-year-old by "forcing him from their home and unnecessarily and unmercifully exposing him to the inclemency of the weather, without furnishing him with sufficient clothing or nourishment, and from which said neglect and treatment the said Eugene Beasley did die."[80] However, the boy had a history of staying out all night and leaving home when he pleased. One Sunday evening in late January 1936, he left the house at 6 P.M. and was not seen again until his brother found him sitting under a tree, his feet frozen, on Monday morning. Eleven days later, the boy died of moist gangrene.

The Commonwealth of Kentucky's theory was that the boy returned home on Sunday night but was either denied entry to the house or was driven out into the cold by his parents. At trial, the parents were convicted of voluntary manslaughter and sentenced to 5 years. The Court of Appeals overturned the conviction for lack of evidence that the 13-year-old boy was denied access to the house or that his parents sent him out into the cold. The court's opinion noted that "one is often held criminally liable on the ground that he must have intended the natural consequences of a particular act, but it can hardly be said that death from freezing is the natural consequence of driving out into the cold a boy who is mentally and physically capable of looking after himself and finding shelter only a few yards away [at one of the neighbors' homes]. However reprehensible may have been the conduct of [the parents], we are constrained to the view that they were not guilty of murder, or any degree thereof."[81]

Historically, a husband has had a duty to provide care for his wife. Under modern law, this has changed to a spousal care rule; instead of the husband having a duty to provide the wife with the necessities of life, spouses have a duty to provide care to each other. Under the current standard, criminal liability in the form of a misdemeanor will only attach if the spouse persistently fails to provide the support he can provide and that he knows he has a duty to provide.[82]

In the late 1800s, a husband's duty to care for his wife was a clearly stated legal duty. The husband was to provide his wife with "necessary clothing, shelter, and protection from the frost, cold and inclemency of the weather";[83] if the wife died because of the husband's failure to provide these necessities of life, the husband could be convicted for murder or manslaughter as two husbands found out. Hugh Smith's wife Lucy was known to be insane and unable to provide for herself. In the winter of 1875, Smith housed Lucy in an open room in the house with a broken window pane, without a stove, with no clothing, with no bed but "husks and rags in a filthy condition," and with no covering but a piece of canvas. When she was found by neighbors in early February 1875, her feet and hips were "badly frozen, swollen and discolored" and gangrene had set in. On May 5, 1875, Lucy died.

As his defense at trial, Smith claimed he did not know that she was in bad condition even though he had gone through the room every night but one from January 19 to February 9. He admitted that he knew the condition of the room, had provided a stove in the room in prior winters, and had not checked his wife's condition during those weeks except to see if the canvas still covered her. The Supreme Judicial Court of Maine upheld his conviction for manslaughter in the death of his wife by exposing her to inclement weather, saying, "It is settled beyond a question that the naked negligent omission of a known duty, when it causes or hastens the death of a human being, constitutes manslaughter."[84]

About 10 years later, a Montana husband and wife walked to town and drank together until they were "more or less drunk." On their way home, as they neared their house, the wife fell down on the ice. Even though it was late February or early March, the husband went on without his wife, leaving her outside all night, "poorly clad, exposed to the cold."[85] The next day, the husband and his hired man carried the wife into the house but did not get a doctor; she died from exposure. The court repeated the rule regarding duty: "wherever there is a legal duty, and death comes by reason of any omission to discharge it, the party omitting it is guilty of felonious homicide." The court continued on to substitute the husband in the place of the cold as the cause of death. Because of his legal duty to protect his wife, by refusing to come to her aid, it was as if he personally used the forces of the elements and "hence is responsible for the death [the elements] immediately caused." The husband was found guilty of murder in the second degree and sentenced to 20 years in the penitentiary.[86]

In the nineteenth century, husbands and parents were also responsible if their wives or children "fled from home, to escape [defendants'] rage and violence, and died from exposure."[87] In Kentucky in the winter of 1885–1886, a husband and his pregnant wife had a brawl over a sow coming into the house after they had gone to bed. Both were getting in physical blows on each other but, when the husband threatened to get his knife and cut her throat, the wife ran out of the house, barefoot and with very little clothing. The husband shut the door behind her, propped the door with a stick of wood, and went back to bed. The next morning, the daughter found her mother lying face down in snow about 18" deep. The weather had been extremely cold that night and the wife had frozen to death.

While the jury convicted the husband of manslaughter, the appellate court reversed and called for a new trial. The decision of the appellate court was based on the instruction to the jury that led the jury to consider only if the wife left the house from fear of death or great bodily harm, not to consider if her fear was well-grounded and reasonable. If the wife's fear was not well-grounded and reasonable, Hendrickson should not be held responsible for his wife's death because he could not be regarded as having forced her to leave her shelter and go into the extremely cold night dressed only in her nightclothes.[88] The court refers to a North Carolina case from 1856 in which the wife left the house after her husband "desisted from beating" her and stayed outside even though her husband did not prevent her from going back into the house. The North Carolina court found that the husband could not be held responsible for the wife's death because she had exposed herself to the elements unnecessarily, but "if, to avoid the rage of a brutal husband, a wife is compelled to expose herself, by wading through a swamp, or jumping into a river, the husband is responsible for the consequences."[89]

Child cruelty and abuse statutes and cases consider exposure to the weather to be abuse. Even in the 1950s, when spanking was the norm and "Spare the rod, spoil the child" was still taken to heart, statutes included provisions prohibiting infliction of unnecessary pain or suffering, either mental or physical, on a child and prohibiting exposure of a child to unnecessary hardship, fatigue or mental or physical strains that may injure the health, or physical or moral well-being of that child.[90] In 1958, the Indiana Supreme Court upheld the guilty verdict of a father charged with child cruelty. The father was charged on December 10, 1956 when his children (Darlene, age 5; William, age 4; and, Raymond, age 1) were found in an unheated car in 28° F weather. The children were left in the car on Main Street in Wabash, Indiana, for about 2.5 hours from 3:30 P.M. to 6 P.M. while the father went to a tavern for some beer. The case reports that "[t]he children were not warmly dressed and when they were found by the police the five year old girl and the four year old boy were shivering and the baby was cold and 'sopping wet from its waist down.'" The Supreme Court held that leaving children in an unheated car met the statutory requirements; a jury could decide that children in these circumstances had been exposed to an unnecessary hardship that might injure their health. [91]

The duty of care for a minor extends to those who stand in the place of the parents as guardians and caregivers. Recently, the director and staff members of an Arizona "tough love" boot camp were criminally charged in the death of a 14-year-old boy who was forced to stand in heat of over 110° for 5 hours. The boy reportedly wanted to leave the camp and was being punished for being a quitter.[92] The director was charged with second-degree murder for the death of the boy[93] and with eight counts of child abuse for disciplining other campers by forcing them to sit in the sun without adequate water.[94] Two other camp supervisors were also arrested, one of whom pled guilty to negligent homicide in the teen's death.[95] The camp director was ultimately convicted of reckless manslaughter for the death of the 14-year-old.[96]

Child endangerment charges have been filed against parents, foster parents, guardians, and babysitters for leaving children unattended in car seats. Children, of course, sometimes enter a vehicle by themselves and become trapped,[97] either in the car itself or in the trunk.[98] But, frequently, these tragedies are the result of the adult who had responsibility for the baby or small child forgetting about the child[99] or deliberately leaving the child in the vehicle. The law has tended to treat the situation of the forgetful adult as an accident, even if the result is death for the child. For example, when a 3-month-old baby girl died in 1996 after being left in the car in Las Vegas for more than half a day, the death was ruled accidental and no charges were filed. Prosecutors based the decision not to press charges on the fact that the mother had "simply forgotten [the baby] was there" because the car seat was rear-facing, the baby was quiet, and the mother had "her mind elsewhere that morning."[100] However, two years later, prosecutors in Las Vegas charged a mother and her boyfriend with second-degree murder and felony child abuse for the death of a 7-month-old boy. This couple was driving around town collecting bottles and cans to recycle for money for about 4 hours on a July afternoon. The van they were driving did not have air-conditioning and had only one operational window that was open only a crack. The district attorney found that, unlike the mother who "simply forgot" that her baby was still in the car, this couple saw the child every time they got in and out of the car yet did nothing to protect him from the heat.[101] The couple pled guilty to child abuse and neglect and received suspended sentences.[102]

To prevent child endangerment and to educate parents and other caregivers on the dangers of leaving children unattended in motor vehicles, several states have enacted legislation that prohibits a parent, guardian, or other responsible person from leaving a young child unattended in a motor vehicle on public highways, roadways, and other public places such as parking lots. The limitations of the laws vary from state to state. Some states specify a time limit of 10 to 15 minutes as the maximum time to leave a child unattended under the statute while others indicate that there is no length of time that is acceptable for leaving a child unattended in a motor vehicle if the child might be endangered.[103] Many states limit liability to unattended children under the age of 6;[104] Washington state, however, specifies 16.[105] The term "unattended" is also defined in different ways by different states. "Unattended" can mean: (1) out of sight,[106] (2) without the supervision of an older minor such as a 12-year-old[107] or a 14-year-old,[108] or (3) more than a certain distance away and unable to continuously observe the child in the vehicle.[109] The penalties range from warnings to fines and imprisonment. The classifications of the offenses range from traffic infraction to misdemeanor with felony status for subsequent violations.

A father who left his 4-month-old baby in the car in winter weather while he ran into the campus bookstore tested the validity of the Illinois child endangerment statute in court. The infant was left bundled in a full body jumpsuit, a hood, and gloves and was covered with a thick wool blanket over a small sheet. The temperature outside was 22°F with a wind-chill of 12°F. The witness for the prosecution could not tell the temperature inside the car but knew that he could see his breath when he rescued the baby. He also did not have the exact length of time that the baby was left unattended but estimated it to be 40 minutes. The Supreme Court of Illinois upheld the father's conviction for child endangerment while it simultaneously struck down as unconstitutional the presumption written into the statute. That statutory presumption allowed the jury or judge to infer violation of the endangerment statute from mere proof that a child under the age of 6 was left unattended in a motor vehicle for more than 10 minutes. However, even without the presumption to support a finding of guilt, the Illinois Supreme Court found that the evidence against this father was strong enough to convict him of knowingly endangering his baby girl's life or health by leaving her unattended in his vehicle in a parking lot in extremely cold weather.[110]

Deliberately leaving children unattended and locked in a vehicle in the heat can bring not only child abuse and neglect charges, but also manslaughter or murder charges. Two Arkansas men, one of whom was the father, were charged with first-degree murder[111] in 1998 for strapping two girls into their car seats, rolling up the vehicle windows, locking the car, and heading off to search for arrowheads and mushrooms for 8 hours.[112] The girls, one 16-months-old and the other 4-months-old, were "cooked to death" in their father's car on a day when the temperature was just 79°F.[113] In a similarly heart-breaking tale from 2002, a 3-year-old boy tried to help his 10-month-old baby sister survive the smothering heat inside a locked vehicle. On a sunny, 86°F afternoon in Detroit, their mother had left the two children in the car for 3.5 hours while she went to the hair-dresser. The little boy managed to unbuckle his sister and get her down from her car seat. Investigators found mouth prints on the inside glass of the car, apparently where the children tried to get a breath of air. When the mother returned to the car, she found the children "covered in vomit, dead [from hyperthermia] inside a car parked baking in the sun." The mother was charged with two counts of felony murder and two counts of first-degree child abuse.[114] She pled guilty to second-degree murder and was sentenced to 12-1/2 to 60 years.[115]

The adults who locked the children in the car and deliberately walked away, leaving the children to suffer and die in the heat while the adults went looking for mushrooms or got their hair done, are easy cases for prosecution. And, the mother or grandmother or babysitter or father who tragically forgot that the baby was still in the car seems less culpable and more deserving of sympathy than criminal charges. But what of the case of the foster mother in Los Angeles County who said she had forgotten to take the two boys out of her SUV when she arrived at her day-care center? The 5-year-old and 3-year-old boys were left unattended, strapped in their car seats for 5 hours in 100°F heat. In this case, the prosecutors originally filed child abuse charges but then, based on a theory of intentional act, added murder charges for the deaths. The deputy district attorney in charge of the case explained that the claim was not that the foster mother intended to leave the children in the car for 5 hours, but that she intended to leave them in the car for some period of time. She "intentionally left them in the car when she walked away and subsequently forgot about them. She got distracted and forgot to go back."[116] This woman was charged with felony murder and child abuse; she ultimately pleaded no contest[117] to involuntary manslaughter and was sentenced to 6 months in jail.[118]

Why was the foster mother subject to criminal charges when she simply "forgot" the children? Why is this different than the mother who forgot her 3-month-old baby? Unlike the mother noted above whose baby was quiet and not immediately visible in a rear-facing car seat or the UC Irvine professor who did not realize he had left his 10-month-old son in the car,[119] the difference in the case of this foster mother seems to be the reasonableness of the forgetfulness. While the accidental deaths focus on the fact that the adults forgot that the children were even in the car, the foster mother made a decision to leave the boys in the car and then forgot to go back to get them when she got distracted. It is more likely and possibly more reasonable to forget a sleeping infant when all you see is the back of the car seat and you hear no noise than it is to claim to forget a toddler and a preschooler who are facing forward in their seats and, as any parent knows, are not likely to be sitting quietly and unobtrusively as you leave the car. The foster mother's decision to leave the children in the car makes her forgetfulness about taking the children out of the car more blameworthy than that of the parents who forgot the children were in the car at all, even as they locked the door and left the vehicle in the heat and sun.

Exposure to extreme weather conditions can result not just in unnecessary hardship but also in death for small children and babies. When the doctor at the University of Illinois Hospital examined 16-month-old Veronica on the night of December 22, 1986, he found her body frigid to the touch; her body temperature was so low the hospital's instruments could not measure it. After 45 minutes in the hospital, her temperature *rose* to 78 degrees. The baby was suffering from severe dehydration and lack of protein as if she had been starved over a long period of time and her blood would not clot. Veronica died 6 hours after entering the hospital. The autopsy showed the immediate cause of death to be hypothermia due to neglect.

Veronica lived in her mother's boyfriend's apartment in Chicago with her mother, her 2.5-year-old brother and her 5-year-old sister. The boyfriend was the stay-at-home caregiver for the three children while their mother went to work. In addition to not feeding the children regularly, the boyfriend kept the children in an unheated room in the apartment, frequently with an open window in the middle of winter, without blankets, and without proper clothing. The doctor who treated Veronica testified at trial that the "profound hypothermia was consistent with the child's having been kept in a room with the window open when the outside temperature was between 20 and 40 degrees for several days."[120]

The boyfriend attempted to argue that he did not have a legal duty to provide the 16-month-old child with basic necessities such as clothing, adequate shelter, and food because he was not the baby's father and, without such a duty, there was no crime in failing to act to prevent the harm. The Supreme Court ruled that the conviction was not for failing to act but for committing overt acts such as depriving the baby of food, clothing, and shelter, keeping her in a cold room, and exposing her to the inclemency of the weather. The boyfriend was convicted of murder and sentenced to death for Veronica's murder.[121] On January 12, 2003, Governor George Ryan commuted the sentence to life in prison.[122]

While the person who fails to fulfill a parental or spousal duty can be held criminally liable, the cases involving parents and spouses generally do not show an intent to kill. But, sometimes the weather is intentionally used as a murder weapon. In a 1970 Nevada case, the defendant argued that she should not have been charged with murder. She claimed that the murder charge was based on speculation and that there was no evidence to prove that her 1-year-old daughter died from anything other than natural means.

The little girl was found in her mother's car, which the mother (the defendant) had left in an acquaintance's parking lot for five days in May[123] before the body was found. After the car was reported to the police as being suspicious, the responding officer smelled the odor of decomposing human flesh and forced open a window of the locked car. The officer found the dead body of the 1-year-old girl under two suitcases lying on the right front floorboard. The cause of death was determined to be "heat prostration and dehydration, which can cause death in infants and small children within a very short length of time, as little as a few hours."

The Nevada Supreme Court held that the defendant's claim that she was improperly charged because of lack of proof that the death was not caused by natural means was untenable. The Court explained, that in this situation where "the victim is a child one year of age, under the circumstances that existed here[,] [a]t such an age a child is almost totally dependent upon the person having its care and custody, and what might reasonably be found to be a natural cause of death in an adult [such as heat prostration and dehydration] can just as reasonably be found to be an unnatural death,…where the victim is a child so dependent upon others."[124]

## "THE WEATHER MADE ME DO IT": WEATHER AS CRIMINAL DEFENSE

In criminal law, a defendant may claim the defense alternatively known as "choice of evils," "competing harms," or necessity. While the defense is defined differently in different states, generally these defenses are applicable if there is imminent harm to person (either self or other) or to property such that the person must choose between breaking the law and preventing the harm. A distinction has been made between the "choice of evils" defense and the necessity defense. "Choice of evils" relates to committing a crime to protect person, animal, or property while the necessity defense is a defense only against a crime committed to protect a person or an animal.[125]

Defendants have claimed that weather events or extreme weather conditions have made them trespass, steal,[126] violate environmental laws, and drive without a license.[127] Under normal circumstances, these actions would have penalties but the necessity defense may justify the actions, allowing the person to go free. The defense does require, however, that the defendant did not have a role in the creation of the imminent danger and did not recklessly place himself in harm's way, that he had no reasonable legal alternative to avoid the danger to himself or others, and that he reasonably believed that his criminal action would directly result in avoidance of the harm.

Necessity can not succeed as a defense where the defendant had a reasonable, legal course of action he could have taken. While being hunted by the police, James Willott broke into a cabin on the Salmon River. At his trial, his attorney tried to assert a necessity defense based on the weather, saying that the defendant went into the cabin to "escape the cold and rainy weather and thereby save his life." The California court refused to allow the necessity defense for Mr. Willott, finding that he was out in the weather and facing the emergency situation by his own doing; he was trying to evade the police. Basically, he could have avoided the dangerous weather and the necessity of breaking in to a building to find shelter by turning himself in to the police.[128]

Necessity also can not succeed as a defense where the defendant's actions or failure to act substantially contributed to the emergency. In 1995, after a period of heavy rains in San Luis Obispo County, the owner of the Buena Vista Mines lowered the level of the company's holding pond by pumping off 180,000 gallons of highly acidic water into Las Tablas Creek in violation of California's Water Code. The owner asserted a necessity defense, testifying that he pumped the water out of the pond to prevent the environmental disaster that would result if the pond's wall burst and 1.5 million gallons of contaminated water was released into the creek. The appellate court ruled that a necessity defense was not available because the owner "substantially contributed to the emergency by storing contaminated water in an inadequately sized open pond." The court also found that the defendant owner did not use the reasonable legal alternatives that were available to him, such as installing a treatment plant or building an overflow pond, well before the March rains. The court also noted that he did not have to pump out water when he did because he waited until it had stopped raining, when the danger of an overflow or wall collapse was no longer imminent; the court said that the "prospect of future rain did not give him a license to continue pumping once the rain stopped." His testimony that he lowered the pond by 18 inches, rather than a lesser amount, so he would not have to pump again for 3 or 4 days probably did not help his case.[129]

The difference between "competing harms" and "choice of evils" is the object of the imminent harm. "Competing harms" defense will only be allowed where the imminent danger is proven to be physical harm to self or another, not harm to property. Aaron Greenwald, whose license had been suspended for a series of moving violations, drove his car to get kerosene for a portable heater. He tried to use the "competing harms" defense to prove that he was justified in driving without a license. His argument included the facts that, on December 27, 1980, his household included his wife and two young children, Ms. Greenwald was incapacitated by illness, their house was old with poor insulation, the furnace in the Greenwald's home was not working, the weather was exceptionally cold,[130] his pipes were on the verge of freezing, and he was unable to reach his sister-in-law to ask her to help get the kerosene. The court reviewed the evidence presented and determined that the defendant had not proven there was in fact a threat of imminent physical harm to him or his family, that the only threat of harm proven was to his pipes, so the "competing harms" defense did not apply. The court also noted that the defendant made no efforts to find someone other than his sister-in-law to help him get the kerosene so it is likely that, even if he had proven imminent danger of harm to himself or his family, he did not use other reasonable legal options to avoid the imminent harm and could not have succeeded with the defense.[131]

The crime of looting, one frequently associated with weather disasters, might be defended as necessity where the "looter" was seeking food or medicine to keep self or others alive. Should this activity even be considered looting? Prosecutors can decide not to pursue charges against those people who are themselves victims of a weather disaster and who are simply trying to survive. For example, in the aftermath of Hurricane Katrina, 290 people were arrested and booked for looting by law enforcement officials in Jefferson Parish between August 27 and November 30, 2005.[132] Prosecutors looked over the cases and reportedly decided not to press charges against 84 of the accused. The District Attorney is quoted as saying, "We wanted to make sure if someone was arrested on the street in possession of those types of items [food], they weren't charged with a crime. They were just trying to survive."[133] An example of one such case is that of a 73-year-old woman who was arrested with $63.50 worth of sausage and beer.[134] Even had the prosecutor decided to proceed with these cases, people who were caught stealing food for themselves and their families, and possibly those who took cars from dealerships to get from their flooded homes to an evacuation site outside of New Orleans,[135] would be able to assert the defense of necessity at trial and would probably not be convicted by a jury. By deciding not to prosecute those people who took small amounts of food and beverage, as opposed to gangs that reportedly took the food stores from a nursing home,[136] the District Attorney was not only being efficient and economical but was also acknowledging the difficulties of those stranded without food, water, and electricity for weeks.

## CONCLUSION

Weather can be an important factor in criminal prosecutions. A person may intentionally expose someone to inclement weather, causing the victim's death, in which case the weather is simply the instrument used to effect a criminal result. In this type of case, the criminal prosecution will proceed no differently than with any other instrumentality. The weather may be the motivating factor for the crime, such as schemes to defraud the government or victims of disasters, or for the enactment of criminal statutes or the increase of criminal penalties, such as the establishment of curfews or the institution of stiffer penalties for looting during emergencies. The weather can also serve as a defense to criminal charges, especially where the person charged with a crime is affected by the weather disaster and must choose crime to locate the necessities of food, water, and shelter.

# CHAPTER 6

# Weather and the Justice System

*The tenants filed the complaint in U.S. District Court in Louisiana. They had escaped Hurricane Katrina by leaving New Orleans, expecting to return to their apartments when the disaster was over. When they did return, many found eviction notices tacked to their apartment doors. Although Louisiana law allows notice of eviction by "tacking," displaced tenants who could not get to their apartments really had no effective notice of the landlords' eviction efforts. No attempts had been made to notify them directly in their locations out of the city, even when landlords knew where tenants had gone for safety.*

*One tenant, who had gone back to her New Orleans apartment in early October and who had found the contents in place, returned in early November to find an eviction notice on her door with a court date that had passed. She "also found her door opened, mildew in her apartment, her televisions missing, and furniture strewn throughout the apartment."*

*The justice system had continued as if nothing had happened, with eviction processes occurring as if Hurricane Katrina had not affected thousands of people. The tenants fought back using that same justice system to require adjustments for the displaced persons.*[1]

T he U.S. judicial and criminal justice systems, including law enforcement, can be affected by the weather. Evidence of the weather may be presented in court to establish an alibi or to provide physical proof. Access to justice can be limited if courts close due to extreme weather conditions or if those in need of access cannot get to the courthouse to protect their rights. Corrections facilities, jails, and prisons may be caught in flood waters, requiring prompt action to ensure the safety of the inmates, the staff, and the public. Records related to both courts and criminal justice institutions may be inaccessible, lost, or damaged as the result of severe weather and weather disasters. And, police officers and other law enforcement staffing may be needed in greater force during certain types of events or certain types of weather.

## CRIMINAL JUSTICE

From evidence of crime to defenses against criminal charges, weather plays a part in the criminal justice process. Statistics, case law, and special studies provide examples of the impact of weather on crime and, more generally, on the legal system. Forensic scientists may find evidence more or less perceptible because of the weather. Accused persons may assert defenses such as necessity or accident due to weather. Even court operations can be affected by weather events, which make it impossible for judges to get to court or which make the courthouses physically inaccessible.

### Impact of Weather on Crime and Crime Rates

> I pray thee, good Mercutio, let's retire:
> The day is hot, the Capulets abroad,
> And if we meet, we shall not 'scape a brawl,
> For now, these hot days, is the mad blood stirring.
> —William Shakespeare, *Romeo and Juliet*, Act III, scene 1

Scientists have established that the weather has an impact on the human body and psyche. Researchers have undertaken studies on the specific impact of heat on human aggression and of extreme weather on crime rates. Although modern interest in the weather's effect on human behavior, particularly on aggression and crime, appeared in a number of books written in the 1970s, probably as a result of the riots in the summers of the late 1960s, interest in the phenomenon of weather's affect on human behavior had been evidenced in studies and articles much earlier[2] and continues today. Studies have concluded that heat increases aggression,[3] high barometric pressure is associated with depression,[4] and winds affect judgment.[5] These reactions to the weather can result in behavior with legal consequences; increased aggression can lead to violent crimes, depression can lead to suicide,[6] and poor judgment can lead to criminal actions that a person would not normally take.

Both urban legend and scientific studies tell us that crime rate and weather are related. For example, it is commonly believed that certain types of weather patterns such as heat waves increase aggressiveness and increase the crime rate. During the 1967 riots, violence first erupted on days where the temperature was quite high.

An argument could be made that the correlation is not between heat and aggression but between proximity of people and aggression. The National Advisory Commission on Civil Disorders report noted that the high temperatures on the most violent days "contributed to the size of the crowds on the street, particularly in areas of congested housing."[7] In addition, police officers generally would rather work their shifts in cold, miserable weather because few people are on the streets. These two assertions regarding proximity and public congestion due to high temperatures might support the argument regarding proximity and aggression. However, further scientific study has shown a connection between aggression and temperatures.

Scientists assert connections between heat waves and increases in aggression and crimes such as assault, rape, and murder.[8] But, they disagree as to the significance of the correlation and as to the type of effects various types of weather have on crime rates. James Rotton and James Frey studied crime data from Dayton, Ohio, for the 2 years between January 1, 1975, and December 31, 1976. Their results indicated that there is, indeed, a correlation between ozone levels and violent crimes but that the more significant factors were wind levels and temperature. The researchers found that family and household disturbances were most frequent when wind levels were low and temperatures were high and that assaults were more frequent on warm, dry days that had been preceded by days of low wind. Rotton and Frey noted that further study was needed and that some results were not clearly established. They also noted that the relationship might be between behavior and air pollution levels as affected by weather and not strictly related to weather; for example, since wind removes pollution from the air and humidity precedes or follows rain that clears the air, pollution might be the true factor to consider, not the weather itself.[9]

The FBI's annual crime data reports indicate that crime rates differ by month. In 2001, the FBI reported that, based upon data from the National Incident-Based Reporting System (NIBRS), thefts of motor vehicles occur more frequently during the second half of the year.[10] The agency's press release notes that this means that the theft rate is higher during warmer summer months of July and August and during the last quarter of the year when new models are released and end of year holiday season when property crime rates tend to be higher than other times during the year.[11] Perhaps this has to do with weather or perhaps it simply has to do with school not being in session since the largest number of motor vehicle theft arrests are of those between the ages of 12 and 17 years.

Efforts have been made to use weather data to predict crime. In 1991, the Waco (Texas) Police Department entered into a project with professors at Baylor University to develop a "statistical-based model using crime reports, weather data, census data, unemployment data, school attendance records, and the lunar calendar" to forecast crime. In one demonstration of the model, police officers identified the most likely times and place for auto thefts.[12] Weather was only one factor in the database model, but it was recognized as an important factor.

While data is still inconclusive as to the exact correlations, the research does show a connection between weather and crime rates. Theoretically, this data could be used to predict crime and to prevent or reduce crime or change sentencing rules. For example, communities could increase police presence during certain types of weather. Perhaps, once people are educated about the effect of the weather on their behavior, they can take steps to resist violent urges spawned by feeling hot and irritable. And, perhaps, as the research develops more fully, the person who commits a crime may be able to make a successful argument in favor of a lighter sentence or have the behavior excused because the "weather made him do it."

## WEATHER AS EVIDENCE

Information about weather conditions is often submitted as evidence in court. Weather data from the federal government and testimony from meteorologists is admissible in court in both civil and criminal trials. Weather data can be presented as evidence at trial to illustrate the conditions in which an event took place. This evidence might then serve as excuse or as corroboration of fault. Weather-related evidence may also convince a jury of a witness's credibility.

While a collision in white-out conditions may be more defensible than one on a sunny, clear day with dry roads, bad weather can also be a factor showing recklessness. The driver of a fully-loaded semi-trailer truck appealed his conviction for "aggravated homicide by vehicle," arguing that his actions did not constitute driving in a reckless manner. [13] In early November 1991, the truck driver, who had 40 years of experience, was traveling from Laramie to Cheyenne along I-80 in southeastern Wyoming. On the stretch of road between mile markers 334 and 335, four young men had pulled their car about 10 to 15 feet off the road because of deteriorating weather conditions and sat in the white-out with their hazard lights on. The driver of the semi-trailer acknowledged that between those same mile markers, he felt a bump, reportedly as if "something or someone hit me, or I ran over a stone or something."[14] The investigation of the scene and the vehicles led to the conclusion that the truck driver had veered off the road, hit or run over the car with the four boys, veered back up on to the highway, back down the slope off the road, and finally up onto I-80, where he continued on for a mile or so until his truck was unable to continue. Following the collision, one of the young men was trapped inside the car and died as the result of a skull fracture. The truck driver stated that his speed was 50–55 mph in blowing snow on the snow-covered highway. He also stated that the weather deteriorated as he got further from Laramie.

The driver argued that these facts did not support a finding of reckless operation of his vehicle beyond a reasonable doubt; however, the appellate court found that the evidence was sufficient to find his actions reckless and, thus, to support his conviction for aggravated homicide with a vehicle. The court's holding was based upon the fact that "as an experienced interstate truck driver, [he] was well aware of the dangerousness of the winter weather conditions on this section of I-80, yet he pushed his 80,000 pound semi at unsafe speeds."[15]

Evidence regarding weather may also throw into question a witness's credibility or may make a witness's testimony more credible. In a Massachusetts case involving a conviction for rape and assault and battery,[16] the defense had prepared its case based upon the victim's statements that the rape occurred on a Sunday evening in September 1992 when it was raining very hard. The defense investigated the weather for all Sundays in September 1992 and found that there were no rainy Sundays that month. The defense intended, then, to present this weather evidence at trial and argue that the "complainant's claim of rape was only as reliable as her memory of the weather."[17] At trial, however, the prosecution's witnesses, the victim and the victim's boyfriend, were less certain as to the month and year of the assault. This left the defense without weather evidence to demonstrate that the victim's memory was faulty.

On appeal, the defense tried to show that this change in witness' testimony prejudiced the defense's case, that if the defendant had known that the victim was going to testify that the alleged rape could have taken place in September or October of 1991 or 1992, he would have investigated all of the weather reports for those months and would have been able to question the witness' credibility. After the trial, when the defense did have the opportunity to collect the weather information for the 17 Sundays in September and October of 1991 and 1992, it found that only 4 Sundays had rain and none of those rainy Sundays had a downpour. The defense requested a new trial, claiming that, if it had been notified that the witness' testimony might vary as to the date of the assault, it could have shown that the complaining witness' testimony that she was walking home in a "downpour" did not fit with the weather; this would have cast doubt on her claim that she innocently accepted a ride from a stranger because of the rain. In denying the motion for a new trial, the court focused on the defense's "vigorous and extensive" cross-examination of the witness that focused on the unexpected change in her testimony about the month and year. While the court found that the lack of evidence about the weather in all the possible months did not prejudice the defendant's case, the efforts made by the defense to offer such testimony show the value of documented weather data as evidence of witness credibility in court.

In another case, a police officer testified that he saw the defendant's concealed weapon when the wind lifted the defendant's coat. The role of the wind is important because, if police do not have a credible reason to search a suspect, such as evidence that is in plain view or evidence that is in a place where the suspect has no expectation of privacy, the evidence can be suppressed and the charges dismissed because of an illegal search and seizure. Following the arrest for criminal possession of a weapon, the defense moved for suppression of the gun that police found on the suspect, questioning the visibility of a gun under the suspect's jacket. The police officer was on patrol on a rainy and very windy evening in the Bronx when the wind reportedly caught the defendant's jacket just as he was pulling up his hood and zipping the jacket. The officer reported that the combination of defendant's movement and the wind caused the jacket to "'ride up,' revealing the butt of a gun protruding from the small of the defendant's back." In its motion for suppression of the gun, the defense argued that the lifting of the jacket by the wind at just the right moment was a physical impossibility. To make a determination on the suppression motion, the court visited the scene to observe the lighting and visibility and contacted the National Climatic Data Center to get documentary evidence of the weather on the evening of the arrest.[18] Based on its observation of the street and the weather information, the court determined that the officer's account of the events was credible.

Interestingly, neither the prosecution nor the defense offered documentary evidence of the weather on the date of the arrest and the defense did not refute the officer's testimony that the night was windy and rainy. So, the court itself sought out that information for the federal government. How much of the court's decision was based upon this information about the weather and how much was based on the judge's own weather experience is debatable. The court stated, "Such finding [that the officer's testimony was credible] is additionally confirmed by the common human experience of walking down a street on a windy day and having one's open outer garment, such as a jacket, blown up, as well as having umbrellas turned inside out by a gust of wind."[19]

## Forensics and Weather

Weather can establish a time frame for evidence. In a 1994 murder case, the victim was found by firefighters who were called to a truck fire. The victim was lying on the seat of a water department truck, with one gunshot wound. The police found evidence implicating the defendant, including a latent palm print on the truck door near the door handle. In the 1996 trial, the prosecution's finger print expert testified that the latent palm print found on the truck door of the murdered man had to have been made near the door handle on the day of the murder. How did the expert determine when the print was left? The water department truck was stored outdoors and exposed to the weather. It had rained in Kansas City on November 13, 1994, the day before the murder. If the print had been on the door before the day of the murder, the rain would have washed the print from the truck.[20]

Weather also provides cover for some crimes or possibly serves as a planned get-away device. In 2005, a bank robber in Charleston, West Virginia, was able to escape when a heavy downpour destroyed the scent that the K9 Unit was following. The man, waving a fake gun, jumped on the counter in a Branch Banking and Trust Co. (BB&T), grabbed cash from the money drawers, and ran out the door of the bank. The K9 Unit had just picked up his trail when the rain started and washed out the scent trail.[21] In another case, an unknown bank robber who is still at large has committed a series of bank robberies in the Chicago suburbs since 2002. This bank robber escapes on foot and, according to the FBI wanted poster, the majority of his robberies have taken place during rainy or snowy weather.[22] Perhaps this tactic serves to cover his tracks.

**Admissibility of Weather Reports and Records**

A weather report concerning road conditions or the records of rainfall, snowfall, temperature, or wind velocity can be important to the outcome of a lawsuit. The law requires that government officials and employees create certain weather reports and records. These reports and records can be admitted in court under an exception to the general hearsay rule.[23] When these reports and records are submitted as evidence, they are being admitted as proof of the facts that are contained in the report or records. For example, in an action against a crop duster for harm to plants in an adjoining field caused by overspraying with chemicals, wind speed and direction can be important facts to establish; the federal government's records of wind conditions in a particular location at a particular time of a particular day can be critical evidence. The report of that data is being admitted by the court as proof of that data.

The ways that weather evidence is handled varies among the courts based on the facts of the case and the value of the information. Courts have refused to admit weather reports in cases where the reports are based on conditions at a site, like an airport, that is miles away from the location of the accident or injury or where the reports include the opinions of the preparer of the reports, not just factual statements regarding the weather. Courts also have refused to admit reports where the information in the report in unclear regarding the dates and times involved in the incident at issue in the case. Some courts, however, have taken the position that the reports are admissible and that issues such as remoteness of locations only affect the weight that the jury should give to the report. If the weather reports are admitted as evidence, the courts usually allow better weather evidence, such as credible local data or eyewitness testimony regarding the weather, to be admitted to refute the governmental reports. To locate copies of weather reports and records that can be authenticated and admitted as evidence in court, you can go to the National Climatic Data Center.[24] You can also obtain data on specific types of weather events and related injuries from special weather service publications.[25]

As discussed above, we now have rules of evidence that specifically allow government records such as weather reports to be admitted as evidence in court. This was not always the case. The U.S. Supreme Court weighed in on the issue of admissibility of weather records in 1878, 8 years after the start of the U.S. Signal Service. In April 1873, a woman in Evanston, Illinois, a town outside Chicago, put her foot through a hole in a make-shift sidewalk, causing serious injury to her back and hip. While she was aware that the hole was there because she had used the sidewalk before she was hurt, on the day of the injury, she was unable to see the hole because of snow. To establish the presence of snow, the woman presented the Chicago office of the U.S. Signal Service record of wind direction and velocity and snowfall for the evening before and for the day of the injury. Over objection of the defendant that there was no law that allowed the record to be accepted as evidence, the trial court in Illinois allowed the record to be read in court and allowed testimony that Evanston is 10 miles from Chicago.

On appeal of the decision in favor of the injured woman, the U.S. Supreme Court held that weather records kept by "a person employed by the Unites States Signal Service at Chicago" were admissible because the records of the meteorological observations were created by a person who had a public duty to "record truly the facts stated."[26] The Supreme Court's decision noted that Signal Service rules require extreme accuracy in both the weather observations and the recording of the observations and that, because the records are kept for public purposes and are in the public eye, any inaccuracies would be spotted and commented on immediately. So, because of the duty to record the facts accurately and the public checks to ensure accurate reporting, the records were deemed admissible.

This view of the accuracy of the weather records kept by the federal government was confirmed in a 1943 decision. Although weather forecasts are predictions and opinions and are not statements of fact, the court in *Fowel v. Insurance Bldg.* held that the official report of the Weather Bureau was "in no sense speculative, for its official character removed it from that status."[27]

The types of weather testimony that will be allowed in court have been limited by the courts. While the courts have said that records are admissible because they are the official record of facts collected by public employees and because the records are not speculative, the courts have also ruled that, while the parts of the report that are factual such as amount of rain or snow or other information related to particular weather events are admissible, any collateral facts noted by the weather observer are not admissible. For example, in 1901 and 1902, when the lands of a man named Hufnagle were flooded, he claimed that the flooding was the result of run-off and dams created by the railroad. At trial, the railroad attempted to introduce testimony from the U.S. Weather Bureau on the weather conditions during the flood seasons of 1901 and 1902. The Weather Bureau official read from the Bureau records, testifying to the temperature and precipitation at the times of the floods. The defendant railroad then tried to have the official read from a journal. The court ruled that the journal information was not admissible where the answers to questions "did not contain exact data, but stated facts concerning the weather at a certain time, namely, that it had caused the rivers and streams to rise rapidly and to overflow low lying adjacent lands, that certain lives had been lost, and 'had it not been for the warning to prepare for floods and the snow melting rapidly the loss of life and damage would doubtless have been greater.'" The court declared the information in the journal to be opinion as opposed to the "regular official record of the Weather Bureau as to the amount of precipitation each day." A major factor in the court's decision was the fact that the official who was testifying did not write the journal entries and did not observe the events recorded. While the official could give temperature and precipitation data for the relevant dates and could offer his professional opinion about what would be "extraordinary precipitation," he could not offer his opinion on the flooding.[28]

In a similar case in 1958, the court considered the admissibility of a "State Climatologist's Evaluation of Storm" that was presented on a U.S. Department of Commerce Weather Bureau form. The defense tried to use the evidence to show that the storm was so violent that, even if the defendant city had taken all precautions to safeguard the plaintiff's airplane, nothing could have been done to prevent damage to the plane. The "Climatologist's Evaluation" contained conclusions and opinions of the climatologist based on his review of newspaper clippings, reports of untrained witnesses, and reports of a weather bureau meteorologist who visited the storm area. All of these sources constituted hearsay evidence. While the climatologist who signed the report was a qualified expert witness, he could not testify to the conclusions and opinions he reached based on hearsay information.[29]

Another limitation imposed by the courts on admission of weather reports as evidence occurs when the reports are deemed confusing. For example, in December 1958, when one of the parties in an auto accident in Cicero, Illinois, tried to introduce a weather report from the U.S. Weather Bureau, the court held the report inadmissible because the report was unclear about the weather at noon on December 19th in that part of Cicero. In describing the report's coverage, the court stated that the three-page report had only one page about Cicero and that the timing for the report was 7 P.M. to 7 P.M. instead of midnight to midnight, making it difficult to determine when the precipitation occurred. The two drivers had completely different stories about the road conditions, one saying that the weather was dry with no snow on the ground while the other said that the street was a "little slick" and covered with "a little ice" with snow banks against the curbs. Without good information on the timing of the precipitation, the weather report did not add clarity to the case; it simply added confusion.[30]

Government officials from the weather service are not the only meteorologists allowed to testify in court. Attorneys are turning to meteorological consultants who have access to complex information and the ability to make sense of the weather data to make their cases in court. These expert witnesses may be local celebrities that also may, for good or ill, affect the jury's belief of the testimony.[31]

## WEATHER'S IMPACT ON ACCESS TO JUSTICE

The displacement of people in the wake of evacuation and the devastating aftermath of weather-related disasters raises many legal issues. Access to the judicial system can be impeded by many factors: social, economic, racial, and even physical. People need access to the courts, to lawyers, and to sources of official documents lost in the disaster. Weather events can impede the operation of the justice system, from snowstorms and flooding that prevent judges and citizens from getting to the courthouse to disasters that destroy evidence, court records, and attorneys' files. Weather events can prevent timely filing of motions and pleadings, prevent the release of the accused on bail, and affect surveillance activities allowed by court order. Weather events can disrupt jail functions and require the creation of alternative locations for incarceration. Weather can affect issues of jurisdiction over a person; jurisdiction is the ability of a court to hear a case or of law enforcement personnel to make an arrest and is based upon the person's connections to the state or locality such as the location of a crime, the person's residence, or the state in which a contract is to be enforced. Weather can also affect service of process, the delivery of papers in person, by mail, or otherwise to notify a person that he is being sued.

One of the first steps in a lawsuit is notification of the person being sued. Notification can happen by directly handing papers to the person. Weather conditions can, of course, impede access to the person's home or workplace. Another method of providing notice is to tack the notice on the person's door. Landlords in Louisiana used this approach to notify tenants of eviction following Katrina. The problem was that the tenants had no notice of the eviction proceedings because they were not physically present, having evacuated to another location for safety and shelter. In November 2005, a lawsuit was filed against parish and city officials who handle eviction proceedings in Orleans and Jefferson Parishes to ensure notice would reach the people being evicted.[32] A settlement was approved by the court about 2 weeks after the lawsuit was filed, providing that eviction hearings could not be held for 45 days after the notice were mailed. Also, the Federal Emergency Management Agency (FEMA) agreed to provide court clerks and other officials with the evacuees' current addresses so notices could be mailed to them. This settlement helped to provide tenants with access to the courts and the opportunity to defend themselves against the evictions.[33]

The lawsuit settlement placed greater reliability on the mail delivery of the eviction notices than on posting the notices on the front doors of the properties. While this may or may not be a misplaced notion, keep in mind that, despite beliefs to the contrary, the motto of the U.S. Postal Service is *not* "[n]either snow nor rain nor heat nor gloom of night stays these couriers from the swift completion of their appointed rounds"; the Postal Service does not have a motto. This saying, inscribed on the General Post Office at 8th Avenue and 33rd Street in New York City, is attributed to Herodotus from about 500 B.C. [34]

In fact, postal service has reportedly slowed down or stopped due to severe weather. A corporation mailed its required 24f-2 registration to the U.S. Securities Exchange Commission (SEC) 7 days before the filing deadline but the mailing did not reach the SEC in time to meet the deadline. The corporation claimed that the delay was caused by the "comparatively poor" performance of the U.S. Postal Service in delivering mail due, in part, to "extreme weather conditions in the early part of the year."[35]

Weather conditions may prevent courts from operating or prevent judges from signing essential orders. To ensure due process and access to justice during a weather disaster, courts must be available for bail hearings, arraignments, and trials. Those who have litigation pending or who want to file lawsuits do not want to delay their proceedings due to the weather, especially if filing deadlines may pass during the court closure. And, law enforcement needs to be able to continue operations such as surveillance, searches, and arrests that require judicial approval.

Arrangements for alternate locations for courts may be one solution. In the aftermath of Hurricane Katrina, judges heard cases in the New Orleans bus and train station. Between the time Katrina hit New Orleans on August 29, 2005 and October 14, 2005, 1,100 people had been arrested, many of whom had bail hearings in the station.[36] Holding court in a train station is certainly not the ideal situation but is better than the alternative of denying access to the courts.

Weather can affect the ability of the government to provide a speedy trial. Both under the 6th Amendment of the U.S. Constitution and under procedural laws, a defendant has a right to a speedy trial. Under the federal Speedy Trial Act,[37] the government is required to act within certain time limits to complete various procedural steps. If the time limits are not met, the court can dismiss the complaint against the defendant. When a major snowstorm in the Portland area prevented the government from presenting its case to the grand jury within the 30 days allowed for filing an indictment, the defendant moved for dismissal of drug trafficking charges based on failure to meet the Speedy Trial Act requirements. The government had previously filed a motion claiming excludable delay under the interest of justice exclusion of the Speedy Trial Act. In its motion, the government claimed that, because of the "extreme adverse weather conditions," the Grand Jury was not able to form a quorum from the 19th of December, the date the government's case was originally scheduled to be presented to the Grand Jury, until the 27th of December, a day after the 30-day deadline for filing an indictment. The court granted the government's motion for an exception to the timing requirements because the interest of justice outweighed the public's and the defendant's interest in a speedy trial and because the weather made the proceedings impossible.[38]

Weather can also prevent law enforcement from obtaining judicial approval of surveillance orders but, as with the speedy trial example above, the weather circumstances can be a controlling factor in a motion for dismissal of the charges or for suppression of evidence. The defendant in an excise tax evasion case asked the court to suppress evidence that was collected as a result of an eavesdropping order signed and extended several times. Under normal circumstances, when an eavesdropping order expires, the eavesdropping must stop and the device used for the eavesdropping must be deactivated as soon as practicable.[39] However, when the order in this case expired on Friday, September 27, 1985, the government had already begun the process for another extension and simply needed to meet with the judge on Friday morning to get the surveillance order extended again. Early Friday morning, Hurricane Gloria hit Long Island, causing extensive flooding and power outages.

As a result of the storm, the Suffolk County courthouse was closed, making it impossible to meet with the judge to get the order signed. The

Assistant District Attorney had difficulty reaching the judge at his home by phone. Even after he did connect with the judge, he learned that flooding on the way to the judge's house made it impossible to get to the judge that day. The judge approved an extension of the order over the phone on Friday; an oral extension can be held valid under emergency circumstances. The prosecutors continued to try to get to the judge over the weekend and even tried to contact other judges but their efforts failed. The judge signed the extension on Monday, the 30th.

The defendant argued that the extension was not effective and, when an order expires, the government is required to deactivate the eavesdropping device. In its review of the case, the federal district court emphasized the unusual weather circumstances and held that the government could not be expected to immediately deactivate the equipment when its personnel were off trying to locate the judge and get his approval of the extension. The court also noted that, even if they should have deactivated instantaneously, the storm made it infeasible to find proper personnel to make the necessary technological arrangements to disconnect the equipment.[40] Here, the important factors seem to be the significant efforts made by the prosecution to get the extension of the order and the impediments imposed on their efforts by Hurricane Gloria's aftermath.

Lawyers are a crucial part of the justice system. They assist with both civil and criminal matters, ensuring defense of Constitutional rights such as due process and equal protection, preservation of the adversary system, and protection of financial and domestic interests such as child custody, insurance, and property matters. However, during an evacuation or storm, lawyers also are affected personally, limiting their abilities to help clients. A weather-related disaster will affect lawyers' offices along with dwellings, businesses, and other structures. Critical documents and client records can be destroyed by a weather event or its aftermath. Storms such as blizzards, hurricanes, and massive rainstorms with flooding can prevent lawyers from getting to court or to meetings with clients just as they can prevent judges and parties from getting to the courthouse.

The aftermath of Hurricane Katrina illustrates the problems presented by a lack of access to lawyers.[41] Thousands of criminal defendants were in jail awaiting trial or hearings. The public defenders in Louisiana are funded with fines and fees for convictions, primarily from traffic tickets. In the aftermath of Katrina, with courts not functioning and limited traffic, this funding source was depleted. The public defenders' office had no money to operate, leaving defendants without representation. The public defenders' office, which pre-Katrina had only 42 lawyers to represent thousands of indigent criminal defendants, was reduced to 6 attorneys following Katrina.[42]

Without lawyers, these prisoners, who were evacuated to facilities around the state, were basically lost in the system, stuck "doing Katrina time."[43] Many defendants were transferred without their records; records may have been destroyed or lost in the storm or simply not been delivered along with the prisoner. Information about trials, lawyers, time limitations for charges, and release dates was not readily available or not reviewed, leaving prisoners in jail in a location outside New Orleans without family or lawyer to contact for help. Some were in jail awaiting trial for a longer period than if they had been convicted. According to news reports, 9 months after Katrina, "more than a thousand jailed defendants [had] had no access to lawyers."[44]

At least one judge took action to deal with the lack of defense attorneys. Judge Arthur Hunter of New Orleans suspended prosecutions in most cases where public defenders were involved and, by May 2006, was moving toward letting some of the inmates who did not have lawyers out of jail. The judge had attempted to locate private firms to represent the indigent defendants but had not been successful. While prosecutors objected to the release of prisoners, the judge placed his actions in the context of the Constitutional duty to provide a speedy trial and to ensure adequate representation.[45]

Not only were there too few defense attorneys for the number of defendants in need of representation, there were no jurors, lack of access to witnesses, loss or contamination of evidence, and an inadequate number of courtrooms, all of which limited access to justice in the wake of the storm. These conditions affected both civil and criminal actions.

While both civil and criminal cases suffer from the problems related to evidence, witnesses, jurors, and courtrooms in the aftermath of a natural disaster, efforts can be made in civil cases to secure the parties' procedural rights and to locate attorney assistance. Procedural issues related to filing deadlines following Katrina were handled by Governor Blanco's Executive Orders suspending "deadlines in legal proceedings in courts, administrative agencies, and boards" for civil cases from September 6, 2005 until November 25, 2005.[46] Just as defendants in eviction cases were assured access to justice and their opportunity to oppose the eviction, parties in other civil actions were provided with a period of time to recover from the storm and its aftermath and to try to locate evidence, documents, filings, and witnesses needed to initiate or continue a lawsuit for a civil matter.

Another method for providing access to justice is to allow attorneys from other states to provide services in the disaster area. An agreement between the FEMA and the Young Lawyers Division of the American Bar Association (ABA) in 1992 allows FEMA to request volunteer attorneys to assist victims of disasters via a hotline.[47] The hotline is made available to people without access to lawyers. Also, state supreme courts can authorize practice of law for attorneys from other states. Following Hurricanes Katrina and Rita, the Supreme Court of Mississippi issued an order allowing attorneys in good standing in other states to provide "temporary emergency *pro bono* legal assistance to persons residing in Mississippi on August 29, 2005, arising out of or related to rights, remedies, claims, defenses, injury or damages resulting from hurricane Katrina or its aftermath or evaluation pursuant to official warnings regarding hurricane Katrina."[48] The out-of-state attorneys can not provide legal services for a general clientele in Mississippi or for the full range of legal issues. They are limited to clients who were in Mississippi when the storm hit Mississippi and who have legal issues directly resulting from Katrina. This type of order ensures that parties can locate counsel even in the situation where in-state lawyers have lost their offices and their records or have left the state or are coping with their own disaster recovery. On the opposite tack, the Supreme Court of Texas authorized practice in Texas by attorneys displaced by Hurricane Katrina or Hurricane Rita who were licensed in Louisiana, Mississippi, or Alabama but who were living in Texas. This order ensures that these lawyers will not be subject to prosecution for unauthorized practice of law.[49]

Weather disasters also affect the arrest and jail detention components of the criminal justice system. Issues of prisoner evacuation, housing of those arrested in the disaster area, and conditions in jails and prisons in the affected area all were raised in the aftermath of Hurricane Katrina. Inmates in prisons and defendants in jail were trapped by the flooding in New Orleans post-Katrina. Prisoners reported filthy living conditions, lack of food and water, and the fear of being trapped. When they were finally evacuated, they were spread throughout the State of Louisiana, frequently without access to a lawyer or their records.

Equal access to justice has long been associated with civil rights and social justice. Weather can disrupt and often remove the veneer of social equality, especially equality under the law. The conditions in U.S. jails and the holding facilities for arrestees post-Katrina led various bodies to comment on the plight of prisoners and defendants in the United States.

With jails flooded, law enforcement must turn to other locations to house suspects and those accused of crimes such as looting. For example, the New Orleans bus terminal was turned into a "makeshift city jail known as 'Camp Greyhound.'"[50] The American Civil Liberties Union (ACLU) National Prison Project reported on the conditions for prisoners in the Orleans Parish Prison (OPP).

> During the storm, and for several days thereafter, thousands of men, women, and children were abandoned at OPP. As floodwaters rose in the OPP buildings, power was lost, and entire buildings were plunged into darkness. Deputies left their posts wholesale, leaving behind prisoners in locked cells, some standing in sewage-tainted water up to their chests. Over the next few days, without food, water, or ventilation, prisoners broke windows in order to get air, and carved holes in the jail's walls in an effort to get to safety.[51]

In July 2006, the United Nations Human Rights Committee issued a report on U.S. compliance with the International Covenant on Civil and Political Rights (ICCPR). The report, which criticized Louisiana officials for their actions during Katrina, included reference to the failure to evacuate prisoners from OPP after the flooding associated with Hurricane Katrina and focused attention on the "racial profiling and racial disparities in prosecutions and sentencing in the criminal justice system."[52]

The weather has also been a factor in determining the fines to be imposed upon a defendant, dating back hundreds of years. During the reign of Charlemagne in eighth-century Frisia,[53] the criminal law was recorded in the Lex Frisionum or Frisian book of law. Under this Germanic legal system, fines were increased three times if the victim of an assault has recurring pain from heat and cold sensitivity at the site of the injury. One translation of the provision in the Lex Frisionum states, "If a man is hit on the head by another man, and through the sensitivity of the wound he can endure neither cold nor heat, three times 4 *solidi* must be paid."[54] This rule may be the precursor to the thirteenth and fourteenth-century law levying penalty taxes based on weather-sensitivity of scar wounds.[55] In modern times, this may equate more to the civil remedies that take into account the victim's pain and suffering. For example, in a recent automobile accident case, the victim received $175,000 for future physical and mental pain and suffering. The victim had had surgery that had improved his condition but he continued to suffer from pain, particularly in cold weather.[56]

## CONCLUSION

Access to justice and the impact that the weather can have on the processes, proof, and penalties are critical points for crisis planning and emergency management. Without access to courts and lawyers and without the ability to assert their rights, those people who have already been victimized by a weather disaster or event may be further victimized. Programs and orders that allow adjustments in normal court and criminal justice operations to meet the needs of the accused, the lawyers, law enforcement and the courts ensure continued access to justice despite the weather.

# CHAPTER 7

# Future of Weather and the Law

Three issues will drive the intersection of weather and law in the future. First, the global nature of weather will draw more international law into the discussion. Second, increased accuracy of forecasting and data collection tools have the potential to alter the face of litigation on liability issues. And, third, warning systems and relief in the face of weather disasters will demand new approaches rather than repetition of the methods that have failed us in the past.

## GLOBALIZATION OF WEATHER LAW

Issues such as global warming and weaponization of weather are weather-related legal issues with international impact. The issues of greenhouse gases and global warming that other countries are addressing and tackling together have an impact on the United States. Several states, led by Massachusetts, are pursuing legal action against the U.S. Environmental Protection Agency to force action by the federal government on emissions of greenhouse gases and global warming. The U.S. Supreme Court heard oral arguments in the case on November 29, 2006. The states argued that the greenhouse gases have already caused and are causing states, cities, and individuals injuries. The states claimed that:

> rising temperatures have injured petitioners in the following specific and concrete ways: coastal States have lost and are losing land to rising sea levels...; ground-level ozone (smog) is exacerbated by rising temperatures, leading to adverse health effects and costly efforts on the part of States to address the problem...; glaciers are melting, causing distinct injuries to particular individuals.... These injuries span a broad range, from the Commonwealth of Massachusetts losing coastal land to [one of the petitioners] no longer being able to hike on the Alaskan glaciers he used to enjoy.[1]

The outcome of this case could have major consequences for the ability of the United States to be involved in the international discussions on climate change.

Weaponization of weather is another issue that will be arising in the next few years. Weather modification is on an increase after a lull of three decades. New techniques and products are increasing the possibility of success in rainmaking and hurricane or hail suppression. The consequence to neighboring property owners is one piece of the discussion. The global element of the discussion, however, is the concern that weather modification will have a worldwide impact or, at least, an bilateral impact with the U.S.'s neighbor countries.

The potential global effects of technologies that the United States is using for research also are controversial. One example is the High-frequency Active Auroral Research Program (HAARP) that is designed to study the ionosphere. The site, based in Alaska, houses a high-power transmitter that operates in the high-frequency range. Opponents of the research claim that the facility will alter the ionosphere in a way that will affect weather patterns and block global communications.

## CAUSES OF ACTION

In litigation parlance, the overall claim that is made in a lawsuit is known as the cause of action. Under current law, a weather forecaster is not held liable for negligence for inaccurate weather forecasts either because no duty is owed to person harmed or because the forecaster is a governmental employee and protected by sovereign immunity. However, in the absence of these two defenses, another defense is possible—the inaccurate weather forecast is as accurate as a prediction can get.

But, what if the level of certainty of a weather forecast increased? With greater computing capacity and with better weather-related data from satellites observing the earth, forecasters may be able to develop more accurate, more definite, and more long-term forecasts. If forecasts are more accurate, the forecaster can not claim that an inaccurate forecast is the best that can be done.

Another type of forecasting may lead to a new medical malpractice claim. Failure to consider biometeorology in diagnosis may someday rise to a level of negligent medical care. Biometeorology is the study of the interactions between human behavior or physical health and the atmosphere. Basically, biometeorology recognizes that the weather has an impact on the human body and psyche. For example, in the physical realm, high barometric pressure, which occurs when the weather is calm and no storm is brewing, reportedly will decrease symptoms of gallstones or glaucoma whereas similar pressure conditions will increase symptoms of the flu.[2] Studies have concluded that heat increases aggression,[3] high barometric pressure is associated with depression,[4] and winds affect judgment.[5] The study of meteorotropism and biometeorology continues today with studies on panic anxiety,[6] strokes,[7] and other illnesses, both physical and psychological.

Although the results of the research are sometimes inconsistent and are still inconclusive, the correlations found between weather and medical conditions raise the prospect for physicians to identify patients with specific weather sensitivities and to adjust treatment accordingly. In fact, in Europe and the United Kingdom, governments are providing health forecasts in addition to weather forecasts to help doctors and patients develop treatment plans and to allow hospitals, clinics, and emergency rooms to anticipate patient loads.

Germany's system was one of the earliest and most comprehensive programs for health forecasting or bioprognosis. In the 1970s, West Germany had a service to link medical practice and weather forecasting. Subscribing doctors could call in for a detailed description of the weather forecast followed by a description of the subjective and physical impacts on patients with various illnesses. Today, Germany's national meteorological service, the Deutscher Wetterdienst, notes that part of its mission is to provide "advice on how to reduce health risks caused by weather."[8]

Although the connection between weather and health has been confirmed by research and has led other countries to make use of the connection in health forecasting, doctors in the United States are not using this information in diagnosing and treating patients. As the data becomes more fully developed, weather sensitivities may be identified as syndromes or disorders that should be treated in specific ways or doctors may be able to develop accurate diagnostic tools for weather-related medical problems. If diagnostic tools become available, physicians may find themselves liable for negligence if they do not make use of this information to benefit their patients.

The impact of weather on individuals may have applications in other areas of the law. Criminal defense lawyers might want to consider the impact of the weather on their clients' behavior and use that information in defense or as a mitigating factor for sentencing. Or, perhaps individuals should consider the impact of the weather on them and not enter contracts or preside in court or enact laws on the "bad weather" days.

## HISTORY REPEATING ITSELF

The review of past weather disasters demonstrates that governments and societies take the same approaches to problems over and over, even if the result was not completely satisfactory the first time. The United States has suffered floods, hurricanes, tornadoes, and other weather disasters frequently in its history. Yet, when you look at the actions taken and the relief provided to victims, similarities emerge. And, the responses of those harmed by the event often lead them to rebuild in the same location subject to a similar storm in the future. To avoid the continuing cycle of predictable responses, governments and individuals must look for new ways to respond.

# Notes

## CHAPTER 1: WEATHER FORECASTING AND WARNING SYSTEMS

1. *Encyclopaedia Britannica Dictionary of Arts, Sciences and General Literature*, R.S. Peale Reprint (Chicago, IL: The Werner Co., 1894), s.v. "Blizzard." For the complete story of the January 1888 blizzard in the Midwest, see David Laskin, *The Children's Blizzard* (New York: HarperCollins, 2004).

2. Roberta Carkeek Cheney, *Sioux Winter Count: A 131-Year Calendar of Events* (Happy Camp, CA: Naturegraph Publishers, Inc., 1998) (originally published: Big Missouri Winter Count [1979]). Dragging meat p. 22, girls p. 47, boys p. 48.

3. See Chapter 2 for information on inventions and technology.

4. Patrick Hughes, *A Century of Weather Service: A History of the Birth and Growth of the National Weather Service, 1870–1970* (New York: Gordon and Breach, 1970), 14.

5. Ibid., 12.

6. U.S. Department of Agriculture Weather Bureau, *Report of the Chief of the Weather Bureau, 1923–1924*, House Document No. 446, 68th Cong., 2d sess. (Washington, DC: Government Printing Office, 1925), 14–15.

7. United States National Oceanic and Atmospheric Administration. National Weather Service (Norman, OK), "An Introduction to Storm Observation and Reporting," at http://www.srh.noaa.gov/oun/stormspotting/.

8. Mel Goldstein, *The Complete Idiot's Guide to Weather*, 2nd ed. (Indianapolis, IN: Alpha, 2002), 298–300.

9. Alan Ward, "The Past, Present, and Future of the Landsat Program," *The Earth Observer* 18, no. 6 (Nov.–Dec. 2006): 4.

10. American Society for Photogrammetry and Remote Sensing and American Bar Association, *Earth Observation Systems: Legal Considerations for the '90s* (Bethesda, MD: American Society for Photogrammetry and Remote Sensing, 1990).

11. For more information about the satellites used in weather forecasting, see Goldstein, *The Complete Idiot's Guide to Weather*, 300–301.

12. Res. No. 12, 41st Cong., 2d sess., 16 Stat. 369, February 9, 1870.

13. c. 415, s. 1, June 10, 1872, in Revised Statutes of the United States Passed at the First Session of the Forty-Third Congress, 1873–'74, section 222.

14. Donald R. Whitnah, *A History of the United States Weather Bureau* (Urbana, IL: University of Illinois Press, 1965), 10.

15. U.S. Congress, House of Representatives, *Estimates for the Army—For the Year 1841*, Doc. No. 47, 26th Cong., 2d sess. (Washington, DC: 1841), 17.

16. The synoptic chart is a short-hand method for presenting weather data such as high and low pressure fronts for a large geographic area; the weather map in the newspaper is a synoptic chart.

17. Whitnah, *History of the United States Weather Bureau*, 12–13.

18. United States National Oceanic and Atmospheric Administration, "Signal Service Years," Stories and Tales of the Weather Service, at http://www.history.noaa.gov/stories_tales/evolut.html.

19. *Report of the Joint Commission to Consider the Present Organizations of the Signal Service, Geological Survey, Coast and Geodetic Survey, and the Hydrographic Office of the Navy Department*, 49th Cong., 1st sess., 1886, S. Rep. 1285, 1.

20. U.S. Congress, 51st Cong., 1st sess., chap. 1266, October 1, 1890; U.S. Congress. House of Representatives, *Transfer of Weather Service*, H. Rep. 1043, 51st Cong., 1st sess., March 25, 1890.

21. *United States Code*, title 5, Appendix, Reorganization Plan No. 2 of 1965.

22. Lyndon B. Johnson, Message of the President, May 13, 1965, *United States Code*, title 5, Appendix, Reorganization Plan No. 2 of 1965.

23. United States National Oceanic and Atmospheric Administration, "NOAA—At It's [sic] Creation: The Environmental Science Services Administration," A History of NOAA, at http://www.history.noaa.gov/legacy/noaahistory_7.html.

24. United States National Oceanic and Atmospheric Administration, "National Weather Service Celebrates 125th Anniversary," NOAA History, at http://www.history.noaa.gov/legacy/nws125/html.

25. House Committee on Science, Space, and Technology, *The Modernization of the Weather Service: Hearing*, 100th Cong., 2d sess., 1988.

26. "Modernization of the National Weather Service," *Code of Federal Regulations* title 15, sections 946.1 et seq.; United States General Accounting Office, "National Weather Service Modernization and NOAA Fleet Issues," Testimony, GAO/T-AIMD/GGD-99-97 (1999); United States General Accounting Office, "National Weather Service Modernization and Weather Satellite Program," Testimony, GAO/T-AIMD-00-86 (2000).

27. Certified Consulting Meteorologist Jan Null of Golden Gate Weather Services has examined the weather predictions of *The Old Farmer's Almanac* for accuracy. His comparison of the predictions against the actual weather data for San Francisco indicates that the predictions were incorrect over 60% of the time

during the period examined. See Jan Null, Review of *1999–2000 Farmer's Almanac*, at http://ggweather.com/almanac/farmers.htm.

28. A secret formula can be protected by state law protecting trade secrets. For a description of trade secret law, see http://en.wikipedia.org/wiki/Trade_secret.

29. "History of the *Old Farmer's Almanac:* How the Almanac Got Off to a Good Start," at http://www.almanac.com/history.

30. Whitnah, *A History of the United States Weather Bureau*, 22–23.

31. "The Weather: Events and Probabilities," *New York Times*, May 5, 1872.

32. United States Department of Agriculture, *Annual Reports of the Department of Agriculture for the Year Ended June 30, 1910* (Washington, DC: Government Printing Office, 1911), 39.

33. Frederick K. Lutgens and Edward J. Tarbuck, *The Atmosphere*, 10th ed. (Upper Saddle River, NJ: Pearson Prentice Hall, 2007), 364.

34. Richard A. Kerr, "Man and Machine Forecast Big Snow," *Science*, New Series 235, no. 4795 (March 20, 1987): 1461.

35. John Pain, "Federal Forecasters Got Hurricane Right," *Associated Press*, September 16, 2005.

36. Whitnah, *History of the United States Weather Bureau*, 12.

37. United States National Oceanic and Atmospheric Administration, "National Weather Service Celebrates 125th Anniversary," NOAA History, at http://www.history.noaa.gov/legacy/nws125/html.

38. U.S. Department of Agriculture, Weather Bureau, *Report of the Chief of the Weather Bureau, 1923–1924*, House Document No. 446, 68th Cong., 2d sess. (Washington, DC: Government Printing Office, 1925), 6.

39. United States National Oceanic and Atmospheric Administration, "National Weather Service Celebrates 125th Anniversary," NOAA History, at http://www.history.noaa.gov/legacy/nws125/html.

40. *Report of the Secretary of War, Volume IV*, Ex. Doc. 1, part 2, 47th Cong., 1st sess. (Washington, DC: Government Printing Office, 1881), 52–53.

41. P.L. 4, 60 Stat. 4, February 12, 1946.

42. P.L. 691, 60 Stat. 944, August 8, 1946.

43. Utah Department of Transportation Avalanche Forecaster Job Announcement, September 19, 2006, at http://www.avalanche.org/special.htm.

44. D. Grifoni, G. Carreras, F. Sabatini, and G. Zipoli, "UV Hazard on a Summer's Day Under Mediterranean Conditions, and the Protective Role of a Beach Umbrella," *International Journal of Biometeorology* 50 (November 2005): 75.

45. *Code of Federal Regulations* title 15, section 946.4(d), (e), (f), (g), (h), and (i).

46. U.S. Department of Commerce National Oceanic and Atmospheric Administration, "Agriculture, Fire Weather Service and Marine Radiofax Privatization Questions and Answers," at http://www.nws.noaa.gov/im/agfirqa.htm.

47. *National Weather Services Duties Act of 2005*, S. 786, 109th Cong., 1st sess., April 14, 2005.

48. Dawn Withers, "Bill Curbs Access to National Weather Service: Senator Supports Private Companies," *Albuquerque Journal*, May 30, 2005.

49. United States National Oceanic and Atmospheric Administration, "Policy on Partnerships in the Provision of Environmental Information," January 2006, at http://www.weather.gov/partnershippolicy/FinalClarifiedPolicy011906.pdf.

50. *United States Code*, title 18, section 2074.

51. "Censorship Code Issued for Press," *New York Times*, January 15, 1942; "Text of War News Code of Office of Censorship," *New York Times*, December 11, 1943.

52. "History of the *Old Farmer's Almanac*: How the Almanac Got Off to a Good Start," at http://www.almanac.com/history; "The Old Farmer," *New York Times*, November 12, 1944.

53. "First Lady is Censored," *New York Times*, August 18, 1942.

54. "Airmen Must Tell Weather in Code," *New York Times*, March 21, 1942.

55. *United States v. Dellarosa*, 30 M.J. 255 (1990).

56. "From the China Meteorological Administration," *Weatherwise* 59, no. 1 (January 1, 2006): 14.

57. c. 9, section 1, 1st Cong., 1st sess., August 7, 1789.

58. c. 17, section 2, 2d Cong., 1st sess., April 12, 1792.

59. c. 9, section 3, 1st Cong., 1st sess., August 7, 1789.

60. c. 112, sections 8 and 12, 32d Cong., 1st sess., August 31, 1852.

61. Michigan Lighthouse Conservancy, "Lighthouses: A Brief Administrative History," The United States Lighthouse Service, at http://www.michiganlights.com/lighthouseservice.htm.

62. The Weather Doctor, "Two Flags Flying," Weather Almanac for October 1999, at http://www.islandnet.com/~see/weather/almanac/arc_1999/alm99oct.htm.

63. "Coastal Warning Display Towers," at http://www.unm.edu/~rowlett/lighthouse/storm_warning_towers.htm.

64. U.S. National Oceanic and Atmospheric Administration, "National Weather Service Retires Its Coastal Warning Display Program," Marine Forecasts, at http://www.weather.gov/om/marine/cwd.htm.

65. United States Department of Agriculture and United States Department of Commerce Federal Emergency Management Agency, *Saving Lives with an All-Hazard Warning Network* (Washington, DC: 1999), 7.

66. Emergency Alert System, *Code of Federal Regulations* title 47, sections 11.1 and 11.11.

67. "International Storm Signals," H.R. Ex. Doc. 288, 51st Cong., 2d sess., February 26, 1891.

68. United States Department of Commerce. National Oceanic and Atmospheric Administration, National Weather Service Weather Glossary, at http://www.weather.gov/glossary/.

69. United States Department of Commerce National Climatic Data Center, "The Northeast Snowfall Impact Scale (NESIS)," at http://www.ncdc.noaa.gov/oa/climate/research/snow-nesis/.

70. See National Science and Technology Council, *Effective Disaster Warnings* (2000).

## CHAPTER 2: "TAMING THE WEATHER" THROUGH SCIENCE AND TECHNOLOGY

1. Anthony Ripley, "Flood Kills 155 in South Dakota; 5,000 Homeless," *New York Times*, June 11, 1972.

2. "Cloud-Seeding for Rain Called Dakota 'Success,'" *New York Times*, January 9, 1963.

3. *Lunsford v. United States*, 570 F.2d 221 (8th Cir. 1977).

4. Patent protection is provided by federal statute. Patent Act, *U. S. Code* 35, §§ 1-376.

5. The large number of patents issued makes it impossible to provide a comprehensive list of devices, methods, and processes that have been invented to try to tame the weather. To search for other patents related to the weather, see the United States Patent and Trademark Office Web site at www.uspto.gov.

6. The construction of the thermometer in the early 1600s is attributed to Galileo Galilei, the Italian astronomer. Storm Dunlop, *A Dictionary of Weather* (Oxford: Oxford University Press, 2001, reissued 2005), s.v. "Galilei, Galileo."

7. The mercury-in-glass barometer is attributed to Italian philosopher and mathematician Evangelista Torricelli in mid-1600s. Ibid., s.v. "Torricelli, Evangelista."

8. Use of the weather vane to determine wind direction traces back to fifth century B.C. Greece. Donald R. Whitnah, *A History of the United States Weather Bureau* (Urbana, IL: Illinois University Press, 1965), 1.

9. An 18" bowl was used to measure rainfall in India in 400 B.C. Ibid.

10. "U.S. Military Using Kestrel® Pocket Weather™ Meters for Efforts in Afghanistan," http://www.nkhome.com/press/press8.html.

11. Richard Kellerman. 1999. Vane anemometer with thermally isolated sensors. US Patent 6,257,074, filed May 27, 1999, and issued July 10, 2001.

12. Henry Frank and Michael Frank Johnnie. 1999. Tornado alarm system. US Patent 6,034,608, filed June 22, 1999, and issued March 7, 2000.

13. Ronald R. Moore and Michael D. Collins. 2004. Personal severe weather warning microchip and pressure sensor. US Patent 7,066,020, filed May 20, 2004, and issued June 27, 2006.

14. Donald S. Frankel and James S. Draper. 1992. Neural network for predicting lightning. US Patent 5,140,523, filed December 14, 1990, and issued August 18, 1992.

15. Takashi Kiyohara. 1993. Disposable foot warmer. US Patent 5,331,688, filed March 12, 1993, and issued July 26, 1994.

16. Geoffrey L. Dodge. 2003. Disposable rainwear. US Patent 6,658,665, filed August 24, 2001, and issued December 9, 2003.

17. "Battelle, R.G. Barry Develop 'Heat Seat,' Cushion Keeps You Toasty Warm Up to 8 Hours," Press Release (1995), http://www.battelle.org/news/95/p4seat.stm; Gideon Salee. 1995. Microwaved-activated thermal storage material; and method. US Patent 5,424,519, filed September 21, 1993, and issued June 13, 1995.

18. See Chapter 5 on crime for more information about penalties for child death from hyperthermia.

19. Teresa Riordan, "Patents; A Car Temperature Alarm is Designed to Cry Out to Save the Life of a Child Who Cannot," *New York Times*, August 30, 2004; Carolyn M. Thornton. 1998. Child alert system for automobiles. US Patent 5,793,291, filed May 13, 1996, and issued August 11, 1998.

20. Marc A. Rossi. Warning system for detecting presence of a child in an infant seat. 2000. US Patent 6,104,293, filed September 7, 1999, and issued August 15, 2000.

21. Sandra Blake Toles. Child safety seat alarm system and method therefore. 2005. US Patent 6,909,365, filed January 6, 2003, and issued June 21, 2005.

22. Paul D. Kalce. Infant alarm system for an automobile. 2006. US Patent 6,998,988, filed April 21, 2004, and issued February 14, 2006.

23. Teresa Riordan, "Patents; A Car Temperature Alarm is Designed to Cry Out to Save the Life of a Child Who Cannot," *New York Times*, August 30, 2004; Mark S. Pelletier. Motor vehicle occupancy and high temperature alarm module. 2005. US Patent 6,940,400, filed March 16, 2004, and issued September 6, 2005.

24. "The windshield on every motor vehicle as defined by subdivision § 32-3-1(11) except farm tractors and motorcycles, shall be equipped with a device for cleaning rain, snow, or other moisture from the windshield, which device shall be operated by the driver of the vehicle. No person may operate a motor vehicle upon the highways unless such vehicle shall be equipped with such device in good working order capable of cleaning the windshield thereof and which device shall provide the driver a clear view of the highway." *South Dakota Statutes* § 32-15-7.

25. U.S. Department of Transportation, National Highway Traffic Safety Administration, "Federal Motor Vehicle Safety Standards: Interior Trunk Release," *Federal Register* 66 (August 17, 2001): 43113-01, codified at *Code of Federal Regulations* tit. 49, § 571.401.

26. Joseph Ferro. Emergency trunk interior release latch. 1995. US Patent 5,445,326, filed December 21, 1993, and issued August 29, 1995. This patent expired on August 29, 2003 for failure to pay maintenance fees.

27. *Cameron Gulbransen Kids and Cars Safety Act of 2005*, HR 2230, 109th Cong., 1st sess., May 10, 2005, http://thomas.loc.gov/cgi-bin/query/z?c109:H.R.2230:.

28. UNESCO, Expenditure on R&D [by country], 1996–2002, http://www.uis.unesco.org/TEMPLATE/html/Exceltables/science/R&DTables.xls.

29. Whitnah, *History of the United States Weather Bureau*, 10–11, citing Joseph Henry, *Annual Report of the Board of Regents of the Smithsonian Institution, for 1853* (Washington, DC: n.p., 1854), 238.

30. Ibid., 71–72, citing R.G. Dyrenforth, *Report of Department of Agriculture for Experiments in Rainmaking*, S. Exec. Doc. No. 45, 52d Cong., 1st sess., 1892.

31. Senate Select Committee on Small Business, *Government Patent Policies in Meteorology and Weather Modification—1962: Hearings*, 87th Cong., 2d sess., 1962, p. 4.

32. Whitnah, *History of the United States Weather Bureau*, 238.

33. U.S. National Aeronautics and Space Administration, *NASA: Supporting Earth System Science 2006*, http://nasadaacs.eos.nasa.gov/pdf/annual_2006.pdf.

34. Whitnah, *History of the United States Weather Bureau*, 233.

35. National Science Foundation, Annual Solicitation for Research in Support of the National Space Weather Program (NSWP), http://www.nsf.gov/pubs/2007/nsf07520/nsf07520.htm.

36. Government contract law and procurement is a complex, highly regulated area of law that will not be explained in detail in this book. For further

information on federal procurement law, see Federal Acquisitions Rules (FAR), http://www.acquisition.gov/.

37. Janet M. Carter, Joyce E. Williamson, and Ralph W. Teller, "The 1972 Black Hills-Rapid City Flood Revisited," *USGS Fact Sheet FS-037-02* (Washington, DC: U.S. Geological Survey, April 2002), http://pubs.usgs.gov/fs/fs-037-02/.

38. Rapid City, South Dakota Code of Ordinances § 17.28.010 et seq.

39. John A. Dracup, Edmond D.H. Cheng, Joanne M. Nigg, and Thomas A.Schroeder, *The New Year's Eve Flood on Oahu, Hawaii, December 31, 1987-January 1, 1988*, Natural Disaster Studies 1 (Washington, DC: National Academy Press, 1991), 51.

40. U.S. Senate Committee on Claims, *Relief of Sufferers in New Mexico Due to the Overflow of the Rio Grande and Its Tributaries*, 69th Cong., 1st sess., 1926, Rpt. No. 128; U.S. House of Representatives Committee on Claims, *Relief of Sufferers in New Mexico Due to the Overflow of the Rio Grande and Its Tributaries*, 69th Cong., 1st sess., 1926, Rpt. No. 1552.

41. "An Act to Authorize Federal Assistance to States and Local Governments in Major Disasters, and for Other Purposes," P.L. 81-875, 64 Stat. 1109, 81st Cong., 2d sess., September 30, 1950.

42. *Pacific Northwest Disaster Relief Act of 1965*, Public Law 89-41, 89th Cong., 1st sess, 1965.

43. *The New Year's Eve Flood on Oahu, Hawaii*, 51, citing Federal Disaster Protection Act of 1973, P.L. 93-234.

44. Bunning-Bereuter-Blumenauer Flood Insurance Reform Act of 2004, Public Law 108-264, 108th Cong., 2d sess, 2004.

45. *Flood Insurance Reform and Modernization Act of 2006*, H.R. 4973, introduced March 16, 2006.

46. *Coastal Barrier Resources Act*, Public Law 97-348, *U.S. Statutes at Large* 96 (1982): 1653, codified at *U. S. Code* 16, §§ 3501 et seq.

47. U.S. General Accounting Office, *Coastal Barriers: Development Occurring Despite Prohibitions Against Federal Assistance*, Report to the U.S. Senate Committee on Environment and Public Works, GAO/RCED-92-115 (1992): 2.

48. U.S. Fish and Wildlife Service, "What are Coastal Barriers?" http://www.fws.gov/habitatconservation/cbra2.htm.

49. U.S. Fish and Wildlife Services, Division of Federal Program Activities, The Coastal Barrier Resources Act: Harnessing the Power of Market Forces to Conserve America's Coasts and Save Taxpayers' Money (August 2002), http://www.fws.gov/habitatconservation/TaxpayerSavingsfromCBRA.pdf.

50. *"Swamp Lands Act,"* chap. 84, 31st Cong., 1st sess., September 28, 1850.

51. David Ropeik, "Floods Raise Scientific Dilemma: Efforts to Control Rivers Can Make Matters Worse Elsewhere," April 21, 2001, at http://www.msnbc.com/id/3077314/.

52. United States Department of Commerce, National Oceanic and Atmospheric Administration, *National Disaster Survey Report: The Great Flood of 1993* (1994): section 4.6.5, pp. 4–18.

53. 1972 Black Hills-Rapid City Flood Revisited: Photos of the Aftermath, at http://sd.water.usgs.gov/projects/1972flood/photos.html.

54. B. Drummond Ayres, Jr., "Flood-Periled Town Evacuated Infirm," *New York Times*, June 14, 1972.

55. Bruce B. Redpath, *Demolition of Ft. Meade Dam, Sturgis, South Dakota, June 1972* (Defense Technical Information Center, 1973).

56. U.S. Commission on Ocean Policy, *An Ocean Blueprint for the 21st Century: Final Report* (Washington, DC, 2004).

57. Whitnah, *A History of the United States Weather Bureau*, 71.

58. For a more detailed and scientific explanation of the creation of rain drops, see Frederick K. Lutgens and Edward J. Tarbuck, *The Atmosphere: An Introduction to Meteorology, 10th ed.* (Upper Saddle River, NJ: 2007), 143–149.

59. Daniel Ruggles. 1880. Method of precipitating rain-falls. US Patent 230,067, filed February 22, 1879, and issued July 13, 1880.

60. U.S. Department of Health and Human Services Agency for Toxic Substances and Disease Registry, "ToxFAQS for Hexachlorobenzene," CAS # 118-74-1 (September 2002), http://www.atsdr.cdc.gov/tfacts90.html#bookmark02.

61. Robert G. Knollenberg. 1971. Weather modification method. US Patent 3,613,992, filed March 25, 1996, and issued October 19, 1971 (urea); Thomas W. Slusher. 1978. Pyrotechnic cloud seeding composition.1978. US Patent 4,096,005, filed June 13, 1977, and issued June 20, 1978 (hexachlorobenzene); Robert L. Gerber. 1979.Weather modification automatic cartridge dispenser. US Patent 4,141,274, filed October 14, 1977, and issued February 27, 1979.

62. Samuel R. Carter, Jr.1972. Solar temperature inversion device. US Patent 3,666,176, filed March 3, 1970, and issued May 30, 1972.

63. Peter Cordani. 2001. Method of modifying weather. US Patent 6,315,213, filed June 21, 2000, and issued November 13, 2001.

64. U.S. National Oceanic and Atmospheric Administration Atlantic Oceanographic and Meteorological Laboratory Hurricane Research Division, "Subject: C5d) Why don't we try to destroy tropical cyclones by adding a water absorbing substance?" Frequently Asked Questions, http://www.aoml.noaa.gov/hrd/tcfaq/C5d.html.

65. David Longshore, *Encyclopedia of Hurricanes, Typhoons, and Cyclones* (New York: Facts on File, 1998), s.v. "Project Cirrus."

66. Ibid., s.v. "Project Stormfury."

67. "The Rainmakers Combining: Ready to Work on the Credulous Kansas Farmer," *New York Times*, April 12, 1893; "With Kansas Rainmakers: Harder to Down than the Old-Time Lightning-Rod Men," *New York Times*, April 17, 1893.

68. Bob Moen, "Wyoming Scientists to Begin Experimenting with Cloud Seeding," *Deseret Morning News*, December 22, 2005.

69. *Kansas Statutes Annotated* § 19-212f; Oklahoma Weather Modification Act, *Oklahoma Statutes Annotated* 82, §§ 1087.1 et seq.; *Vernon's Texas Statutes and Codes Annotated* 9, §§ 301.001 et seq.

70. Oklahoma Statutes Annotated 82, § 1087.8.

71. National Research Council Committee on the Status and Future Directions in U.S. Weather Modification Research and Operations, *Critical Issues in Weather Modification Research* (Washington, DC: National Academies Press, 2003).

72. *Weather Modification Research and Technology Transfer Authorization Act of 2005*, U.S. Senate, S. 517, reported to Senate as amended, December 8, 2005.

73. Letter from John H. Marburger, III, Director, Office of Science and Technology Policy, Executive Office of the President to Senator Kay Bailey Hutchison, United States Senate, December 13, 2005, http://www.legislative.noaa.gov/viewsletters/marburgerweathermodviewsletter121305.pdf.

74. Public Law 256, *U.S. Statutes at Large* 67 (1953): 559.

75. Public Law 85-510, *U.S. Statutes at Large* 72 (1958): 353, codified at *U. S. Code* 42, § 1862.

76. U.S. Senate, 90th Cong., 2d sess., 1968, S. Rep. 1137, 15.

77. Public Law 92-205, *U.S. Statutes at Large* 85 (1971): 735, codified at *U. S. Code* 15, § 330.

78. Code of Federal Regulations 15, § 908.3(a).

79. Code of Federal Regulations 15, § 908.3(c).

80. *Lunsford v. United States*, 570 F.2d 221 (8th Cir. 1977).

81. *U. S. Code* 33, § 702c.

82. Eric I. Hemel and Clifford G. Holderness, *An Environmentalist's Primer on Weather Modification* (Stanford, CA: Stanford Environmental Law Society, 1977), 71.

83. Ibid.

84. *Pennsylvania Natural Weather Assn. v. Blue Ridge Weather Modification Assn.*, 44 Pa. D. & C. 2d 749, 760 (1968).

85. *Slutsky v. City of New York*, 197 Misc. 730, 97 N.Y.S.2d 238 (Sup. Ct. N.Y. Co. 1950).

86. *Pennsylvania Natural Weather Assn. v. Blue Ridge Weather Modification Assn.*, 44 Pa. D. & C. 2d 749, 756 (1968).

87. *Southwest Weather Research, Inc. v. Duncan*, 319 S.W. 2d 940 (Tex. Civ. App. 1958); *Southwest Weather Research, Inc. v. Rounsaville*, 320 S.W. 2d 211 (Tex. Civ. App. 1958).

88. *Pennsylvania Natural Weather Assn. v. Blue Ridge Weather Modification Assn.*, 44 Pa. D. & C. 2d 749 (1968).

## CHAPTER 3: GOVERNMENTAL LIABILITY FOR INJURY TO INDIVIDUALS

1. *Slevin v. City of New York*, 122 N.Y.S. 2d 228 (City of New York, City Court, 1953).

2. The installation of warning signs such as "Slippery When Wet" and "Bridge Ices Before Road" is a part of highway and road maintenance. The decisions about sign postings are made by the state department of transportation. The design of the signs is mandated by federal law under the Highway Safety Act of 1966. See *United States Code* 23, §§ 109(d) and 402(a); U.S. Department of Transportation Federal Highway Administration, *Manual on Uniform Traffic Control Devices for Streets and Highways, 2003 Edition*, http://mutcd.fhwa.dot.gov/pdfs/2003/pdf-index.htm.

3. *Black's Law Dictionary*, 8th ed., s.v. "Sovereign immunity."

4. The Tucker Act identifies the claims that the federal Court of Claims has jurisdiction to hear. Tucker Act, *United States Code* 28, § 1346(a).

5. The Federal Tort Claims Act identifies the types of tort claims that can be brought against the federal government. It also establishes the exceptions to right

to sue for wrongful acts by the government, such as the prohibition on suit for discretionary functions. Discretionary functions are those that require the government's employees to use their own judgment to implement policy. On the other hand, ministerial functions are those tasks that government agencies and employees are mandated to perform and over which they have no discretion in how they perform the function. Federal Tort Claims Act, *United States Code*, 28, §§ 1346(b) and 2671-2680.

6. *Bradley v. Board of County Commissioners of Butler County*, 20 Kan. App. 2d 602, 890 P. 2d 1228 (1995).

7. *Griffin v. Rogers*, 232 Kan. 168, 175, 653 P. 2d 463 (1982).

8. *Bradley v. Board of County Commissioners of Butler County*, 20 Kan. App. 2d 602, 890 P. 2d 1228 (1995).

9. Study of the incident by a state commission concluded that a design flaw contributed to the collapse of the wall when winds of between 90 and 100 mph hit it. Kevin Sack, "Design Flaw is Cited in School Collapse," *New York Times*, January 11, 1990.

10. Robert D. McFadden, "120 at Lunch When Hurricane-Force Gust Strikes—4 Are Critically Hurt by Flying Debris," *New York Times*, November 17, 1989.

11. *Litchhult v. Reiss*, 149 Misc. 2d 584, 566 N.Y.S. 2d 834 (Sup. Ct. Orange Co. 1991).

12. *Litchhult v. Reiss*, 183 A.D. 2d 1067, 583 N.Y.S. 2d 671 (1992).

13. *Gill v. United States*, 285 F. Supp. 253, 259-260 (E.D. Tex. 1968).

14. Visual Flight Rules (VFR) require a certain flight visibility distance for operation of an aircraft. *Code of Federal Regulations*, 14, § 91.155 (2006).

15. *Gill v. United States*, 429 F. 2d 1072 (5th Cir. 1970).

16. The lighthouse on Chandeleur Island was destroyed by Hurricane Katrina in 2005. Chandeleur Island, LA, at http://www.lighthousefriends.com/light.asp?ID=810.

17. The dissent in the case noted that navigators were warned that the lighthouse on Chandeleur Island was an "unwatched light" by the Coast Guard's *Light List, Atlantic and Gulf Coasts of the United States* (1951). *Indian Towing Co. v. United States*, 350 U.S. 61, 76 S.Ct. 122, 100 L.Ed. 48 (1955).

18. *Schinmann v. United States*, 618 F. Supp. 1030 (E.D. Wash. 1985).

19. Loran L. Lewis, Jr., "The Law of Icy Sidewalks in New York State," *Yale Law Journal* 6, no. 5 (April 1897): 258–262, 258.

20. The government can also claim other defenses such as assumption of risk and open and obvious dangers to prevent liability. See *Wilson v. City of Charlestown*, 90 Mass. 137 (1864) (in holding for the town, the court reasoned that person who knows the way is dangerous cannot look to the town for indemnity if he is injured).

21. New Jersey Tort Claims Act, *New Jersey Statutes* § 59:4-7 (2005); *California Gov. Code* § 831.

22. *Kaveny v. City of Troy*, 108 N.Y. 571, 15 N.E. 726 (1888).

23. See "Nightfall Brings Paralysis to Surface Transportation," *New York Times*, December 27, 1947; "More Heatless Homes Predicted as Snow Impedes Fuel Deliveries," *New York Times*, December 17, 1947; "Fast Rate of Fall: 1888 [Blizzard of 1888] Mark Topped in 12 Hours as City Gets Brunt of Storm," *New York Times*, December 27, 1947; "Note to Big Snow Victims [item explains ticket exchange

policies for Broadway theaters]," *New York Times*, January 11, 1948; Grace Barrett, "Cold of 8.9° Sets Low for Winter; New Wave on Way," *New York Times*, January 16, 1948.

24. "Removal of Big Snow Cost City $6,605,000," *New York Times*, January 16, 1948.

25. See *Rapoport v. City of New York*, 281 A.D. 33, 117 N.Y.S. 2d 408 (1952) (three and one-half days was not a reasonable amount of time for the city to clear all streets and sidewalks).

26. *Slevin v. City of New York*, 122 N.Y.S. 2d 228 (City Court, City of New York, 1953).

27. *Ziencina v. County of Cook*, 188 Ill. 2d 1, 719 N.E. 2d 739 (1999).

28. Ibid.

29. "Snow plowing shall begin when 1 inch of snow has accumulated . . . When snow plowing leaves a glazed or snow covered surface, the plowing shall be accompanied or immediately followed with applications of cinders or mixture of cinders and salt for melting and traction purposes." Columbia (Mo.) Public Works Department, *Snow and Ice Control Operations Manual* (2005): 16.

30. "Rule: If little or no wind and no low clouds are forecast and the expected minimum temperature (at the bridge) is as low or lower than the dew point, and the dew point is below 32 degrees, expect frost to form on the bridge floor." *Hunt v. State of Iowa*, 252 N.W. 2d 715, 719 (Iowa 1977).

31. Ibid.

32. *Reliant Airlines, Inc. v. Broome County (NY)*, No. 96-9419 (2d Cir. July 25, 1997).

33. "Passengers File Suit Over Chicago Runway Accident,' *Aviation Litigation Reporter* 23, no. 23 (January 4, 2006), http://news.findlaw.com/andrews/pl/avi/20060104/20060104bennett.html.

34. A class action lawsuit allows large numbers of people to join together in a single lawsuit to settle common issues of law and fact.

35. *McWaters v. Federal Emergency Management Agency*, Civ. No. 05-5488, Plaintiffs' Memorandum in Opposition to Defendants' Motions to Dismiss, January 30, 2006.

36. Howard Manly, "Lawsuit Alleges Feds Failed Katrina Victims," *Bay State Banner (Boston)*, December 1, 2005.

37. See http://www.centralstate.edu/.

38. Nathaniel Sheppard, Jr., "Xenia, Ohio, Rebuilt After Tornado, Still Faces Problems," *New York Times*, April 10, 1978.

39. Governmental Immunity Act, *Utah Code Annotated* § 63-30-10(11) and (13).

40. *Blackner v. State Department of Transportation*, 48 P.3d 949 (Utah 2002).

41. See David Margolick, "Weighing the Risks and Rights of Homelessness," *New York Times*, December 8, 1985.

42. See New York State's statutory law on civil commitment at *McKinney's Mental Hygiene Law* §§ 9.39 and 9.41.

43. *In the Matter of Webb*, 186 Or. App. 404, 63 P.2d 1258 (2003).

44. Of course, exposure to extreme heat can be as deadly as extreme cold. Phoenix and the surrounding area were reported to have had at least 32 heat-related deaths of homeless people during the summer of 2005. "'All Our Problem

Now': Mentally Ill Homeless Cost the Valley's Cities on Many Levels, From ERs to Parks to Jails," *The Arizona Republic*, September 4, 2005, at http://www.azcentral. com/arizonarepublic/news/articles/0904mhomeless-main04.html.

45. "Rebecca Smith, Who Said No," *New York Times*, January 29, 1982.

46. Other cities also have programs to address the dangers faced by homeless persons in extremely cold weather. The City of Boston has programs to increase the number of shelter spaces available on extremely cold nights by opening expansion facilities. See City of Boston Emergency Shelter Commission, *2005 Extreme Cold Weather Emergency Response*, at http://www.cityofboston.gov/snow/ PDFs/dec05_cold.pdf. Baltimore has "Code Blue," a cold weather emergency response plan, which includes response in emergency situations by a three-person "Death Prevention Team," which can call for mental competence evaluations of individuals who refuse assistance. Baltimore City "Code Blue" Cold Weather Emergency Response Plan, at http://www.baltimorecity.gov/news/codeblue.html.

47. David Margolick, "Weighing the Risks and Rights of Homelessness," *New York Times*, December 8, 1985.

48. Norman Siegel and Robert Levy, "Helping New York City's Homeless; The Real Problem is Housing," *New York Times*, December 17, 1985.

49. New York City Police Department Operations Order No. 111, November 20, 1985 (amended December 19, 1985 and January 16, 1986).

50. Koch's original plan from the previous winter provided for help only on days when the temperature, including wind chill, was 5°F or below. Josh Barbanel, "Saving Homeless from Themselves: A New Policy Creates New Disputes," *New York Times*, December 7, 1985.

51. Luis R. Marcos, Neal L. Cohen, David Nardacci, and Joan Brittain, "Psychiatry Takes to the Streets: The New York City Initiative for the Homeless Mentally Ill," *American Journal of Psychiatry* 147, no. 11 (November 1990): 1557–1561.

52. *Kneipp v. Tedder*, 95 F.3d 1199 (3d Cir. 1996).

53. Flood Control Act of 1928, *United States Code* 33, § 702c.

54. *Corpus Juris Secundum*, s.v. "eminent domain," at § 83 (2005).

55. Disaster Relief and Emergency Assistance Act, *United States Code* 42, §§ 5121 and 5173.

56. *Easton v. Gilbert Southern Corp.*, No. 94-505-CIV-UNGARO-BENAGES (S.D. Fla. November 23, 1994).

## CHAPTER 4: CIVIL LIABILITIES FOR WEATHER-RELATED HARM

1. *Patton v. United States of America Rugby Football Union*, 381 Md. 627, 851 A. 2d 566 (Ct. App. 2004).

2. National Center for State Courts, *Examining the Work of State Courts, 2005: A National Perspective from the Court Statistics Project* (2006), 22, http://www. ncsconline.org/D_Research/csp/2005_files/0-EWWhole%20Document_final_1.pdf.

3. For definitions and basic discussion of tort law, negligence, and duty, see *Black's Law Dictionary*, 8th ed., s.v. "Duty"; and *The Oxford Companion to American Law*, ed. Kermit Hall (Oxford: Oxford University Press, 2002), s.v. "Torts."

4. *Cunningham v. Braum's Ice Cream and Dairy Stores*, 276 Kan. 883, 80 P.2d 35 (2003).

5. A 1907 case did impose a duty of care and shelter for a business invitee. A cattle-buyer fell ill while at a customer's house and asked to stay the night. His request was refused and, instead, he was helped to his horse and cutter and headed on his way home on a January night in Minnesota. He apparently fell from the cutter not far from the defendants' home and was found by a passing farmer nearly frozen to death. The court ruled that humanity demanded that they "minister to plaintiff in his distress" and imposed a legal duty of care. *Depue v. Flatteau*, 100 Minn. 299, 111 N.W. 1 (1907).

6. The comparative negligence doctrine has been adopted by most states. While contributory negligence completely barred recovery for the plaintiff if she had any fault in her injury, comparative negligence or comparative fault doctrine allows a proportional recovery based on the allocated faults of the plaintiff and defendant. For complete discussion of tort law doctrines, see Dan B. Dobbs, *The Law of Torts* (St. Paul, MN: West Group, 2000).

7. *Patton v. United States of America Rugby Football Union*, 381 Md. 627, 632, 851 A.2d 566, 568 (Ct. App. 2004).

8. Perhaps a professional player who is an employee under contract to a team would have greater claim to dependence on the officials calling a game to ensure safety of players from inclement weather. However, as is noted in a later section, professional athletes are covered by workers' compensation laws and cannot avail themselves of tort law claims unless the coach or official intentionally caused harm.

9. *Patton v. United States of America Rugby Football Union*, 381 Md. 627, 851 A.2d 566 (Ct. App. 2004).

10. *Pichardo v. North Patchogue Medford Youth Athletic Association*, 172 A.D. 2d 814, 569 N.Y.S. 2d 186 (1991).

11. After the summer of 2001 saw three deaths from heatstroke in preseason football training, the following two summers had no deaths from heatstroke. Possibly the publicity surrounding the incidents in 2001 affected the way training was handled the following year. National Center for Catastrophic Sports Injury Research, *Annual Survey of Football Injury Research, 1931–2005*, at http://www.unc.edu/depts/nccsi/FootballInjuryData.htm.

12. Thomas R. Hurst and James N. Knight, "Coaches' Liability for Athletes' Injuries and Deaths," *Seton Hall Journal of Sport Law* 13 (2003): 27–51; National Center for Catastrophic Sports Injury Research, *Annual Survey of Football Injury Research, 1931–2005*, at http://www.unc.edu/depts/nccsi/FootballInjuryData.htm.

13. When Stringer arrived at the hospital on the day of his collapse, his core body temperature was 108.8°F. *Stringer v. Minnesota Vikings Football Club*, 705 N.W. 2d 746, 748 (Minn. 2005). "Life threatening hyperthermia typically starts in humans when their temperatures rise to 105–107°F (40.6–41.7°C). Only a few days at this extraordinarily high temperature level is likely to result in the deterioration of internal organs and death." Dennis O'Neil, "Adapting to Climate Extremes," *Human Biological Adaptability: An Introduction to Human Responses to Common Environmental Stresses* (2006), at http://anthro.palomar.edu/adapt/adapt_2.htm.

14. Donald T. Meier, "Primary Assumption of Risk and Duty in Football Indirect Injury Cases: A Legal Workout from the Tragedies on the Training Ground for American Values," *Virginia Sports and Entertainment Law Journal* 2 (2002): 96.

15. *Stringer v. Minnesota Vikings Football Club*, Complaint in Wrongful Death Action, Filed January 14, 2002, Minnesota District Court (Hennepin County), available at http://news.lp.findlaw.com/hdocs/docs/sports/strngrvkngs011502cmp.pdf.

16. *Stringer v. Minnesota Vikings*, Complaint, 4–9.

17. Meier, "Primary Assumption of Risk and Duty in Football Indirect Injury Cases," 96.

18. *Stringer v. Minnesota Vikings Football Club*, 705 N.W. 2d 746 (Minn. 2005).

19. John O. Spengler and Brian P. Burket, "Sport Safety Statutes and Inherent Risk: A Comparison Study of Sport Specific Legislation," *Journal of Legal Aspects of Sport* 11 (2001): 161.

20. *Vermont Statutes Annotated* 12, § 1037.

21. A "double black diamond trail" designation means that the trail is more difficult to ski than those trails designated "most difficult." *Nelson v. Snowridge*, 818 F. Supp. 80, 81 (D. Vt. 1993).

22. Ibid., 83.

23. *Gasper v. Freidel*, 450 N.W. 2d 226 (S.D. 1990) (a high school coach who held a summer conditioning program was not liable for injuries sustained by student athlete because the program was a discretionary element of the coach's duties to condition athletes); *Lupash v. City of Seal Beach*, 75 Cal. App. 4th 1428, 89 Cal. Rptr. 2d 920 (1999) (the city was not liable for injuries sustained by a participant in a junior lifeguard competition allegedly caused by instructor's cajoling of participant to continue despite fatigue).

24. *Stowers v. Clinton Central School Corp.*, 855 N.E. 2d 739 (Ind. Ct. App. 2006). At the close of the new trial that the Court of Appeals has ordered, the jury is to receive specific instructions on assumption of risk (or incurred risk, as it is known in Indiana) and on the required language in a release form to relieve the school of liability for negligence. Given the recentness of this decision, it is not possible to know the ultimate outcome of the case at the time of publication.

25. Indiana High School Athletic Association (IHSAA) rules limit the first 2 days of preseason practice to no more than two 90-minute sessions per day or less with a 2-hour break between sessions. IHSAA Rule 54-4 as cited in *Stowers v. Clinton Central School Corp.*, 855 N.E. 2d 739, 743 (Ind. Ct. App. 2006). The coach's practice sessions in 2001 went for 2.5 hours followed by a 90-minute rest period and 20-minute team meeting in the morning and for 2 hours in the afternoon.

26. *Stowers v. Clinton Central*, at 748.

27. Of course, some coaches in schools and in community activities are volunteers. These coaches are protected in several states by "volunteer statutes" that prevent them from being held liable for injuries that result from negligence in connection with their coaching. Thomas R. Hurst and James N. Knight, "Coaches' Liability for Athletes' Injuries and Deaths," *Seton Hall Journal of Sport Law* 13 (2003): 47. The federal government has also enacted a volunteer protection act that may apply to individuals who coach for organized charitable organizations such as Little League baseball. Volunteer Protection Act of 1997, *United States Code* 42, § 14501 (1997).

28. *Prince v. Louisville Municipal School District*, 741 So. 2d 207 (Miss. 1999).

29. Harry E. Figgie, Jr., "Football Faces a 100-Yard Loss," *New York Times*, October 9, 1988.

30. Joseph J. Tribbia and Richard A. Anthes, "Scientific Basis for Modern Weather Prediction," *Science* 237, no. 4814 (July 31, 1987): 497.

31. This phenomenon, frequently referred to as the "butterfly effect," is discussed in chaos theory. "Specifically, two very similar atmospheric disturbances may, over time, develop into two very different weather patterns. One may intensify, becoming a major disturbance, while the other withers and dissipates." This metaphor and theory are attributed to Edward Lorenz from the Massachusetts Institute of Technology. Frederick K. Lutgens and Edward J. Tarbuck, *The Atmosphere: An Introduction to Meteorology, Tenth Edition* (2007): 355–356. For a demonstration of the Lorenz Attractor, see Michael Cross, "The Butterfly Effect," at http://www.its.caltech.edu/~mcc/chaos_new/Lorenz.html.

32. *Brandt v. The Weather Channel*, 42 F. Supp. 2d 1344 (S.D. Fla. 1999).

33. *In the Matter of Cornfield*, 365 F. Supp. 2d 271, 279 (E.D. N.Y. 2004).

34. Alison O'Leary Murray, "Private Forecasters Help Towns Weather the Storm," *Boston Globe*, January 8, 2006, http://www.boston.com/news/local/articles/2006/01/08/private_forecasters_help_towns_weather_the_storm/.

35. Roberta Klein, "Bad Weather? Then Sue the Weatherman! Part II: Legal Liability for Private Sector Forecasts," *Bulletin of the American Meteorological Society* 83, no. 12 (December 1, 2002): 1801–1807.

36. Steve Levine, "Ill Wind Blows Profits to Private Forecasters," *Wall Street Journal*, October 13, 2005, B1, quoting Ron Sznaider, Vice President, Meteorlogix. See http://www.meteorlogix.com/welcome.cfm for company information.

37. Cheyenne, Wyoming's storm of August 1985 killed 12 people and flooded the city. The storm remained over the city for three hours, pouring down rain and pelting down hail. The city received more than half of its total annual rainfall in 3 hours that day. Most of the lives were lost when an 8-foot-high wall of water plunged down a drainage canal. James Coates, "Terrifying Flood Leaves 11 Dead in Cheyenne," *Chicago Tribune*, August 3, 1985.

38. *Mostert v. CBL & Associates*, 741 P. 2d 1090 (Wy. 1987).

39. The dissenting opinion by Justice Cardine in *Mostert* noted that the extension of liability beyond the business premises subjects the owner to liability for accidents that happen to customers at locations over which she has no control, no ability to correct defects, and no control over the actions or risks undertaken by the customer. *Mostert v. CBL & Associates*, 741 P. 2d 1090, 1104 (Wy. 1987). The Supreme Court of Kansas agreed with Justice Cardine's assessment of the majority ruling in *Mostert*, making clear that Kansas' premises liability did not extend off premises. *Cunningham v. Braum's Ice Cream and Dairy Stores*, 276 Kan. 883, 889-890, 80 P.2d 35, 39–40 (2003).

40. *Dykema v. Gus Macker Enterprises, Inc.*, 196 Mich. App. 6, 492 N.W. 2d 472 (1992).

41. *Hames v. State*, 808 S.W. 2d 41 (Tenn. 1991). Other cases that involve lightning and golf courses have focused on the duty of a golf course to post signs regarding the safety procedures, if any, that the golf course uses to protect golfers from lightning. See *Maussner v. Atlantic City Country Club, Inc.*, 299 N.J. Super. 535, 691 A.2d 826 (1997); *Sall v. T's, Inc.*, 34 Kan. App. 2d 296, 117 P. 3d 896 (2005).

42. *Home Insurance Company and City of Wilmington v. Accu-Weather, Inc.*, Civil Action Number 98C-JN-93 (Superior Court of Delaware, New Castle, May 13, 1992).

43. *Gadowski v. Union Oil of Boston*, 326 F. 2d 524, 525 (1st Cir. 1964).

44. See David H. Estes, *Premises Liability for Owners and Occupiers of Real Property: A Legal Research Guide* (Buffalo, NY: William S. Hein & Co., 2000), 2–3, citing Restatement (Second) of Torts sections 329, 330, and 332 (1965).

45. L.S. Tellier, "Liability for Injury to Person in Street by Glass Falling from Window, Door, or Wall," *A. L. R. 2d* 81 (1993): 897.

46. George L. Blum, "Liability of Owner of Store, Office, or Similar Place of Business to Invitee Falling on Tracked-In Water or Snow," *A.L.R. 5th* 123 (2005 update): section 2a.

47. Dan B. Dobbs, *The Law of Torts*, section 235 at page 605 (2000).

48. *Laurendine v. CCA Associated Limited Partnership*, No. 257775 (Michigan Court of Appeals, March 21, 2006).

49. Ladders are not the only products with labels warning about use during certain weather conditions. Propane tanks have warnings about storage in direct sunlight. *Jone v. Coleman Corp.*, 183 S.W. 3d 600 (Mo. App. 2005). Ski areas place notices about weather conditions on lift tickets. *Gerischer v. Snowstar Corp.*, No. 05-0241 (Iowa Court of Appeals, May 10, 2006). Pesticides include warnings about spraying in windy conditions. *United States v. Wabash Valley Service Co.*, 426 F. Supp. 2d 835 (S.D. Ill. 2006). Although the bottles do not show warning labels, soda bottles exposed to hot weather have been known to explode. *Ruping v. Great Atlantic & Pacific Tea Co.*, 283 A. D. 204, 126 N.Y.S. 2d 687 (1953); *Royal Crown Bottling Co. v. Ward*, 520 S.W. 2d (Tex. Ct. Civ. App. 1975).

50. *Orenski v. Zaremba Management Co.*, No. 80402 (Ohio Ct. App. June 20, 2002).

51. *Selby v. Conquistador Apartments*, 990 P.2d 491 (Wy. 1999).

52. Ibid.

53. *Valance v. VI-Doug, Inc.*, 2002 Wy. 113, 50 P.2d 697 (2002). This case was sent back to the trial court for further action.

54. George L. Blum, "Comparative Negligence, Contributory Negligence and Assumption of Risk in Action Against Owner of Store, Office, or Similar Place of Business by Invitee Falling on Tracked-in Water or Snow," *A.L.R. 5th* 83 (2004 update): section 8.

55. *Cook v. Arrington*, 183 Ga. App. 384, 358 S.E.2d 869 (1987).

56. *Curtis v. Traders Nat. Bank*, 314 Ky. 765, 237 S.W. 2d 76 (1951).

57. *Picariello v. Linares & Rescigno Bank*, 127 N.J.L. 63, 21 A.2d 343 (N.J. Sup. Ct. 1941).

58. Dan B. Dobbs, *The Law of Torts* § 199 (St. Paul, Minn.: West Group, 2000).

59. *Bolson v. Kuhn*, 2003 Westlaw 21458574 (Iowa App. June 25, 2003).

60. *Wiggins v. Goddard*, 1999 Westlaw 33441268 (Mich. App. June 4, 1999).

61. *Levey v. DeNardo*, 555 Pa. 514, 725 A. 2d 733 (1999).

62. *Stober v. McCracken*, 2001 Westlaw 704368 (Mich. App. March 20, 2001), *1.

63. *Black's Law Dictionary*, 6th ed. (St. Paul: WestGroup, 1990), s.v. "act of God," "act of providence."

64. *Jahanger v. Purolator Sky Courier*, 615 F. Supp. 29, 32-33 (1985).

65. *Southern Pacific Co. v. Loden*, 508 P.2d 347 (1973).

66. *Wald v. Pittsburgh, C., C. & St. L. R. Co.*, 35 L.R.A. 356, 162 Ill. 545, 44 N.E. 888, 53 Am. St. Rep. 332 (1896).

67. See Gerald I. Katz and Stephen W. Smith, "Stormy Weather: Material Price Increases and *Force Majeure*," *Construction Accounting and Taxation* 15, no. 6 (2005): 46.

## CHAPTER 5: CRIME AND WEATHER

1. *Simpson v. Sheriff, Clark County*, 86 Nev. 803 (1970).

2. The issue of looting versus finding food needed for survival made the news following Hurricane Katrina. Photo captions were criticized for describing a picture of a person of a color as "looting a grocery store" and a picture of a white person as "finding bread and soda from a local grocery store." See "Some 'loot' food...Others 'find' it" at http://criticalresistance.org/katrina/press-katrinaLoot.html (last visited August 26, 2006).

3. "Police, Residents Loot New Orleans Stores after Storm," *Columbia Daily Tribune*, August 31, 2005, http://archive.columbiatribune.com/2005/aug/20050831news017.asp; "Business Owners Survey Mess Left Behind By Storm, Looters," *Columbia Daily Tribune*, September 18, 2005, http://www.columbiatribune.com/2005/Sep/20050918News009.asp.

4. "Business Owners Survey Mess Left Behind by Storm, Looters," *Columbia Daily Tribune*, September 18, 2005, http://www.columbiatribune.com/2005/Sep/20050918News009.asp.

5. See Miss. Code Ann. § 97-17-65; La. R. S. 14:62.5; N.C. Gen. Stat. § 14-288.6; Cal. Pen. Code § 463; Ill. Con. Stat. 5/42-1; S. C. Code Ann. § 16-7-10. Municipalities may also have legislation criminalizing looting; for example, the City of Camas, Washington, has made looting unlawful and provides a fine and jail sentence for the misdemeanor offense under the Civil Emergency chapter of the Municipal Code. Camas Municipal Code §2.48.100 (2004).

6. Russell Dynes and Enrico L. Quarantelli, "What Looting in Civil Disturbances Really Means," in *Modern Criminals*, 2nd ed., James F. Short, Jr. (ed.) (New Brunswick, NJ: Transaction Books, 1973), 231–246.

7. Roger D. Scott, "Looting: A Proposal to Enhance the Sanction for Aggravated Property Crime," *11 Journal of Law and Politics* (Winter 1995): 129–175.

8. La. R. S. § 14:62.5, amended by Acts 2005, No. 208, § 1.

9. According to the defendants' lawyer, the sentence is being appealed. Associated Press, "Katrina Looters Get 15 Years in Prison," June 29, 2006.

10. For the 27 events recorded in the commission report for the summer of 1967, 74.8% of the arrests were for looting. Robert M. Fogelson and Robert B. Hill, "Who Riots? A Study of Participation in the 1967 Riots" (July 1968), in *Supplemental Studies for the National Advisory Commission on Civil Disorders* (Washington, DC: G.P.O., 1968), 247, table 9.

11. Ibid., 245, table 1.

12. Ibid., 247, table 9.

13. Louis Genevie, Seymour R. Kaplan, Harris Peck, Elmer L. Struening, June E. Kallos, Gregory L. Muhlin, and Arthur Richardson, "Predictors of Looting in

Selected Neighborhoods of New York City During the Blackouts of 1977," *Sociology and Social Research* 71, no. 3 (April 1987): 228–231.

14. "500 Farmers Storm Arkansas Town Demanding Food for Their Children: Drought Sufferers, Many Armed, Get Aid for Hungry Families After Pressing Into Stores—Are Appeased by Red Cross Help—Organization Feeds 100,000 in the State," *New York Times*, January 4, 1931, sec. 1.

15. While news reports do not indicate that this event was related to the weather, Oklahoma was certainly affected by the drought. See "Food Rioters Raid Oklahoma City Store; 500 Dispersed By Police With Tear Gas," *New York Times*, January 21, 1931, sec. 1, p. 1.

16. *State v. Moe*, 174 Wash. 303, 24 P.2d 638 (1933).

17. This type of looting is distinguishable from the looting sometimes identified as social protest, which generally involves large groups of people acting in concert or a mob mentality making it acceptable to members of the group for looting to occur. In a 1995 article, the article's author identifies five categories of looting: pillaging by conquering armies; looting of financial institutions; looting of cultural objects and artifacts; "scavenging of property in the aftermath of disasters, such as hurricanes, earthquakes, and blizzards"; and, "'looting' by large crowds after sporting events, concerts, and during riots attributed to social grievances." The article's author decries the notion of looting as a form of social protest and the tendency of government to respond to looting in protest of an event such as the acquittals in the Rodney King case with increases in social welfare spending rather than criminal sanctions. See Roger D. Scott, "Looting: A Proposal to Enhance the Sanction for Aggravated Property Crime," 11 *Journal of Law and Politics* 129–211 (Winter 1995). This type of group activity, whether considered rioting, looting, or social protest is not discussed in this book; here the focus is on necessity for survival as the result of a weather disaster.

18. Scott's 1995 article identifies six states with specific looting statutes: California, Illinois, Louisiana, Mississippi, North Carolina, and South Carolina. Scott also notes that convictions could not be found under these statutes and that plea bargaining and the efficiency of charging with burglary and larceny made prosecution for the specific crime of looting unlikely. Ibid., 152–157.

19. Ibid., 164.

20. According to some research, looting is not as common as is believed or as is reported. Studies comparing stories of looting with reported incidents show that the view that looting is rampant can not be supported by the evidence and that the evidence may actually indicate that crime rates decline after a major weather disaster. Russell Dynes and Enrico L. Quarantelli, "What Looting in Civil Disturbances Really Means," in *Modern Criminals*, 2d ed., James F. Short, Jr. (ed.) (New Brunswick, NJ: Transaction Books, 1973), 231–246.

21. Frank Charles Tanner was charged with a felony count of Burglary of Inhabited Dwelling on February 24, 2006, according to the criminal defendant report from the St. Tammany Clerk's Web site. See www.sttammanyclerk.org. Tanner allegedly removed $550 worth of personal property from a home in Slidell on January 6th and was caught in the act by the homeowner who had come to see the trailer installation. Associated Press, "FEMA Subcontractor Arrested for Looting Residence," AP Alert—Louisiana, January 9, 2006. While stories report that

Tanner was arrested for looting, the clerk's documents state that Tanner was charged under La. R. S. 14:62.2 (Simple Burglary of an Inhabited Home) that carries a minimum sentence of 1 year. Under Louisiana criminal law, looting carries a penalty of a fine of not more than $10,000 or up to 15 years in prison or both and the crime of looting during the existence of a state of emergency carries the possibility of a five thousand to ten thousand dollar fine and a mandatory prison sentence of not less than 3 years. La. R. S. 14:62.5.

22. Ibid., 137–138.

23. United Press International, "Looters Come By Sea, Land, Car," August 20, 1983.

24. Jennifer K. Elsea, "The Use of Federal Troops for Disaster Assistance: Legal Issues," *CRS Report for Congress* (Washington, DC: Library of Congress Congressional Research Service, August 14, 2006).

25. See U.S. Const. art. IV, § 4.

26. Posse Comitatus Act (PCA), *U.S. Code* 18 (2000), § 1385.

27. Insurrection Act, *U.S. Code* 10 (2000), §§ 331-335. If the President signs the John Warner National Defense Authorization Act for Fiscal Year 2007, the Insurrection Act will be renamed. The heading of chapter 15 of title 10 of the United States Code will change from "Insurrection" to "Enforcement of the Laws to Restore Public Order." The National Defense Authorization Act also expands the coverage of section 333 of the current Insurrection Act to allow the President to use the armed forces in a natural disaster.

28. President, Proclamation, "Law and Order in the Virgin Islands, Proclamation 6023," *Code of Federal Regulations*, title 3 (1990): 113–114.

29. Exec. Order No. 12,690, *Code of Federal Regulations*, title 3 (1990): 236–237.

30. A factor that Scott identifies as relevant to natural disasters is that looting does not occur in every disaster. Where the communities affected by the natural disaster are homogeneous (such as during the 1993 Mississippi River flooding in the Midwest), looting seems to be less than in areas which have "a divided population in which different groups lack respect for the property of others in their community." Scott, "Looting," 138.

31. Associated Press, "New Orleans police abandon rescue efforts as looting escalates; evacuations begin," AP DataStream, September 1, 2005.

32. City of New Orleans Mayor's Office of Communications, "Safety and Security Re-Entry Information: Updated," Press Release, September 28, 2005, http://www.cityofno.com/portal.aspx?portal=1&load=~/PortalModules/ViewPressRelease.ascx&itemid=3150.

33. City of New Orleans, "Post-Katrina FAQ," http://www.cityofno.com/portal.aspx?portal=1&tabid=50 (accessed October 14, 2006).

34. *Moorhead v. Farrelly*, 723 F. Supp. 1109 (D.V.I. 1989).

35. The language being challenged stated that "all persons residing in these areas are commanded to remain in their homes during the hours of the curfew, unless otherwise authorized by Dade County, State of Florida or federal officials." *Smith v. Avino*, 91 F.3d 105, 108 (11th Cir. 1996).

36. Ibid., 109.

37. Unconfirmed reports on the web indicate that, in Palm Beach in 2004 and in New Orleans in 2005, the majority of arrests for curfew violations were

people of color. John Pacenti, Kathleen Chapman, and William M. Hartnett, "Curfew Arrests Show Lopsided Minority Tally," *Palm Beach Post*, September 10, 2004, http://www.palmbeachpost.com/storm/content/south_county/epaper/2004/09/10/s1c_arrests_0910.html; Walidah Imarisha, "New Orleans: Occupied Territory," *The Objector*, Special Issue (January 2006): 9–10, http://www.objector.org.

38. U.S. Department of Justice Hurricane Katrina Fraud Task Force, *First Year Report to the Attorney General, September2006*, http://www.usdoj.gov/katrina/Katrina_Fraud/docs/09-12-06AGprogressrpt.pdf.

39. U.S. Department of Homeland Security Federal Emergency Management Agency, "Scam Artists Are Lurking," Press Release No. 1603-377 (March 1, 2006), http://www.fema.gov/news/newsrelease.fema?id=23958.

40. Emergency and Disaster Assistance Fraud Penalty Enhancement Act of 2005 (H.R. 4356), introduced November 17, 2005, reported out of the Judiciary Committee on May 19, 2006.

41. U.S. House of Representatives Report 109-473, Emergency and Disaster Assistance Fraud Penalty Enhancement Act of 2005, May 19, 2006.

42. Ibid., 18–19.

43. Clark C. Spence, *The Rainmakers: American "Pluviculture" to World War II* (Lincoln, NE: University of Nebraska, 1980), 128.

44. Ibid., 2.

45. For further discussion of weather modification, see Chapter 2 on inventions and technology.

46. Articles in newspapers such as the *New York Times* reported on rainmaking activities in the Midwest and Southwest with a slight tone of skepticism. See "The Rainmakers at Work: 'Trial' Rains Can be Bought for $600 Each," *New York Times*, March 14, 1892.

47. Spence, *The Rainmakers*, 131.

48. See chapter 2.

49. U.S. Department of Homeland Security Federal Emergency Management Agency, "FEMA Inspector General Targets New Disaster Scam," Release Number: 1435-120, November 7, 2002, at http://www.fema.gov/news/newsrelease.fema?id=3767.

50. U.S. Department of Justice Hurricane Katrina Fraud Task Force, *First Year Report to the Attorney General, September 2006*, http://www.usdoj.gov/katrina/Katrina_Fraud/docs/09-12-06AGprogressrpt.pdf, 14.

51. Ibid.

52. U.S. Code, title 18, § 1341.

53. U.S. Code, title 18, § 1343.

54. U.S. Code, title 18, § 1029.

55. U.S. Department of Justice, United States Attorney Southern District of Florida, "Aventura Man Charged with Hurricane Katrina Internet Scam," Press Release, October 3, 2005, www.usdoj.gov/katrina/Katrina_Fraud/pr/press_releases.

56. U.S. Department of Justice Hurricane Katrina Fraud Task Force, *First Year Report to the Attorney General, September 2006*, http://www.usdoj.gov/katrina/Katrina_Fraud/docs/09-12-06AGprogressrpt.pdf, 18.

57. U.S. Department of Justice, "Romanian Nationals Indicted for Running Internet Scam that Purported to Benefit Hurricane Katrina Victims," Press Release, October 6, 2006, http://www.usdoj.gov/usao/cac/.

58. Louisiana Revised Statutes § 9:4814 (civil); Louisiana Revised Statutes §14:202 (criminal).

59. "Mississippi Contractor Arrested in Connection with Kenner Home Repairs," *The Times Picayune*, February 6, 2006, http://www.nola.com/newslogs/tpupdates/index.ssf?/mtlogs/nola_tpupdates/archives/2006_02_06.html.

60. Kenner (Louisiana) Police Department, "Contractor Fraud Arrest," *News Release*, February 6, 2006, http://www.kennerpd.com/Press%20Releases/2006/feb06/contractorfraud2-2-06.htm.

61. Louisiana Revised Statutes § 14:202(C) and (D).

62. See *Georgia Code Annotated*, § 10-1-393.4 for an example of a state law. See www.ftc.gov for materials related to the Federal Trade Commission's efforts to protect consumers in the wake of disasters. According to one commentator, state anti-gouging laws have been classified as percentage price caps, unconscionability laws, or no-increase laws. Geoffrey C. Rapp, "Gouging: Terrorist Attacks, Hurricanes, and the Legal and Economic Aspects of Post-Disaster Price Regulation," *Kentucky Law Journal* 94 (2005/2006): 535–560.

63. *Virgin Islands Code*, title 23, § 1125.

64. *Virgin Islands Code*, title 23, § 1125a.

65. U.S. Department of Justice Antitrust Division, "Criminal Enforcement: Disaster Recovery," http://www.usdoj.gov/atr/disaster.htm (accessed October 16, 2006).

66. U.S. Department of Justice Antitrust Division, "Preventing and Detecting Bid Rigging, Price Fixing, and Market Allocation in Post-Disaster Rebuilding Projects: An Antitrust Primer for Agents and Procurement Officials," http://www.usdoj.gov/atr/public/guidelines/disaster_primer.htm (accessed October 16, 2006).

67. According to studies on heatstroke in children completed by Dr. Oded Bar-Or for GM Canada, within 20 minutes, the air temperature in a previously air-conditioned small car exposed to the sun on a 95°F day exceeded 122°F. Within 40 minutes, the temperature soared to 150°F. A child left in a hot, closed vehicle can suffer injury or death within minutes. Canada Safety Council, "Hot Car Warning,"http://www.safety-council.org/info/child/hotcar.html. See also U.S. Department of Transportation, National Highway Traffic Safety Administration, Data Collection Study: Deaths and Injuries Resulting from Certain Non-Traffic and Non-Crash Events, pp. 22–24 (May 2004); A. Guard and S. S. Gallagher, "Heat Related Deaths to Young Children in Parked Cars: An Analysis of 171 Fatalities in the United States, 1995–2002," *Injury Prevention* 11 (2005): 33–37; Catherine McLaren, Jan Null, and James Quinn, "Heat Stress From Enclosed Vehicles: Moderate Ambient Temperatures Cause Significant Temperature Rise in Enclosed Vehicles," *Pediatrics* 116, no. 1 (2005): 109–112.

68. In addition to child endangerment, neglect, and homicide statutes, advocacy groups and some state legislators are making efforts to enact specific legislation to prohibit leaving children under 14 and companion animals unattended inside closed vehicles in the heat. "Thirteen states currently have laws against

leaving an unattended child in a vehicle, and 12 more states, including Minnesota, are considering such a law." Kyle Johnson, "N.D. Legislature: Lawmakers May Propose Unattended Child Law," GrandForksHerald.com (June 30, 2006). See Kids and Cars, "Unattended Children in Motor Vehicle Safety Act Model Law," http://www.kidsandcars.org/docs/Model%20law2.doc; California State Senate Bill No. 1806 (introduced February 24, 2006); New York State Senate Bill 6289 (introduced January 4, 2006). Animal cruelty statutes and municipal ordinances may include a specific provision creating criminal penalties for leaving an animal unattended in a motor vehicle or transporting an animal without adequate ventilation. See City of New Orleans City Code section 18-2; California Penal Code section 597.7 (added September 22, 2006).

69. To prevent deaths of newborns from exposure to the weather, many states have now passed "Safe Haven" statutes "which provide a defense to abandonment charges when a newborn is abandoned in a hospital or fire station." Ana L. Partida, "The Case for 'Safe Haven' Laws: Choosing the Lesser of Two Evils in a Disposable Society," 28 N. E. J. on Crim. & Civ. Con. 61 (2002).

70. 18 U.S.C. § 1115

71. "If a husband fails to supply his wife with clothing or shelter, thereby causing her death by freezing or exposure, he is guilty of manslaughter. A parent, who fails to supply his minor child with clothing or shelter, is likewise guilty of manslaughter if the child dies by freezing or exposure." Charles E. Torcia, 2 Wharton's Criminal Law § 174 (West 15th ed. 2005 update).

72. Ibid.

73. *Jones v. United States*, 308 F. 2d 307 (D.C. Cir. 1962).

74. *United States. v. McHugh*, 122 F.3d 153 (2nd Cir. 1997).

75. Wharton, Homicide, section 304, cited in *Gibson v. Commonwealth*, 106 Ky. 360 (1899).

76. *Gibson v. Commonwealth*, 106 Ky. 360 (1899).

77. "Proximate cause" is the action or omission which creates the resulting injury. While it is usually the event or omission closest in time to the injury, it need not be.

78. Ga. Code Ann. § 16-5-72. Reckless abandonment of a child

(a) A parent, guardian, or other person supervising the welfare of or having immediate charge or custody of a child under the age of one year commits the offense of reckless abandonment of a child when the person willfully and voluntarily physically abandons such child with the intention of severing all parental or custodial duties and responsibilities to such child and leaving such child in a condition which results in the death of said child.

(b) Any person who violates subsection (a) of this Code section shall be guilty of a felony and shall, upon conviction thereof, be punished by imprisonment for not less than ten nor more than 25 years.

79. *In the Interest of B.L.M.*, 228 Ga. App. 664 (1997).

80. *Pullins v. Commonwealth*, 266 Ky. 637 (1936).

81. Ibid., 641.

82. ULA Model Penal Code, § 230.5.

83. *State v. Smith*, 65 Me. 257 (1876).

84. Ibid.

85. *Territory of Montana v. Manton*, 8 Mont. 95 (1888).

86. Ibid.

87. Charles E. Torcia, 2 Wharton's Criminal Law § 119 (West 15th ed., 2005).

88. *Hendrickson v. Commonwealth*, 85 Ky. 281(1887).

89. *State v. Preslar*, 48 N.C. 421 (1856).

90. See, e.g., Burn's Annotated Indiana Statutes § 10-813.

91. *Helwig v. State*, 238 Ind. 559 (1958).

92. Alisa Blackwood, "Director of Arizona Boot Camp Where 14-Year-Old Died Arrested on Murder Charges," Associated Press State and Local Wire, February 16, 2002.

93. "Director of Boot Camp Can't Reach Settlement with Prosecutors over Youth's Death," Associated Press State and Local Wire, August 21, 2004.

94. Michael Kiefer, "Boot Camp Instructor Convicted; Teen's Death Manslaughter," *Arizona Republic*, January 4, 2005.

95. "Camp Director Accused of Murder Says He Will Be Vindicated," Associated Press State and Local Wire, February 22, 2002.

96. Kiefer, "Boot Camp Instructor Convicted."

97. Marie McCain, "Toddler's Death Considered Tragic Accident," *Desert Sun (Palm Springs, California)*, September 21, 2005.

98. In August, 2001, the National Highway Traffic Safety Administration created a rule establishing a motor vehicle safety standard requiring all passenger cars with trunks to be equipped with a release latch inside the trunk. U.S. Department of Transportation, National Highway Traffic Safety Administration, "Federal Motor Vehicle Safety Standards: Interior Trunk Release," *Code of Federal Regulations*, title 49, part 571.

99. Jan Null of Golden Gate Services, formerly with the National Weather Service, sees a correlation between hyperthermia deaths and the laws that moved children from the front seat of vehicles to avoid air bag injuries. According to Null, there has been a tenfold increase in the car hyperthermia death rates since the changes in the laws about seating arrangements in cars. He is not suggesting that children should be placed in the front seats or that airbags should be disabled; he is merely pointing out that "parents can be more forgetful if the child is not seen." Kat Bergeron, "On the Health Front: Death Can Come Quickly to a Child, Pet in a Parked Car," *Miami (Florida) Herald*, July 4, 2006.

100. Caren Benjamin, "Mother, Boyfriend Face Second-Degree Murder Charges in Infant's Death," *Las Vegas (Nevada) Review-Journal*, July 8, 1998.

101. Ibid.

102. Glenn Puit, "Couple Faces Charges in Child's Drowning," *Las Vegas (Nevada) Review-Journal*, October 4, 2001.

103. See West's Anno. Cal. Vehicle Code section 15600-15630; West's Florida Statutes Annotated section 316.6135.

104. Pennsylvania, California, Florida, and Louisiana have specified 6 years old. Rhode Island has specified 7 years old. California's statute was named "Kaitlyn's Law" in memory of the 6-month-old girl who "died of hyperthermia after

her babysitter left her unattended in a van for more than two hours in over one-hundred-degree weather." Jaeson D. White, "Sit Right Here Honey, I'll Be Right Back: The Unattended Child in Motor Vehicle Safety Act," *McGeorge Law Review* 33 (2001–2002): 343–353.

105. West's Revised Code of Washington Annotated, title 46, section 46.61.685(1) (enacted 1961).

106. Purdon's Pennsylvania Statutes and Consolidated Statutes Annotated, title 75, section 3701.1(a) (enacted 1991).

107. West's Annotated California Vehicle Code section 15620 (enacted 2001).

108. Illinois Compiled Statutes, 720 ILCS 5/12–266. Declared presumption unconstitutional. *People v. Jordan*, 218 Ill. 2d 255 (2006).

109. Louisiana specifies a distance greater than 10 feet. West's Louisiana Statutes Annotated, title 32, section 295.3(B) (enacted 2003) (LSA-R.S. 32-295.3).

110. The father had been charged, convicted, and sentenced to 3 months of court supervision in 2003. His supervision was discharged by the circuit court in April 2004. *People v. Jordan*, 218 Ill. 2d 255, 843 N.E. 2d 870, 300 Ill. Dec. 2770 (2006).

111. Under Arkansas statutory law, knowingly causing the death of a person under the age of 14 under circumstances manifesting extreme indifference to the value of human life is treated as capital murder. Capital murder is punishable by death or life imprisonment without parole. West's Arkansas Code Annotated § 5-10-101(a)(9)(A).

112. "Arkansas Tragedy; Laws Can't Prevent Irresponsibility," *Tulsa (Oklahoma) World*, April 30, 1998.

113. Glenn Puit, "Hot Weather Elicits Calls of Warning," *Las-Vegas (Nevada) Review-Journal*, May 11, 1998.

114. John Masson, "Mom Faces Murder Charges in Car Deaths; Detroit Woman Leaves Kids in Hot Auto to Get Hair Done," *Ventura County (California) Star*, July 2, 2002. *People v. Maynor*, 256 Mich. App. 238, 662 N.W. 2d 468 (2003).

115. Jennifer Chambers, "Contrite Mom Draws Prison Term," *Detroit News*, September 23, 2004.

116. Karen Maeshiro, "Plea Spares Foster Mom; Smoot Avoids Life Sentence," *Daily News of Los Angeles*, February 6, 2004.

117. A plea of "no contest" does not admit guilt or innocence. The defendant is simply electing not to dispute the charges.

118. Troy Anderson, "Parents of Foster Boys File Lawsuit over Deaths," *Daily News of Los Angeles*, April 27, 2004. The parents also sued one of the insurance companies that insured the foster mother. The insurance company had refused coverage based on the insurance policy's exclusion for injuries arising out the use of an automobile. The trial court and appellate court found in favor of the insurance company. *Prince v. United National Insurance Company*, 142 Cal. App. 4th 233, 47 Cal. Rptr. 3d 727 (2006). For opposite result, see *Mount Vernon Fire Insurance Co. v. Heaven's Little Hands Day Care*, 343 Ill.App. 3d 309, 795 N.E. 2d 1034, 277 Ill. Dec. 366 (2003).

119. "Hot, Parked Cars Can Be Deadly," *Pasadena (California) Star-News*, August 11, 2003.

120. *People v. Banks*, 161 Ill. 2d 119, 127 (1994).

121. *People v. Banks*, 161 Ill. 2d 119 (1994).

122. Death Penalty Information Center, "Illinois Death Row Inmates Granted Commutation by Governor George Ryan on January 12, 2003," http://www.deathpenaltyinfo.org/article.php?scid=13&did=485.

123. The average minimum and maximum temperatures in Las Vegas, Nevada, in May 1970 were 40.06°F and 89.87°F, respectively. "Las Vegas FAA Airport, Nevada: Monthly Average Minimum Temperature (Degrees Fahrenheit)," Associated Press State and Local Wire, http://www.wrcc.dri.edu/cgi-bin/cliMONtmnt.pl?nmlasv. "Las Vegas WSO Airport, Nevada: Monthly Average Maximum Temperature (Degrees Fahrenheit)," http://www.wrcc.dri.edu/cgi-bin/cliMONtmxt.pl?nvlasv.

124. *Simpson v. Sheriff, Clark County*, 86 Nev. 803 (1970). The testimony from Simpson's former husband and from two other witnesses who had heard Simpson threaten the little girl's life constituted probable cause sufficient to hold Simpson for trial.

125. *Corpus Juris Secundum*, Criminal Law, § (2006).

126. The courts do not accept economic necessity as a defense to a criminal charge, although it may serve as a mitigating factor in sentencing. For example, in September 1932, a large number of the unemployed marched to the Red Cross commissary in Anacortes, Washington, as a demonstration to demand a larger ration of flour from the relief committee. When their demand was denied, some members of the group (anywhere from 40 to 75 according to estimates) went to a local store and helped themselves to food without paying. The defendants who were convicted of grand larceny and rioting wanted to claim conditions of poverty as justification for the raid on the store. The court declared that "[e]conomic necessity has never been accepted as a defense to a criminal charge.... [If it were], it would leave to the individual the right to take the law into his own hands." *State v. Moe*, 174 Wash. 303, 24 P. 2d 638 (1933), at 640.

127. Cannibalism is probably the most extreme example of a crime defended by a survival or necessity defense. One of the most frequently referenced examples of cannibalism is the story of the Donner party, who were stranded by snow in the high Sierra Nevada Mountains in the winter of 1846–1847 while traveling from Illinois to California. 36 members of the party died. While cannibalism and possibly murder were reported, no legal proceedings were undertaken against the survivors. A recent 3-year study of the encampment of the Donner family by archeologists failed to locate physical evidence of cannibalism. See A. W. Brian Simpson, *Cannibalism and the Common Law: The Story of the Tragic Lost Voyage of the* Mignonette *and the Strange Legal Proceedings to Which It Gave Rise* (Chicago, IL: The University of Chicago Press, 1984), 150; Eric Bailey, "No Proof Found of Donner Cannibalism: Delayed by Axle Trouble, Brothers' Group Camped Separately," *San Francisco Chronicle*, January 13, 2006, at http://www.sfgate.com/cgi-bin/article.cgi?f=/c/a/2006/01/13/MNG29GMOV91.DTL.

128. *People v. Willott*, 2002 Westlaw 1057490 (Cal. App. May 28, 2002).

129. *People v. Buena Vista Mines, Inc.*, 60 Cal. App. 4th 1198, 71 Cal. Rptr. 2d 101 (1998).

130. According to the NOAA NCDC collection data form for Corinna, Maine, for December 1980, the high on December 27, 1980 was 11°F and the low was −8°F. Corinna is in Penobscot County, Maine, the location of Mr. Greenwald's trials.

131. *State v. Greenwald*, 454 A. 2d 827 (Maine 1982).

132. Paul Purpura, "Charges Dropped in 84 of 290 Jefferson Looting Cases," *The Times-Picayune*, February 6, 2006, www.nola.com/newslogs/tpupdates/index.ssf?/mtlogs/nola_tpupdates/archives/2006_02_06.html.

133. Ibid.

134. Ibid.

135. Michelle Hunter, "275 Booked with Looting in Jeff," *The Times-Picayune*, September 30, 2005, http://www.nola.com/weblogs/print.ssf?/mtlogs/nola_Times-Picayune/archives/print084045.html (accessed October 13, 2006).

136. Mona Charen, Commentary, "Looters Should Face Threat of Being Shot," *Columbia Daily Tribune*, September 3, 2005, http://www.columbiatribune.com/2005/Sep/20050903Comm003.asp.

## CHAPTER 6: WEATHER AND THE JUSTICE SYSTEM

1. *Sylvester v. Boissiere*, Complaint, U.S. District Court, Eastern District of Louisiana, Docket No. 05-0527, n.d., at http://newstandardnews.net/content/documents/nola_evictions_complaint.pdf.

2. According to Professor of Criminology Frank Leishman, in his speech to the Southampton Institute in November 2002, Adolphe Quetelet formulated his Thermic Law of Criminality in 1842. In this Thermic Law, Quetelet "specified that 'crimes against property reach a maximum in winter months, and crimes against the person and against morals, in the summer months.'" Frank Leishman, "Elemental, My Dear Watson? The Weather, Crime and Criminology," Inaugural Professorial Lecture, Southampton Institute, November 14, 2002, at page 6. Also see, for example, Edwin G. Dexter, "Ethics and the Weather," *International Journal of Ethics* 11, no. 4 (July 1901): 481–492; and Gerald J. Falk, "The Influence of the Seasons on the Crime Rate," *The Journal of Criminal Law, Criminology, and Police Science* 43, no. 2 (July/August 1952): 199–213.

3. Craig A. Anderson, "Temperature and Aggression: Ubiquitous Effects of Heat on Occurrence of Human Violence," *Psychological Bulletin* 106, no. 1 (1989): 74–96.

4. Bruce Palmer, *Body Weather: How Natural and Man-Made Climates Affect You and Your Health* (Harrisburg, PA: Stackpole Books, 1976), 25.

5. Stephen Rosen, *Weathering: How the Atmosphere Conditions Your Body, Your Mind, Your Moods, and Your Health* (New York: M. Evans, 1979): 36.

6. While suicide is not illegal, attempted suicide is still illegal in some states and subjects the person to psychiatric commitment based on danger to self.

7. National Advisory Commission on Civil Disorders, *Report of The National Commission on Civil Disorders, March 1, 1968* (Washington, DC: GPO., 1968), 71. "Eighteen disorders for which temperature information was available occurred at the end of a day in which the temperature had reached a high of at least 79 degrees. In nine cases the temperature had reached 90 degrees or more during the day (Atlanta, Cambridge, Cincinnati, the June Dayton disturbance, Newark, Paterson, Phoenix, Tampa, and Tucson;...); in eight cases the temperature had been in the 80s (Detroit, Elizabeth, Englewood, Grand Rapids, Jersey

City, New Brunswick, New Haven, and Rockford; . . . ), and in one city the high temperature was 79 degrees (Milwaukee; . . . )." Punctuation as in original. fn. 53, page 327.

8. See Craig A. Anderson, "Temperature and Aggression: Effects on Quarterly, Yearly, and City Rates of Violent and Nonviolent Crime," *Journal of Personality and Social Psychology* 52, no. 6 (1987): 1161–1173; Ellen G. Cohn and James Rotton, "Assault as a Function of Time and Temperature: A Moderator-Variable Time-Series Analysis," *Journal of Personality and Social Psychology* 72, no. 6 (1997): 1322–1334; and James Rotton and Ellen G. Cohn, "Weather, Disorderly Conduct, and Assaults: From Social Contact to Social Avoidance," *Environment and Behavior* 32, no. 5 (September 2000): 651–673.

9. James Rotton and James Frey, "Air Pollution, Weather, and Violent Crimes: Concomitant Time-Series Analysis of Archival Data," *Journal of Personality and Social Psychology*, 49, no. 5 (1985): 1207–1220.

10. U.S. Department of Justice, Federal Bureau of Investigation, *Crime in the United States 2000: Uniform Crime Reports* (Washington, DC: GPO, 2001).

11. U.S. Department of Justice, Federal Bureau of Investigation, Press Release, October 22, 2001, "NIBRS and NCIC Data used in the CIUS, 2000," http://www.fbi.gov/pressrel/pressrel01/sec5cius2000.htm.

12. Kent Borowick, "Baylor Model Helps Predict Crime in the City of Waco," *Baylor Business Review* 12, no. 2 (Fall 1994): 6–7.

13. Wyoming's aggravated homicide by vehicle statute includes provision for operation or driving of a vehicle in a reckless manner where that conduct is the proximate cause of the death of another person. *Wyoming Statutes* § 6-2-106(b)(ii).

14. *Relish v. State of Wyoming*, 860 P.2d 455, 457 (Wy. 1993).

15. Ibid., 462.

16. *Commonwealth of Massachusetts v. Nurse*, Nos. CRIM. A. 98932, CRIM. A. 98934, 1997 Westlaw 805466 (Mass. Super. November 11, 1997).

17. Ibid., 2.

18. According to the case report, the information provided by the National Climatic Data Center (NCDC) showed that between 11 P.M. and midnight in New York City on the arrest date, there was approximately 1.37 inches of rain and winds with a high of 33 mph (originally stated by the NCDC in knots).

19. *People v. Diaz*, 163 Misc. 2nd 390, 625 N.Y.S. 2nd 388 (1994).

20. *State v. Hudson*, 950 S.W.2d 543 (Mo. Ct. App. 2006).

21. "Sudden Rain Helps Brazen Bank Robber: Man Escapes on Foot After Grabbing Cash from West Side Bank," *Charleston Daily Mail* (Charleston, W.Va.), July 20, 2005.

22. United States Federal Bureau of Investigation, Wanted Poster, http://www.fbi.gov/wanted/unkn/illinoisbank.htm.

23. When a person testifies to something he has been told as opposed to something he witnessed, the person is offering hearsay testimony. Under most circumstances, hearsay testimony is not allowed but there are some exceptions. The public records and reports exception to the hearsay rule allows authenticated public records to be admitted in court if the agency had a statutory duty to observe and report on particular matters. Federal Rules of Evidence §803(8). The states each

have their own version of this rule. In addition, a federal statute provides for admissibility of government records and papers. *U.S. Code* 28, § 1733.

24. Dennis H. McCarthy, "Weather Records and Expert Testimony for Courts of Law," *Journal of the Missouri Bar* 41, no. 7 (October/November 1985): 457–458.

25. See U.S. Department of Commerce National Oceanic and Atmospheric Administration, National Severe Storms Laboratory, "Lightning Fatalities, Injuries, and Damage Reports in the United States from 1959-1994," NOAA Technical Memorandum NWS SR-193, October 1997, http://www.nssl.noaa.gov/paper/techmemos/NWS-SR-193/techmemo-sr193.html.

26. *Evanston v. Gunn*, 99 U.S. 660, 666 (1878), citing *Revised Statutes* §§221 and 222.

27. *Fowel v. Insurance Bldg., Inc.*, 32 A.2d 100 (D.C. App. 1943).

28. *Hufnagle v. Delaware & H. Co.*, 227 Pa. 476 (1910).

29. *City of Enid v. Reeser*, 330 P.2d 198 (Okla. 1958).

30. The court also noted that the report only talked about trace precipitation on the 19th. The report described a "trace" as "an amount too small to measure," to which the court responded parenthetically, "What is an amount too small to measure is not stated, but the report does show that precipitation can be measured if it amounts to as much as one one-hundreth (0.01) of an inch." *Fedors v. O'Brien*, 39 Ill. App. 2d. 407, 409-410 (1963).

31. See Barry Grossman and Peter Muldavin, "Weather Experts Join the Law Team," *NBA: National Bar Association Magazine* 7 (September/October 1993): 16–17; George L. Sanepietro and Steve Cascione, "Weather Witnesses: Meteorologists as Experts," *Rhode Island Bar Journal* 45 (November 1996): 9–10.

32. *Sylvester v. Boissiere*, Complaint, U.S. District Court, E.D. La., Docket no. 05-0527, http://newstandardnews.net/content/documents/nola_evictions_complaint.pdf.

33. Gwen Filosa, "Settlement Gives Renters Respite: Evictions on Hold; Notices to be Mailed," November 23, 2005, http://www.nola.com/printer/printer.ssf?/base/news-11/1132747306303880.xml.

34. United States Postal Service, "History of the U.S. Postal Service, 1775-1993: Postal Insignia," http://www.usps.com/history/his8.htm.

35. Practising Law Institute, "Regulation of Investment Companies and Investment Advisors," *The SEC Speaks in 1995*, Corporate Law and Practice Course Handbook Series (March 1995): 349–350.

36. Christopher Drew, "Courts' Slow Recovery Begins at Train Station in New Orleans," *New York Times*, October 14, 2005.

37. Speedy Trial Act, *U. S. Code*, 18, § 3161.

38. *U.S. v. Paschall*, 988 F. 2d 972 (9th Cir. 1993).

39. *New York C.P.L.* § 700.35(2).

40. *U.S. v. Levine*, 690 F. Supp. 1165 (E.D. N.Y. 1988).

41. Various data sources reflect a reduction in the number of New Orleans attorneys post-Katrina. The Louisiana Bar Association reported that, as of October 24, 2006, New Orleans showed a loss of over 750 lawyers from the pre-Katrina number. Pre-Katrina, New Orleans had 5,400 attorneys; post-Katrina, New Orleans has 4,648. Phone interview with Kim Lane, Member Records Coordinator, Louisiana Bar Association, by Daniel Marquez, on October 24, 2006.

42. Laura Parker, "Lack of Public Defenders May Free Accused Felons," *USA Today*, February 14, 2006, http://www.usatoday.com/news/nation/2006-02-14-free-felons_x.htm.

43. Phrase "doing Katrina time" used in Andrew Cohen, "The Battle of New Orleans," *CBS News*, May 25, 2006, http://www.cbsnews.com.

44. Leslie Eaton, "Judge Steps in for Poor Inmates without Justice since Hurricane," *New York Times*, May 23, 2006.

45. Ibid.

46. State of Louisiana, Governor Kathleen Blanco, Executive Order No. KBB 2005-32 (September 6, 2005); Executive Order No. KBB 2005-48 (September 23, 2005); Executive Order No. KBB 2005-67 (October 19, 2005).

47. American Bar Association Young Lawyers Division, Letter to membership, September 15, 2005, http://www.abanet.org/yld/disaster.html.

48. Supreme Court of Mississippi, Rules of Professional Conduct, Order No. 89-R-99018-SCT (September 9, 2005).

49. Supreme Court of Texas, "Amended Emergency Order Permitting Lawyers Displaced by Hurricane Katrina or Hurricane Rita to Continue Representing Clients from Temporary Offices in Texas," Misc. Docket No. 05-9171 (October 11, 2005).

50. Jerry Seper, "'Camp Greyhoud' Home to 220 Looting Suspects," *The Washington Times*, September 9, 2005, http://washingtontimes.com.

51. American Civil Liberties Union National Prison Project, *Abandoned and Abused: Orleans Parish Prisoners in the Wake of Hurricane Katrina* (2006): 9.

52. American Civil Liberties Union, "U.N. Human Rights Body Slams Louisiana Actions During Katrina," Press Release, July 28, 2006, http://www.aclu.org/intlhumanrights/gen/26273prs20060728.html.

53. Frisia was comprised of the lands along the northern coast of Europe "from Flanders, through Holland, to North Germany." http://www.keesn.nl/lex/intr_en.htm.

54. Lex Frisionum Add.III.22, http://www.keesn.nl/lex/lex_en4.htm#AIII22A.

55. Rosen, *Weathering*, p. 280, appendix A.

56. *Robin v. Allstate Indem. Co.*, 889 So. 2d 450 (La. App. 2004).

## CHAPTER 7: FUTURE OF WEATHER AND THE LAW

1. *Massachusetts v. Environmental Protection Agency*, No. 05-1120, United States Supreme Court, Oral Argument Transcript, November 29, 2006.

2. Stephen Rosen, *Weathering: How the Atmosphere Conditions Your Body, Your Mind, Your Moods—And Your Health* (New York: M. Evans and Company, Inc., 1979), 40.

3. Craig A. Anderson, "Temperature and Aggression: Ubiquitous Effects of Heat on Occurrence of Human Violence," *Psychological Bulletin* 106, no. 1 (1989): 74–96.

4. Bruce Palmer, *Body Weather: How Natural and Man-Made Climates Affect You and Your Health* (Harrisburg, PA: Stackpole Books, 1976), 25.

5. Rosen, *Weathering*, 36.

6. A. Bulbena, G. Pailhez, R. Acena, J. Cunillera, A. Rius, C. Garcia-Ribera, J. Gutierrez, and C. Rojo, "Panic Anxiety, Under the Weather?" *International Journal of Biometeorology* 49, no. 4 (March 2005): 238–243.

7. Petar Reiae, "The Relationship between Transient Ischemic Attacks and Meteorological STRE," at http://www.mzos.hr/svibor/3/01/229/proj_e.htm.

8. Deutscher Wetterdienst,"The Weather and Human Health," http://www.dwd.de/en/SundL/Gesundheit/Gesundheit.htm.

# Glossary of Weather Terms

The selected definitions of weather-related terms found in this glossary are taken verbatim from the U.S. Department of Commerce National Oceanic and Atmospheric Administration's National Weather Service Web site at http://www.weather.gov/glossary/. The author chose those terms from the National Weather Service glossary most relevant to this book, focusing on the terms related to meteorology, weather forecasting, weather data collection, special weather warnings, and environmental issues of most general interest.

**Acid Precipitation.** Precipitation, such as rain, snow or sleet, containing relatively high concentrations of acid-forming chemicals that have been released into the atmosphere and combined with water vapor; harmful to the environment.

**Advisory (Abbrev. ADVY).** Highlights special weather conditions that are less serious than a warning. They are for events that may cause significant inconvenience, and if caution is not exercised, it could lead to situations that may threaten life and/or property.

**Aeroallergens.** Any of a variety of allergens such as pollens, grasses, or dust carried by winds.

**Air Pollution Potential.** The meteorological potential for air pollution problems, considered without regard to the presence or absence of actual pollution sources.

**Air Stagnation Advisory.** This National Weather Service product is issued when major buildups of air pollution, smoke, dust, or industrial gases are expected near the ground for a period of time. This usually results from a stagnant high pressure system with weak winds being unable to bring in fresh air.

**ALERT.** Automated Local Event Reporting in Real Time. Network of automatic rain gauges that transmit via VHF radio link when precipitation occurs. Some sites are also equipped with other sensors such as temperature, wind, pressure, river stage or tide level.

**Algorithm.** A computer program (or set of programs) which is designed to systematically solve a certain kind of problem. WSR-88D radars (NEXRAD) employ algorithms to analyze radar data and automatically determine storm motion, probability of hail, VIL, accumulated rainfall, and several other parameters.

**Anemometer.** An instrument used for measuring the speed of the wind.

**Aneroid Barometer.** An instrument for measuring atmospheric pressure in which a needle, attached to the top of an evacuated box, is deflected as changes in atmospheric pressure cause the top of the box to bend in or out.

**Angels.** Radar echoes caused by birds, insects, and localized refractive index discontinuities.

**Atmosphere.** The air surrounding and bound to the Earth.

**Atmospheric Pressure.** The pressure exerted by the earth's atmosphere at any given point, determined by taking the product of the gravitational acceleration at the point and the mass of the unit area column of air above the point.

**Automated Surface Observing System (ASOS).** The ASOS program is a joint effort of the National Weather Service (NWS), the Federal Aviation Administration (FAA), and the Department of Defense (DOD). Completed in the mid-1990s, the ASOS systems serve as the nation's primary surface weather observing network. ASOS is designed to support weather forecast activities and aviation operations and, at the same time, support the needs of the meteorological, hydrological, and climatological research communities.

**Avalanche.** A mass of snow, rock, and/or ice falling down a mountain or incline. In practice, it usually refers to the snow avalanche. In the United States, the term snow slide is commonly used to mean a snow avalanche.

**Avalanche Advisory.** A preliminary notification that conditions may be favorable for the development of avalanches in mountain regions.

**Barometer.** An instrument that measures atmospheric pressure.

**Barometric Pressure.** The pressure of the atmosphere as indicated by a barometer. Measured in *Inches of Mercury* (or in Hg) in the United States. The term "inches of mercury" comes from the use of mercurial barometers which equate the height of a column of mercury with air pressure. One inch of mercury is equivalent to 33.86 millibars or 25.40 millimeters. First divised [*sic*] in 1644 by Evangelista Torricelli (1608–1647), an Italian physicist and mathematician, to explain the fundamental principles of hydromechanics.

**Beaufort Scale.** A scale assigned to wind force:

| Force | Wind Speed (kts) | Description |
|---|---|---|
| 0 | 0 | Calm |
| 1 | 1–3 | Light Air |
| 2 | 4–6 | Light Breeze |
| 3 | 7–10 | Gentle Breeze |
| 4 | 11–16 | Moderate Breeze |
| 5 | 17–21 | Fresh Breeze |
| 6 | 22–27 | Strong Breeze |
| 7 | 28–33 | Near Gale |
| 8 | 34–40 | Gale |
| 9 | 41–47 | Strong Gale |
| 10 | 48–55 | Storm |
| 11 | 56–63 | Violent Storm |
| 12 | 64+ | Hurricane |

**Black Ice.** (1) Slang reference to patchy ice on roadways or other transportation surfaces that cannot easily be seen. (2) In hydrologic terms, transparent ice formed on rivers and lakes.

**Blizzard Warning.** Issued for winter storms with sustained or frequent winds of 35 mph or higher with considerable falling and/or blowing snow that frequently reduces visibility to $1/4$ of a mile or less. These conditions are expected to prevail for a minimum of 3 hours.

**Blowing.** A descriptor used to amplify observed weather phenomena whenever the phenomena are raised to a height of 6 feet or more above the ground.

**Blowing Snow Advisory.** Issued when wind driven snow reduces surface visibility, possibly, hampering traveling. Blowing snow may be falling snow, or snow that has already accumulated but is picked up and blown by strong winds.

**Blue Watch or Blue Box.** [Slang], a severe thunderstorm watch.

**Blustery.** Same as *Breezy* [and *Brisk*]: 15 to 25 mph winds.

**Bright Band.** A distinct feature observed by a radar that denotes the freezing level of the atmosphere. The term originates from a horizontal band of enhanced reflectivity that can result when a radar antenna scans vertically through precipitation. The freezing level in a cloud contains ice particles that are coated with liquid water. These particles reflect significantly more radiation (appearing to the radar as large raindrops) than the portions of the cloud above and below the freezing layer. The bright band can affect the ability of the NEXRAD algorithms to produce accurate rainfall estimates at far ranges because the algorithm may interpret reflectivity from the bright band as an overestimate of precipitation reaching the surface.

**Calm.** A weather condition when no air motion (wind) is detected.

**Chance.** A National Weather Service precipitation descriptor for 30, 40, or 50 percent chance of measurable precipitation (0.01 inch). When the precipitation is convective in nature, the term scattered is used.

**Climate.** The composite or generally prevailing weather conditions of a region, throughout the year, averaged over a series of years.

**Climate Change.** A non-random change in climate that is measured over several decades or longer. The change may be due to natural or human-induced causes.

**Climatology.** The science that deals with the phenomena of climates or climatic conditions.

**Coastal Flooding.** The inundation of land areas along the coast caused by sea water above normal tidal actions.

**Coastal Forecast.** A forecast of wind, wave and weather conditions between the coastline and 60 miles offshore.

**Coastal Waters.** Includes the area from a line approximating the mean high water along the mainland or island as far out as sixty nautical miles including the bays, harbors, and sounds.

**Cold Front.** A zone separating two air masses, of which the cooler, denser mass is advancing and replacing the warmer.

**Congressional Organic Act of 1890.** The act that assigned the responsibility of river and floor forecasting for the benefit of the general welfare of the Nation's people and economy to the Weather Bureau, and subsequently the National Weather Service.

**Crest.** In hydrologic terms,

1) The highest stage or level of a flood wave as it passes a point.
2) The top of a dam, dike, spillway, or weir, to which water must rise before passing over the structure.

**Cyclone (Abbrev. CYC).** A large-scale circulation of winds around a central region of low atmospheric pressure, counterclockwise in the Northern Hemisphere, clockwise in the Southern Hemisphere.

**Daily Climatological Report.** As the name indicates, this climatological product is issued daily by each National Weather Service office. Most of the climatological data in this report are presented in a tabular form; however, some narrative statements may also be used in the product. The report is organized so that similar items are grouped together (i.e., temperature, precipitation, wind, sunrise and sunset times, etc.).

**Dam Failure.** In hydrologic terms, catastrophic event characterized by the sudden, rapid, and uncontrolled release of impounded water.

**Dense Fog Advisory.** Issued when fog reduces visibility to $1/8$ mile or less over a widespread area.

**Desertification.** A tendency toward more prominent desert conditions in a region.

**Direct Flood Damage.** In hydrologic terms, the damage done to property, structures, goods, etc., by a flood as measured by the cost of replacement and repairs.

**Direct Runoff.** In hydrologic terms, the runoff entering stream channels promptly after rainfall or snowmelt. Superposed [sic] on base runoff, it forms the bulk of the hydrograph of a flood.

**Doppler Radar.** Radar that can measure radial velocity, the instantaneous component of motion parallel to the radar beam (i.e., toward or away from the radar antenna).

**Drifting Snow.** Drifting snow is an uneven distribution of snowfall/snow depth caused by strong surface winds. Drifting snow may occur during or after a snowfall. Drifting snow is usually associated with blowing snow.

**Drizzle.** Precipitation consisting of numerous minute droplets of water less than 0.5 mm (500 micrometers) in diameter.

**Drought.** Drought is a deficiency of moisture that results in adverse impacts on people, animals, or vegetation over a sizeable area. NOAA together with its partners provides short- and long-term Drought Assessments.

**Drought Index.** In hydrologic terms, computed value which is related to some of the cumulative effects of a prolonged and abnormal moisture deficiency. (An index of hydrological drought corresponding to levels below the mean in streams, lakes, and reservoirs.)

**Dust Storm.** A severe weather condition characterized by strong winds and dust-filled air over an extensive area.

**EBS.** Emergency Broadcast System.

**El Niño.** A warming of the ocean current along the coasts of Peru and Ecuador that is generally associated with dramatic changes in the weather patterns of the region; a major El Niño event generally occurs every 3 to 7 years and is associated with changes in the weather patterns worldwide.

**Emergency Services.** In hydrologic terms, services provided in order to minimize the impact of a flood that is already happening. These measures are the responsibility of city, or county emergency management staff and the owners or operators of major, or critical facilities. Some examples of emergency services are flood warning and evacuation, flood response, and post flood activities.

**Ensemble Forecast.** Multiple predictions from an ensemble of slightly different initial conditions and/or various versions of models. The objectives are to improve the accuracy of the forecast through averaging the various forecasts, which eliminates non-predictable components, and to provide reliable information on forecast uncertainties from the diversity amongst ensemble members. Forecasters use this tool to measure the likelihood of a forecast.

**Excessive Heat.** Excessive heat occurs from a combination of high temperatures (significantly above normal) and high humidities. At certain levels, the human body cannot maintain proper internal temperatures and may experience heat stroke. The "Heat Index" is a measure of the effect of the combined elements on the body.

**Excessive Heat Outlook.** This CPC [Climate Prediction Center of the National Weather Service] product, a combination of temperature and humidity over a certain number of days, is designed to provide an indication of areas of the country where people and animals may need to take precautions against the heat during May to November.

**Excessive Heat Warning.** Issued within 12 hours of the onset of the following criteria: heat index of at least 105°F for more than 3 hours per day for 2 consecutive days, or heat index more than 115°F for any period of time.

**Excessive Heat Watch.** Issued by the National Weather Service when heat indices in excess of 105°F (41°C) during the day combined with nighttime low temperatures of 80°F (27°C) or higher are forecast to occur for two consecutive days.

**Extended Forecast Discussion.** This discussion is issued once a day around 2 PM EST (3 PM EDT) and is primarily intended to provide insight into guidance forecasts for the 3- to 5-day forecast period. The geographic focus of this discussion is on the United States (including Alaska and Hawaii). Although portions of this narrative will parallel the Hemispheric Map Discussion, a much greater effort is made to routinely relate the model forecasts and necessary modifications to weather forecasts, mainly in terms of temperature and precipitation.

**Fair.** It is usually used at night to describe less than $^3/_8$ opaque clouds, no precipitation, no extremes of visibility, temperature or winds. It describes generally pleasant weather conditions.

**FEMA.** Federal Emergency Management Agency. An agency of the federal government having responsibilities in hazard mitigation; FEMA also administers the National Flood Insurance Program.

**Flash Flood.** A flood which is caused by heavy or excessive rainfall in a short period of time, generally less than 6 hours. Also, at times a dam failure can cause a flash flood, depending on the type of dam and time period during which the break occurs.

**Flash Flood Guidance.** Forecast guidance, often model output, specific to the potential for flash flooding (e.g., how much rainfall over a given area will be required to produce flash flooding).

**Flash Flood Table.** In hydrologic terms, a table of pre-computed forecast crest stage values for small streams for a variety of antecedent moisture conditions and rain amounts. Soil moisture conditions are often represented by flash flood guidance values. In lieu of crest stages, categorical representations of flooding, e.g., minor, moderate, etc. may be used on the tables.

**Flash Flood Warning.** Issued to inform the public, emergency management, and other cooperating agencies that flash flooding is in progress, imminent, or highly likely.

**Flash Flood Watch.** Issued to indicate current or developing hydrologic conditions that are favorable for flash flooding in and close to the watch area, but the occurrence is neither certain or imminent.

**Flood.** The inundation of a normally dry area caused by an increased water level in an established watercourse, such as a river, stream, or drainage ditch, or ponding of water at or near the point where the rain fell.

**Flood Control Storage.** In hydrologic terms, storage of water in reservoirs to abate flood damage.

**Flood Crest.** Maximum height of a flood wave as it passes a certain location.

**Flood/Flash Flood Watch.** Issued to inform the public and cooperating agencies that current and developing hydrometeorological conditions are such that there is a threat of flooding, but the occurrence is neither certain nor imminent.

**Flood Loss Reduction Measures.** In hydrologic terms, the strategy for reducing flood losses. There are four basic strategies. They are prevention, property protection, emergency services, and structural projects. Each strategy incorporates different measures that are appropriate for different conditions. In many communities, a different person may be responsible for each strategy.

**Flood Potential Outlook.** In hydrologic terms, an NWS outlook that is issued to alert the public of potentially heavy rainfall that could send area rivers and streams into flood or aggravate an existing flood.

**Flood Prevention.** In hydrologic terms, measures that are taken in order to keep flood problems from getting worse. Planning, land acquisition, river channel maintenance, wetlands protection, and other regulations all help modify development on floodplains and watersheds to reduce their susceptibility to flood damage. Preventive measures are usually administered by the building, zoning, planning and/or code enforcement offices of the local government.

**Flood Problems.** In hydrologic terms, problems and damages that occur during a flood as a result of human development and actions. Flood problems are a result from:

1) Inappropriate development in the floodplain (e.g., building too low, too close to the channel, or blocking flood flows);
2) Development in the watershed that increases flood flows and creates a larger floodplain, or;
3) A combination of the previous two.

**Floodproofing.** In hydrologic terms, the process of protecting a building from flood damage on site. Floodproofing can be divided into wet and dry floodproofing. In areas subject to slow-moving, shallow flooding, buildings can be elevated, or barriers can be constructed to block the water's approach to the building. These techniques have the advantage of being less disruptive to the neighborhood. It must be noted that during a flood, a floodproofed building may be isolated and without utilities and therefore unusable, even though it has not been damaged.

**Flood Stage.** A gage height at which a watercourse overtops its banks and begins to cause damage to any portion of the defined reach. Flood stage is usually higher than or equal to bankful stage.

**Flood Statement (FLS).** In hydrologic terms, a statement issued by the NWS to inform the public of flooding along major streams in which there is not a serious threat to life or property. It may also follow a flood warning to give later information.

**Flood Warning (FLW).** In hydrologic terms, a release by the NWS to inform the public of flooding along larger streams in which there is a serious threat to life or property. A flood warning will usually contain river stage (level) forecasts.

**Flurries.** Snow flurries are an intermittent light snowfall of short duration (generally light snow showers) with no measurable accumulation (trace category).

**Fog (Abbrev. F).** Fog is water droplets suspended in the air at the Earth's surface. Fog is often hazardous when the visibility is reduced to $1/4$ mile or less.

**Forecast.** A statement of prediction.

**Forecast Guidance.** Computer-generated forecast materials used to assist the preparation of a forecast, such as numerical forecast models.

**Forecast Periods.** Official definitions for NWS products:

Today ................................................. Sunrise to sunset
This afternoon ................................... noon till 6 p.m.
This evening ...................................... 6 p.m. till sunset
Tonight ............................................. sunset till sunrise
Tomorrow .......................................... sunrise to sunset of the following day

**Freeze.** A freeze is when the surface air temperature is expected to be 32°F or below over a widespread area for a climatologically significant period of time. Use of the term is usually restricted to advective situations or to occasions when wind or other conditions prevent frost. "Killing" may be used during the growing season when the temperature is expected to be low enough for a sufficient duration to kill all but the hardiest herbaceous crops.

**Freezeup date.** In hydrologic terms, the date on which the water body was first observed to be completely frozen over.

**Freeze Warning.** Issued during the growing season when surface temperatures are expected to drop below freezing over a large area for an extended period of time, regardless whether or not frost develops.

**Freezing Drizzle.** A drizzle that falls as a liquid but freezes into glaze or rime upon contact with the cold ground or surface structures.

**Freezing Drizzle Advisory.** Issued when freezing rain or freezing drizzle is forecast but a significant accumulation is not expected. However, even small amounts of freezing rain or freezing drizzle may cause significant travel problems.

**Freezing Fog.** A suspension of numerous minute ice crystals in the air, or water droplets at temperatures below 0° Celsius, based at the Earth's surface, which reduces horizontal visibility; also called ice fog.

**Freezing Rain.** Rain that falls as a liquid but freezes into glaze upon contact with the ground.

**Freezing Rain Advisory.** Issued when freezing rain or freezing drizzle is forecast but a significant accumulation is not expected. However, even small amounts of freezing rain or freezing drizzle may cause significant travel problems.

**Freshet.** The annual spring rise of streams in cold climates as a result of snow melt; freshet also refers to a flood caused by rain or melting snow.

**Front.** A boundary or transition zone between two air masses of different density, and thus (usually) of different temperature. A moving front is named according to the advancing air mass, e.g., cold front if colder air is advancing.

**Frontal Inversion.** A temperature inversion that develops aloft when warm air overruns the cold air behind a front.

**Frost (Abbrev. FRST).** Frost describes the formation of thin ice crystals on the ground or other surfaces in the form of scales, needles, feathers, or fans. Frost develops under conditions similar to dew, except the temperatures of the Earth's surface and earthbound objects falls below 32°F. As with the term "freeze," this condition is primarily significant during the growing season. If a frost period is sufficiently severe to end the growing season or delay its beginning, it is commonly referred to as a "killing frost." Because frost is primarily an event that occurs as the result of radiational cooling, it frequently occurs with a thermometer level temperature in the mid-30s.

**Frost Advisory.** Issued during the growing season when widespread frost formation is expected over an extensive area. Surface temperatures are usually in the mid 30s Fahrenheit.

**Frostbite.** Human tissue damage caused by exposure to intense cold.

**Fujita Scale (or F Scale).** A scale of tornado intensity in which wind speeds are inferred from an analysis of wind damage:

| Rating | Wind, Damage |
| --- | --- |
| F0 (weak) | 40–72 mph, light damage |
| F1 (weak) | 73–112 mph, moderate damage |
| F2 (strong) | 113–157 mph, considerable damage |
| F3 (strong) | 158–206 mph, severe damage |
| F4 (violent) | 207–260 mph, devastating damage |
| F5 (violent) | 260–318 mph (rare), incredible damage |

All tornadoes, and most other severe local windstorms, are assigned a single number from this scale according to the most intense damage caused by the storm.

**Gage.** In hydrologic terms: A device for indicating the magnitude or position of a thing in specific units, when such magnitude or position undergoes change, for example: The elevation of a water surface, the velocity of flowing water, the pressure of water, the amount or intensity of precipitation, the depth of snowfall, etc.

**Gaging Station.** In hydrologic terms, a particular site on a watercourse where systematic observations of stage/and or flow are measured.

**GEMPAK.** General Environmental Meteorological Package (programing language).

**General Circulation.** The totality of large-scale organized motion for the entire global atmosphere.

**General Circulation Models (GCMs).** These computer simulations reproduce the Earth's weather patterns and can be used to predict change in the weather and climate.

**General Wind.** Land management agency term for winds produced by synoptic-scale pressure systems on which smaller-scale or local convective winds are superimposed.

**Geostationary Satellite.** A satellite that rotates at the same rate as the earth, remaining over the same spot above the equator.

**GFS.** The Global Forecast System (360-hour numerical model of the atmosphere). Previously known as the AVN and MRF.

**GIS.** Geographic Information System. A computer-based graphics program that allows the superposition of plan-maps of thematic elements, such as roads, rivers, land use patterns, and the like to aid in local or regional planning activities.

**Global Temperature Change.** The net result of four primary factors including the greenhouse effect, changes in incoming solar radiation, altered patterns of ocean circulations, and changes in continental position, topography and/or vegetation. Three feedback mechanisms which affect global temperature change include cloud height and amount, snow and ice distribution, and atmospheric water vapor levels.

**Global Warming.** An overall increase in world temperatures which may be caused by additional heat being trapped by greenhouse gases.

**GOES.** Geostationary Operational Environmental Satellite. Satellites orbiting at 22,370 miles above the Earth's surface with the same rotational velocity as the Earth; therefore, the satellite remains over the same location on the Earth 24 hours a day. Besides sending back satellite pictures to earth, it also relays the DCPs river and rainfall data back to the ground.

**Greenhouse Effect.** Atmospheric heating caused by solar radiation being readily transmitted inward through the earth's atmosphere but longwave radiation less readily transmitted outward, due to absorption by certain gases in the atmosphere.

**Greenhouse Gases.** The gases that absorb terrestrial radiation and contribute to the greenhouse effect; the main greenhouse gasses are water vapor, methane, carbon dioxide, and ozone.

**Ground Blizzard Warning.** When blizzard conditions are solely caused by blowing and drifting snow.

**Ground Clutter.** A pattern of radar echoes from fixed ground targets (buildings, hills, etc.) near the radar. Ground clutter may hide or confuse precipitation echoes near the radar antenna.

**Ground Fog (Abbrev. GF).** Fog produced over the land by the cooling of the lower atmosphere as it comes in contact with the ground. Also known as radiation fog, and in parts of California as tule fog.

**Ground receive sites.** In hydrologic terms, a satellite dish and associated computer which receives signals from the GOES satellite, decodes the information, and transmits it to a another [sic] site for further processing. The GOES satellite ground-receive site is located at Wallops Island, VA; and the information is relayed to a mainframe computer at NWSH for processing.

**Growing Degree Day.** The number of degrees that the average temperature is above a baseline value. For example, 40 degrees for canning purposes; 45 degree for potatoes; and 50 degrees for sweet corn, snap beans, lima beans, tomatoes, grapes, and field corn. Every degree that the average temperature is above the baseline value becomes a growing degree day. Agricultural related interests use growing degree days to determine planting times.

**Growing Season.** The period of time between the last killing frost of spring and the first killing frost of autumn.

**Gunge.** Slang for anything in the atmosphere that restricts visibility for storm spotting, such as fog, haze, precipitation (steady rain or drizzle), widespread low clouds (stratus), etc.

**Gust (Abbrev. G).** A rapid fluctuation of wind speed with variations of 10 knots or more between peaks and lulls.

178

**Hail.** Showery precipitation in the form of irregular pellets or balls of ice more than 5 mm in diameter, falling from a cumulonimbus cloud.

**Hail Contamination.** A limitation in NEXRAD rainfall estimates whereby abnormally high reflectivities associated with hail are converted to rainfall rates and rainfall accumulations. These high reflectivity values are mistaken by the radar for extremely heavy rain, thus "contaminating" (inflating) its estimation of how much rain has fallen over the affected area.

**Hail Index.** An indication of whether the thunderstorm structure of each storm identified is conducive to the production of hail.

**Hail Size.** Typically refers to the diameter of the hailstones. Warnings and reports may report hail size through comparisons with real-world objects that correspond to certain diameters:

| Description | Diameter (inches) |
| --- | --- |
| Pea | 0.25 |
| Marble or Mothball | 0.50 |
| Penny or Dime | 0.75 |
| Nickel | 0.88 |
| Quarter | 1.00 |
| Half Dollar | 1.25 |
| Walnut or Ping Pong Ball | 1.50 |
| Golfball | 1.75 |
| Hen's Egg | 2.00 |
| Tennis Ball | 2.50 |
| Baseball | 2.75 |
| Tea Cup | 3.00 |
| Grapefruit | 4.00 |
| Softball | 4.50 |

**Hail Spike.** An area of reflectivity extending away from the radar immediately behind a thunderstorm with extremely large hail. In an area of large hail, radiation from the radar can bounce from hailstone to hailstone before being reflected back to the radar. The time delay between the backscattered radiation from the storm and the bounced and scattered radiation from the large hail causes the reflectivity from the hail to appear to come from a farther range than the actual storm.

**Haines Index.** This is also called the Lower Atmosphere Stability Index. It is computed from the morning (12Z) soundings from RAOB stations across North America. The index is composed of a stability term and a moisture term. The stability term is derived from the temperature difference at two atmosphere levels. The moisture term is derived from the dew point depression at a single atmosphere level. This index has been shown to be correlated with large fire growth on initiating and existing fires where surface winds do not dominate fire behavior. The Haines Indices range from 2 to 6 for indicating potential for large fire growth.

**Hazardous Weather Outlook.** A narrative statement produced by the National Weather Service, frequently issued on a routine basis, to provide information regarding the potential of significant weather expected during the next 1 to 5 days.

**Hazards Assessment.** CPC's Hazards Assessment provides emergency managers, planners, forecasters and the public advance notice of potential hazards related to climate, weather and hydrological events.

**Haze (Abbrev. HZ).** An aggregation in the atmosphere of very fine, widely dispersed, solid or liquid particles, or both, giving the air an opalescent appearance that subdues colors.

**HDRAIN.** An Hourly Digital Rainfall Product of the WSR-88D.

**Heat Advisory.** Issued within 12 hours of the onset of the following conditions: heat index of at least 105°F but less than 115°F for less than 3 hours per day, or nighttime lows above 80°F for 2 consecutive days.

**Heat Exhaustion.** A mild form of heat stroke, characterized by faintness, dizziness, and heavy sweating.

**Heat Index.** The Heat Index (HI) or the "Apparent Temperature" is an accurate measure of how hot it really feels when the Relative Humidity (RH) is added to the actual air temperature.

**Heat Lightning.** Lightning that occurs at a distance such that thunder is no longer audible.

**Heat Stroke.** A condition resulting from excessive exposure to intense heat, characterized by high fever, collapse, and sometimes convulsions or coma.

**Heat Wave.** A period of abnormally and uncomfortably hot and unusually humid weather. Typically a heat wave lasts two or more days.

**Heating Degree Days (Abbrev. HDD).** A form of degree day used to estimate energy requirements for heating. Typically, heating degree days are calculated as how much colder the mean temperature at a location is than 65°F on a given day. For example, if a location experiences a mean temperature of 55°F on a certain day, there were 10 HDD (Heating Degree Days) that day because 65–55 = 10.

**Heavy Snow.** This generally means: (1) snowfall accumulating to 4 inches or more in depth in 12 hours or less; or (2) snowfall accumulating to 6 inches or more in depth in 24 hours or less. In forecasts, snowfall amounts are expressed as a range of values, e.g., "8 to 12 inches." However, in heavy snow situations where there is considerable uncertainty concerning the range of values, more appropriate phrases are used, such as " . . . up to 12 inches . . . " or alternatively " . . . 8 inches or more . . . "

**Heavy Snow Warning.** Issued by the National Weather Service when snowfall of 6 inches (15 cm) or more in 12 hours or 8 inches (20 cm) or more in 24 hours is imminent or occurring. These criteria are specific for the Midwest and may vary regionally.

**High (Abbrev. HI).** In meteorology, a region of high pressure; also known as anticyclone.

**High Risk (of severe thunderstorms).** Severe weather is expected to affect more than 10 percent of the area. A high risk is rare, and implies an unusually dangerous situation and usually the possibility of a major severe weather outbreak.

**High Surf Advisory.** Issued when seas of 7 feet or greater are affecting the coastline.

**High Wind.** Sustained wind speeds of 40 mph or greater lasting for 1 hour or longer, or winds of 58 mph or greater for any duration.

**High Wind Advisory.** This product is issued by the National Weather Service when high wind speeds may pose a hazard. The criteria for this advisory varies from state to state. In Michigan, the criteria is sustained non-convective (not related to thunderstorms) winds greater than or equal to 30 mph lasting for one hour or longer, or winds greater than or equal to 45 mph for any duration.

**High Wind Warning.** This product is issued by the National Weather Service when high wind speeds may pose a hazard or is life threatening. The criteria for this warning varies from state to state. In Michigan, the criteria is sustained non-convective (not related to thunderstorms) winds greater than or equal to 40 mph lasting for one hour or longer, or winds greater than or equal to 58 mph for any duration.

**High Wind Watch.** This product is issued by the National Weather Service when there is the potential of high wind speeds developing that may pose a hazard or is life threatening. The criteria for this watch varies from state to state. In Michigan, the criteria is the potential for sustained non-convective (not related to thunderstorms) winds greater than or equal to 40 mph and/or gusts greater than or equal to 58 mph.

**Hoar Frost.** A deposit of interlocking crystals formed by direct sublimation on objects, usually those of small diameter freely exposed to the air, such as tree branches, plants, wires, poles, etc. The deposition of hoar frost is similar to the process by which dew is formed, except that the temperature of the frosted object must be below freezing. It forms when air with a dew point below freezing is brought to saturation by cooling.

**Hodograph.** A polar coordinate graph which shows the vertical wind profile of the lowest 7,000 meters of the atmosphere. These plots are used to determine the advection patterns aloft, whether a thunderstorm will rotate, and the type of thunderstorms that you will likely see that day.

**Hook Echo.** A radar reflectivity pattern characterized by a hook-shaped extension of a thunderstorm echo, usually in the right-rear part of the storm (relative to its direction of motion). A hook often is associated with a mesocyclone, and indicates favorable conditions for tornado development.

**Hourly Precipitation Data (HPD).** It contains data on nearly 3,000 hourly precipitation stations (National Weather Service, Federal Aviation Administration, and cooperative observer stations) in inches to tenths or inches to hundredths at local standard time. HPD includes maximum precipitation for nine (9) time periods from 15 minutes to 24 hours, for selected stations.

**HPC.** Hydrometeorological Prediction Center.

**HSA (Hydrologic Service Area).** A geographical area assigned to Weather Service Forecast Office's/Weather Forecast Office's that embraces one or more rivers.

**Humidity.** Generally, a measure of the water vapor content of the air. Popularly, it is used synonymously with relative humidity.

**Hurricane (Abbrev. HURCN).** A tropical cyclone with surface winds in excess of 32 m/s (64 knots or 74 mph) in the Western Hemisphere. There are various regional names for these storms.

**Hurricane Local Statement.** A public release prepared by local National Weather Service offices in or near a threatened area giving specific details for its county/parish warning area on:

1) weather conditions
2) evacuation decisions made by local officials
3) other precautions necessary to protect life and property.

**Hurricane Season.** The portion of the year having a relatively high incidence of hurricanes. The hurricane season in the Atlantic, Caribbean, and Gulf of Mexico runs from June 1 to November 30. The hurricane season in the Eastern Pacific basin runs from May 15 to November 30. The hurricane season in the Central Pacific basin runs from June 1 to November 30.

**Hurricane Warning.** A warning that sustained winds 64 kt (74 mph or 119 kph) or higher associated with a hurricane are expected in a specified coastal area in 24 hours or less. A hurricane warning can remain in effect when dangerously high water or a combination of dangerously high water and exceptionally high waves continue, even though winds may be less than hurricane force.

**Hurricane Watch.** An announcement of specific coastal areas that a hurricane or an incipient hurricane condition poses a possible threat, generally within 36 hours.

**Hydrologic Budget.** In hydrologic terms, an accounting of the inflow to, outflow from, and storage in, a hydrologic unit, such as a drainage basin, aquifer, soil zone, lake, reservoir, or irrigation project.

**Hydrologic Equation.** In hydrologic terms, the water inventory equation (Inflow = Outflow + Change in Storage) which expresses the basic principle that during a given time interval the total inflow to an area must equal the total outflow plus the net change in storage.

**Hydrologic Model.** In hydrologic terms, a conceptual or physically-based procedure for numerically simulating a process or processes which occur in a watershed.

**Hydrologic Service Area.** HSA. A geographical area assigned to Weather Service Forecast Office's/Weather Forecast Office's that embraces one or more rivers.

**Hydrology.** The scientific study of the waters of the earth, especially with relation to the effects of precipitation and evaporation upon the occurrence and character of water on or below the land surface.

**Hydrometeorologists.** In hydrologic terms, individuals who have the combined knowledge in the fields of both meteorology and hydrology which enables them to study and solve hydrologic problems where meteorology is a factor.

**Ice Storm.** An ice storm is used to describe occasions when damaging accumulations of ice are expected during freezing rain situations. Significant accumulations of ice pull down trees and utility lines resulting in loss of power and communication. These accumulations of ice make walking and driving extremely dangerous. Significant ice accumulations are usually accumulations of $1/4$ inches or greater.

**Ice Storm Warning.** This product is issued by the National Weather Service when freezing rain produces a significant and possibly damaging accumulation of ice. The criteria for this warning varies from state to state, but typically will be issued any time more than $1/4$ inches of ice is expected to accumulate in an area.

**Infiltration Capacity.** In hydrologic terms, the maximum rate at which water can enter the soil at a particular point under a given set of conditions.

**Infrared Satellite Imagery.** This satellite imagery senses surface and cloud top temperatures by measuring the wavelength of electromagnetic radiation emitted from these objects. This energy is called "infrared." High clouds are very cold, so they appear white. Mid-level clouds are somewhat warmer, so they will be a light gray shade. Low clouds are warmer still, so they appear as a dark shade of gray or black. Often, low clouds are the same temperature as the surrounding terrain and cannot be distinguished at all. The satellite picks up this infrared energy between 10.5 and 12.6 micrometer (um) channels.

**Instrument Shelter.** A boxlike structure designed to protect temperature measuring instruments from exposure to direct sunshine, precipitation, and condensation, while at the same time providing adequate ventilation.

**Intangible Flood Damage.** In hydrologic terms, estimates of the damage done by disruption of business, danger to health, shock, and loss of life and in general all costs not directly measurable which require a large element of judgment for estimating.

**Interception.** In hydrologic terms, the process by which precipitation is caught and held by foliage, twigs, and branches of trees, shrubs, and other vegetation, and lost by evaporation, never reaching the surface of the ground. Interception equals the precipitation on the vegetation minus streamflow and through fall.

**Interpolate.** To estimate a value within an interval between two known values. This technique is sometimes used with computer models for locations in between the model's "gridpoints."

**Inversion (Abbrev. INVRN).** Generally, a departure from the usual increase or decrease in an atmospheric property with altitude. Specifically it almost always refers to a temperature inversion, i.e., an increase in temperature with height, or to the layer within which such an increase occurs. An inversion is present in the lower part of a cap.

**Irrigation Requirement.** In hydrologic terms, the quantity of water, exclusive of precipitation, that is required for crop production. It includes surface evaporation and other economically unavoidable wastes.

**Isentropic Analysis.** A way in which the forecaster can look at the atmosphere in 3-dimensions instead of looking at constant pressure surfaces (such as the 850 mb, 700 mb, 500 mb, etc.) which are in 2-dimensions. In this analysis method, the forecaster looks at constant potential temperature (the temperature that it would take if we compressed or expanded it adiabatically to the pressure of 1000 mb) surfaces. Air parcels move up and down these surfaces; therefore, the forecaster can see where the moisture is located and how much moisture is available.

**Isobar.** A line connecting points of equal pressure.

**Isobaric Chart.** A weather map representing conditions on a surface of equal atmospheric pressure. For example, a 500 mb chart will display conditions at the level of the atmosphere at which the atmospheric pressure is 500 mb. The height above sea level at which the pressure is that particular value may vary from one location to another at any given time, and also varies with time at any one location, so it does not represent a surface of constant altitude/height (i.e., the 500 mb level may be at a different height above sea level over Dallas than over New York).

**Jet Stream (Abbrev. JSTR).** Relatively strong winds concentrated in a narrow stream in the atmosphere, normally referring to horizontal, high-altitude winds. The position and orientation of jet streams vary from day to day. General weather patterns (hot/cold, wet/dry) are related closely to the position, strength and orientation of the jet stream (or jet streams). A jet stream at low levels is known as a low-level jet.

**La Niña.** La Niña, a phase of ENSO, is a periodic cooling of surface ocean waters in the eastern tropical Pacific along with a shift in convection in the western Pacific further west than the climatological average. These conditions affect weather patterns around the world. The preliminary CPC definition of La Niña is a phenomenon in the equatorial Pacific Ocean characterized by a negative sea surface temperature departure from normal.

**Lake Effect Snow.** Snow showers that are created when cold, dry air passes over a large warmer lake, such as one of the Great Lakes, and picks up moisture and heat.

**Lake Effect Snow Advisory.** This product is issued by the National Weather Service when pure lake effect snow (this is where the snow is a direct result of lake effect snow and not because of a low pressure system) may pose a hazard or it is life threatening. The criteria for this advisory varies from area to area.

**Lake Effect Snow Squall.** A local, intense, narrow band of moderate to heavy snow squall that can extend long distances inland. It may persist for many hours. It may also be accompanied by strong, gusty, surface winds and possibly lightning. Accumulations can be 6 inches or more in 12 hours.

**Lake Effect Snow Warning.** This product is issued by the National Weather Service when pure lake effect snow (this is where the snow is a direct result of lake effect snow and not because of a synoptic storm or low pressure system) may pose a hazard or it is life threatening.

**Lake Effect Storm.** A fall or winter storm that produces heavy but localized precipitation as a result of temperature differences between the air over snow-covered ground and the air over the open waters of a lake.

**LALs.** (L)ightning (A)ctivity (L)evels.

LAL 1—No thunderstorms.

LAL 2—Few building cumulus with isolated thunderstorms.

LAL 3—Much building cumulus with scattered thunderstorms. Light to moderate rain.

LAL 4—Thunderstorms common. Moderate to heavy rain reaching the ground.

LAL 5—Numerous thunderstorms. Moderate to heavy rain reaching the ground.

LAL 6—Dry lightning (same as LAL 3 but without the rain).

**Landfall.** The intersection of the surface center of a tropical cyclone with a coastline. Because the strongest winds in a tropical cyclone are not located precisely at the center, it is possible for a cyclone's strongest winds to be experienced over land even if landfall does not occur. Similarly, it is possible for a tropical cyclone to make landfall and have its strongest winds remain over the water. Compare direct hit, indirect hit, and strike.

**Large Scale.** (Synoptic Scale) Size scale referring generally to weather systems with horizontal dimensions of several hundred miles or more. Most high and low pressure areas seen on weather maps are synoptic-scale systems.

**Last Update.** The time and date in which the forecast was issued or updated. The forecast may be updated at any time as weather conditions warrant.

**Layered Haze.** Haze produced when air pollution from multiple line, area or point sources is transported long distances to form distinguishable layers of discoloration in a stable atmosphere.

**LCD (Local Climatological Data).** This National Climatic Data Center (NCDC) publication is produced monthly and annually for some 270 United States cities and it's territories. The LCD summarizes temperature, relative humidity, precipitation, cloudiness, wind speed and direction observation.

**Levee (Dike [or Floodwall]).** In hydrologic terms, a long, narrow embankment usually built to protect land from flooding. If built of concrete or masonry the structure is usually referred to as a flood wall. Levees and floodwalls confine streamflow within a specified area to prevent flooding. The term "dike" is used to describe an embankment that blocks an area on a reservoir or lake rim that is lower than the top of the dam.

**Lifted Index (Abbrev. LI).** A common measure of atmospheric instability. Its value is obtained by computing the temperature that air near the ground would have if it were lifted to some higher level (around 18,000 feet, usually) and comparing that temperature to the actual temperature at that level. Negative values indicate instability—the more negative, the more unstable the air is, and the stronger the updrafts are likely to be with any developing thunderstorms. However there are no "magic numbers" or threshold LI values below which severe weather becomes imminent.

**Lightning (Abbrev. LTNG).** A visible electrical discharge produced by a thunderstorm. The discharge may occur within or between clouds, between the cloud and air, between a cloud and the ground or between the ground and a cloud.

**Likely (Abbrev. LKLY).** In probability of precipitation statements, the equivalent of a 60 or 70 percent chance.

**Line Echo Wave Pattern (Abbrev. LEWP).** A radar echo pattern formed when a segment of a line of thunderstorms surges forward at an accelerated rate.

**Local Convective Wind.** In fire weather terminology, local thermally driven winds arising over a comparatively small area and influenced by local terrain. Examples include sea and land breezes, lake breezes, diurnal mountain wind systems and columnar convective currents.

**Long Term Retention.** Retention of data for 5 years to satisfy requirements for local studies and to support litigation.

**Low.** A region of low pressure, marked as "L" on a weather map. A low center is usually accompanied by precipitation, extensive cloudiness, and moderate winds. See Cyclone.

**Lowland Flooding.** In hydrologic terms, inundation of low areas near the river, often rural, but may also occur in urban areas.

**Low Pressure System.** An area of a relative pressure minimum that has converging winds and rotates in the same direction as the earth. This is counterclockwise in the Northern Hemisphere and clockwise in the Southern Hemisphere. Also known as a cyclone, it is the opposite of an area of high pressure, or a anticyclone.

**Macroscale.** Large scale, characteristic of weather systems several hundred to several thousand kilometers in diameter.

**Major Flooding.** A general term including extensive inundation and property damage. (Usually characterized by the evacuation of people and livestock and the closure of both primary and secondary roads.)

**MAREP (short for MArine REPort).** A marine weather report from a vessel which is forwarded to the National Weather Service. Since there are very few weather buoys in the coastal waters, MAREPS are very useful in determining weather conditions for the marine forecaster.

**Marine Prediction Center.** This is one of 9 centers that comprise the National Centers for Environmental Prediction (NCEP, formerly the National Meteorological Center). The Marine Prediction Center (MPC) is an integral component of the National Centers for Environmental Prediction (NCEP). MPC is located at the NOAA Science Center in Camp Springs, MD. The primary responsibility is the issuance of marine warnings, forecasts, and guidance in text and graphical format for maritime users. Also, the MPC quality controls marine observations globally from ship, buoy, and automated marine observations for gross errors prior to being assimilated into computer model guidance. In addition MPC coordinates with the National Hurricane Center (NHC) with forecast points for Tropical Cyclones in the Atlantic Ocean E of 65W. The MPC originates and issues marine warnings and forecasts, continually monitors and analyzes maritime data, and provides guidance of marine atmospheric variables for purposes of protection of life and property, safety at sea, and enhancement of economic opportunity. These products fulfill U.S. responsibilities with the World Meteorological Organization and Safety of Life at Sea Convention (SOLAS). In emergency situations MPC acts as a backup to the Tropical Prediction Center (TPC) taking over the marine functions of TPC.

**Marine Small Craft Thunderstorm Advisory.** A marine warning issued by Environment Canada Atmospheric Environment Branch when the possibility of thunderstorms is greater than 40 percent.

**Marine Small Craft Wind Warning.** A marine warning issued by Environment Canada Atmospheric Environment Branch for winds which are forecasted to be in the 20–33 knot range inclusive.

**Marine Weather Statement.** The National Weather Service will issue this statement:

1) To provide follow-up information on Special Marine Warnings and to cancel all or part of a warning.
2) To describe short duration, nonsevere, but potentially hazardous conditions which sustained winds or frequent gusts are less than 34 knots for 2 hours or less. Short-lived increases in winds, although below threshold for Special Marine Warnings, that may make small craft handling difficult especially for inexperienced boaters.
3) To provide information for a variety of conditions not covered by warnings or routine forecasts (e.g., low water conditions, dense fog, etc.).
4) To discuss increasing or decreasing winds and to convey details on possible later warnings.

**Maximum Temperature.** This is the highest temperature recorded during a specified period of time. Common time periods include 6, 12 and 24 hours. The most common reference is to the daily maximum temperature, or "high."

**Mean Annual Temperature.** The average temperature for the entire year at any given location.

**Mean Areal Precipitation (Abbrev. MAP).** The average rainfall over a given area, generally expressed as an average depth over the area.

**Mean Daily Temperature.** The average of the highest and lowest temperatures during a 24-hour period.

**Medium Range.** In forecasting, (generally) three to seven days in advance.

**Mercury Barometer.** An instrument for measuring atmospheric pressure. The instrument contains an evacuated and graduated glass tube in which mercury rises or falls as the pressure of the atmosphere increases or decreases.

**Mesoclimate.** The climate of a small area of the earth's surface which may differ from the general climate of the district.

**Mesonet.** A regional network of observing stations (usually surface stations) designed to diagnose mesoscale weather features and their associated processes.

**Mesoscale.** Size scale referring to weather systems smaller than synoptic-scale systems but larger than storm-scale systems. Horizontal dimensions generally range from around 50 miles to several hundred miles. Squall lines, MCCs, and MCSs are examples of mesoscale weather systems.

**Mesoscale Discussion.** When conditions actually begin to shape up for severe weather, SPC (Storm Prediction Center) often issues a Mesoscale Discussion (MCD) statement anywhere from roughly half an hour to several hours before issuing a weather watch. SPC also puts out MCDs for hazardous winter weather events on the mesoscale, such as locally heavy snow, blizzards and freezing rain (see below). MCDs are also issued on occasion for heavy rainfall, convective trends, and other phenomena, when the forecaster feels he/she can provide useful information that is not readily available or apparent to field forecasters. MCDs are based on mesoscale analysis and interpretation of observations and of short term, high resolution numerical model output. The MCD basically describes what is currently happening, what is expected in the next few hours, the meteorological reasoning for the forecast, and when/where SPC plans to issue the watch (if dealing with severe thunderstorm potential). Severe thunderstorm MCDs can help you get a little extra lead time on the weather and allow you to begin gearing up operations before a watch is issued. The MCD begins with a numerical string that gives the LAT/LON coordinates of a polygon that loosely describes the area being discussed.

**METAR.** An international code (Aviation Routine Weather Report) used for reporting, recording and transmitting weather observations.

**Meteogram.** A graphical depiction of trends in meteorological variables such as temperature, dew point, wind speed and direction, pressure, etc. The time series meteogram can be constructed using observed data or forecast data.

**Meteorologist.** A person who studies meteorology. There are many different paths within the field of meteorology. For example, one could be a research meteorologist, radar meteorologist, climatologist, or operational meteorologist.

**Meteorology.** The science dealing with the atmosphere and its phenomena. A distinction can be drawn between meteorology and climatology, the latter being primarily concerned with average, not actual, weather conditions.

**Microbarograph.** An instrument designed to continuously record a barometer's reading of very small changes in atmospheric pressure.

**Microburst.** A convective downdraft with an affected outflow area of less than $2^1/_2$ miles wide and peak winds lasting less than 5 minutes. Microbursts may induce dangerous horizontal/vertical wind shears, which can adversely affect aircraft performance and cause property damage.

**Microclimate.** The climate of a small area such as a cave, house, city or valley that may be different from that in the general region.

**Microscale.** Pertaining to meteorological phenomena, such as wind circulations or cloud patterns, that are less than 2 km in horizontal extent.

**Mid-Flame Wind.** Wind measured at the midpoint of the flames, considered to be most representative of the speed of the wind that is affecting fire behavior.

**Minimum Temperature.** This is the lowest temperature recorded during a specified period of time. The time period can be 6, 12 or 24 hours. The most common reference is to the daily minimum temperature, or "low."

**Minor Flooding.** A general term indicating minimal or no property damage but possibly some public inconvenience.

**Mist.** A visible aggregate of minute water particles suspended in the atmosphere that reduces visibility to less than 7 statute miles, but greater than or equal to 5/8 statute miles. It does not reduce visibility as much as fog and is often confused with drizzle.

**Mixed Precipitation.** Any of the following combinations of freezing and frozen precipitation: snow and sleet, snow and freezing rain, or sleet alone. Rain may also be present.

**Model Output Statistics (Abbrev. MOS).** The Hydrometeorological Center (HPC) produces a short range (6 to 60 hours) MOS (Model Output Statistics) guidance package generated from the NGM, GFS, and ETA models for over 300 individual stations in the continental United States. These alphanumeric messages are made available at approximately 0400 and 1600 UTC for the 0000 and 1200 UTC forecast cycles, respectively. Model Output Statistics are a set of statistical equations that use model output to forecast the probability of precipitation, high and low temperature, cloud cover, and precipitation amount for many cities across the U.S.A. The statistical equations were specifically tailored for each location, taking into account factors such as each location's climate.

**Moderate Flooding.** The inundation of secondary roads; transfer to higher elevation necessary to save property—some evacuation may be required.

**Moderate Risk (of severe thunderstorms).** Severe thunderstorms are expected to affect between 5 and 10 percent of the area. A moderate risk indicates the possibility of a significant severe weather episode.

**Monthly Climatological Report.** This climatological product is issued once a month by each National Weather Service office. It is a mix of tabular and narrative information. It is organized so that similar items are grouped together (i.e., temperature, precipitation, wind, heating/cooling degree information, etc.).

**Mostly Clear.** When the predominant/average sky condition is covered $^1/_8$ to $^2/_8$ with opaque (not transparent) clouds. Sometimes referred to as *Mostly Sunny* if this condition is present during daylight hours.

**Mostly Cloudy.** When the predominant/average sky condition is covered by more than half, but not completely covered by opaque (not transparent) clouds. In other words, $^5/_8$ to $^7/_8$ of the sky is covered by opaque clouds.

**Mostly Sunny.** Same as *Mostly Clear*, except only applicable during daylight hours; when the predominant/average sky condition is covered $^1/_8$ to $^2/_8$ with opaque (not transparent) clouds.

**MRF.** Medium Range Forecast model, the medium-range computer model run by the United States (NOAA). The output from this model is part of what is now known as the GFS model, so the term MRF is no longer widely used.

**Mud Slide.** Fast moving soil, rocks and water that flow down mountain slopes and canyons during a heavy downpour of rain.

**Muggy.** A subjective term for warm and excessively humid conditions.

**Multiple Doppler Analysis.** The use of more than one radar (and hence more than one look angle) to reconstruct spatial distributions of the 2D or 3D wind field, which cannot be measured from a single radar alone. Includes dual Doppler, triple Doppler, and overdetermined multiple Doppler analysis.

**National Ambient Air Quality Standards.** In the United States, national standards for the ambient concentrations in air of different air pollutants designed to protect human health and welfare.

**National Climatic Data Center.** The agency that archives climatic data from the National Oceanic and Atmospheric Administration, as well as other climatological organizations.

**National Fire Danger Rating System.** A uniform fire danger rating system used in the United States that focuses on the environmental factors that impact the moisture content of fuels. Fire danger is rated daily over large administrative areas, such as national forests.

**National Flood Summary.** This NWS daily product (abbreviated FLN) contains nationwide information on current flood conditions. It is issued by the Hydrometeorological Information Center of the Office of Hydrology.

**National Hurricane Center.** One of three branches of the Tropical Prediction Center (TPC). This center maintains a continuous watch on tropical cyclones over the Atlantic, Caribbean, Gulf of Mexico, and the Eastern Pacific from May 15 through November 30. The Center prepares and distributes hurricane watches and warnings for the general public, and also prepares and distributes marine and military advisories for other users. During the "off-season" NHC provides training for U.S. emergency managers and representatives from many other countries that are affected by tropical cyclones. NHC also conducts applied research to evaluate and improve hurricane forecasting techniques, and is involved in public awareness programs.

**National Severe Storms Laboratory.** This is one of NOAA's internationally known Environmental Research Laboratories, leading the way in investigations of all aspects of severe weather. Headquartered in Norman OK with staff in Colorado, Nevada, Washington, Utah, and Wisconsin, the people of NSSL, in partnership with the National Weather Service, are dedicated to improving severe weather warnings and forecasts in order to save lives and reduce property damage.

**National Weather and Crop Summary.** A product of the National Agricultural Statistics Service, Agricultural Statistics Board, and U.S. Department of Agriculture. It contains weekly national agricultural weather summaries, including the weather's effect on crops; summaries and farm progress for 44 states and New England area.

**NCAR.** National Center for Atmospheric Research.

**NCDC.** National Climatic Data Center.

**NCEP.** National Centers for Environmental Prediction. A part of the National Weather Service which provides nationwide computerized and manual guidance to Warning and Forecast Offices concerning the forecast of basic weather elements.

**NESDIS.** National Environmental Satellite, Data, and Information Service. NESDIS collects, processes, stores, analyzes, and disseminates various types of hydrologic, meteorologic, and oceanic data. NESDIS is also responsible for the development of analytical and descriptive products so as to meet the needs of it's users.

**Net Rainfall.** In hydrologic terms, the portion of rainfall which reaches a stream channel or the concentration point as direct surface flow.

**NEXRAD.** NEXt Generation RADar. A NWS network of about 140 Doppler radars operating nationwide.

**NGM.** The Nested Grid Model, a 48-hour numerical model of the atmosphere run twice daily by NCEP.

**NHC.** National Hurricane Center. One of three branches of the Tropical Prediction Center (TPC). This center maintains a continuous watch on tropical cyclones over the Atlantic, Caribbean, Gulf of Mexico, and the Eastern Pacific from May 15 through November 30. The Center prepares and distributes hurricane watches and warnings for the general public, and also prepares and distributes marine and military advisories for other users. During the "off-season" NHC provides training for U.S. emergency managers and representatives from many other countries that are affected by tropical cyclones. NHC also conducts applied research to evaluate and improve hurricane forecasting techniques, and is involved in public awareness programs.

**NMC.** National Meteorological Center.

**NOAA.** National Oceanic and Atmospheric Administration

**NOAA Weather Radio (Abbrev. NWR).** "The voice of the National Weather Service"—NOAA Weather Radio broadcasts National Weather Service warnings, watches, forecasts and other hazard information 24 hours a day. It is provided as a public service by NOAA. The NOAA Weather Radio network has more than 480 stations in the 50 states and near adjacent coastal waters, Puerto Rico, the U.S. Virgin Islands and U.S. Pacific Territories.

**NOAA Weather Wire.** Mass dissemination via satellite of National Weather Service products to the media and public.

**Non-Uniform Sky Condition.** A localized sky condition which varies from that reported in the body of the report.

**Non-Uniform Visibility.** A localized visibility which varies from that reported in the body of the report.

**Normal.** The long-term average value of a meteorological paramater (i.e., temperature, humidity, etc.) for a certain area. For example, "temperatures are normal for this time of year" means that temperatures are at or near the average climatological value for the given date. Normals are usually taken from data averaged over a 30-year period (e.g., 1971–2000 average), and are concerned with the distribution of data within limits of common occurrence.

**Nowcast.** A short-term weather forecast, generally out to six hours or less. This is also called a Short Term Forecast.

**NSSFC.** National Severe Storm Forecast Center.

**NSSL.** National Severe Storms Laboratory. This is one of NOAA's internationally known Environmental Research Laboratories, leading the way in investigations of all aspects of severe weather. Headquartered in Norman OK with staff in Colorado, Nevada, Washington, Utah, and Wisconsin, the people of NSSL, in partnership with the National Weather Service, are dedicated to improving severe weather warnings and forecasts in order to save lives and reduce property damage.

**Numerical Forecasting [or Numerical Weather Prediction].** A computer forecast or prediction based on equations governing the motions and the forces affecting motion of fluids. The equations are based, or initialized, on specified weather or climate conditions at a certain place and time.

**NWS.** National Weather Service. An agency of the Federal Government within the Department of Commerce, National Oceanic and Atmospheric Administration, which is responsible for providing observations, forecasts and warnings of meteorological and hydrological events in the interest of national safety and economy.

**Office of Global Programs (OGP).** The Office of Global Programs sponsors focused scientific research, within approximately eleven research elements, aimed at understanding climate variability and its predictability. Through studies in these areas, researchers coordinate activities that jointly contribute to improved predictions and assessments of climate variability over a continuum of timescales from season to season, year to year, and over the course of a decade and beyond.

**Offshore Forecast.** A marine weather forecast for the waters between 60 and 250 miles off the coast.

**100-year Flood.** A statistic that indicates the magnitude of flood which can be expected to occur on average with a frequency of once every 100 years at a given point or reach on a river. The 100-year flood is usually developed from a statistical distribution that is based on historical floods. This is also called a base flood.

**Outlook (Abbrev. OTLK).** An outlook is used to indicate that a hazardous weather or hydrologic event may develop. It is intended to provide information to those who need considerable lead time to prepare for the event.

**Overcast (Abbrev. OVC).** An official sky cover classification for aviation weather observations, when the sky is completely covered by an obscuring phenomenon. This is applied only when obscuring phenomenon aloft are present—that is, not when obscuring phenomenon are surface-based, such as fog.

**Ozone.** A form of oxygen, $O_3$. A powerful oxidizing agent that is considered a pollutant in the lower troposphere but an essential chemical in the stratosphere where it protects the earth from high-energy ultraviolet radiation from the sun.

**Ozone Action Day.** A "heads-up" message issued by the Department of Natural Resources (DNR) through the National Weather Service when ozone levels may reach dangerous levels the next day. This message encourages residents to prevent air pollution by postponing the use of lawn mowing, motor vehicles, boats, as well as filling their vehicle gas tanks.

**Ozone Advisory.** It is issued by the Department of Natural Resources (DNR) through the National Weather Service when ozone levels reach 100. Ozone levels above 100 are unhealthy for people with heat and/or respiratory ailments.

**Ozone Hole.** A severe depletion of stratospheric ozone over Antarctica that occurs each spring. The possibility exists that a hole could form over the Arctic as well. The depletion is caused by a chemical reaction involving ozone and chlorine, primarily from human produced sources, cloud particles, and low temperatures.

**Ozone Layer.** An atmospheric layer that contains a high proportion of oxygen that exists as ozone. It acts as a filtering mechanism against incoming ultraviolet radiation. It is located between the troposphere and the stratosphere, around 9.5 to 12.5 miles (15 to 20 kilometers) above the earth's surface.

**Palmer Drought Severity Index (Abbrev. PDSI).** An index used to gage the severity of drought conditions by using a water balance equation to track water supply and demand. This index is calculated weekly by the National Weather Service.

**Partial Beam Filling.** A limitation of the rainfall estimation techniques used by NEXRAD. At far ranges from the radar, a storm may occupy only a portion of the radar beam (which may be several miles across). However, the radiation received by the radar antenna consists of the average reflectivity across the entire beam, so the reflectivity and associated rainfall rates are underestimated.

**Partly Cloudy.** When the predominant/average sky condition is covered $^3/_8$ to $^4/_8$ with opaque (not transparent) clouds. Same as Partly Sunny.

**Partly Sunny.** When the predominant/average sky condition is covered $^3/_8$ to $^4/_8$ with opaque (not transparent) clouds. Same as Partly Cloudy.

**PC-GRIDDS.** PC-Gridded Interactive Display and Diagnostic System. Allows the forecaster to view fields of gridded model output in contour or vector format.

By doing this, the forecaster can extract relevant information from the numerical model grid-point data.

**PDS Watch.** [Slang] A Severe Thunderstorm Watch or Tornado Watch with *Enhanced Wording* ("THIS IS A PARTICULARLY DANGEROUS SITUATION") issued by the Storm Prediction Center.

**Permafrost.** A layer of soil at varying depths below the surface in which the temperature has remained below freezing continuously from a few to several thousands of years.

**Persistence Forecast.** A forecast that the current weather condition will persist and that future weather will be the same as the present (e.g., if it is raining today, a forecast predicting rain tonight).

**Pervious Zone.** In hydrologic terms, a part of the cross section of an embankment dam comprising material of high permeability.

**Photochemical Smog.** Air pollution containing ozone and other reactive chemical compounds formed by the reaction of nitrogen oxides and hydrocarbons in the presence of sunlight.

**Pilot Balloon (Abbrev. PIBAL).** A small helium-filled meteorological balloon that is tracked as it rises through the atmosphere to determine how wind speed and direction change with altitude.

**Pilot Report (Abbrev. PIREP).** A report of inflight weather by an aircraft pilot or crew member. A complete coded report includes the following information in this order: location and/or extent of reported weather phenomenon: type of aircraft (only with reports of turbulence or icing).

**Plume-dominated Fire.** A fire whose behavior is governed primarily by the local wind circulation produced in response to the strong convection above the fire rather than by the general wind.

**Pluvial.** In hydrology, anything that is brought about directly by precipitation.

**Point Precipitation.** Precipitation at a particular site, in contrast to the mean precipitation over an area.

**Polar Orbiting Satellite.** A weather satellite which travels over both poles each time it orbits the Earth. It orbits about 530 miles (850 km) above the Earth's surface. A satellite with an orbit nearly parallel to the earth's meridian lines which crosses the polar regions on each orbit.

**Precipitation.** The process where water vapor condenses in the atmosphere to form water droplets that fall to the Earth as rain, sleet, snow, hail, etc.

**Precipitation Mode.** The standard, or default, operational mode of the WSR-88D. The radar automatically switches into precipitation mode from clear-air mode if the measured reflectivity exceeds a specific threshold value. The precipitation mode of NEXRAD is more sensitive than previous weather radars. The minimum detectable reflectivity in NEXRAD's precipitation mode is 5 dBZ, compared to 28 dBZ with the old WSR-57.

**Precipitation Processing System.** The WSR-88D system that generates 1-hour running, 3-hourly, and running storm total precipitation accumulations. Five functional steps are performed to calculate the best estimate of precipitation: (1) development of a sectorized hybrid scan, (2) conversion to precipitation rate, (3) precipitation accumulation, (4) adjustment using rain gages, (5) product update.

**Predominant Wind.** The wind that in the forecasters judgment generates (or is expected to generate) the local component of the significant sea conditions across the forecast area. This is the wind included in all marine forecast products.

**Pre-Hurricane Squall Line.** It is often the first serious indication that a hurricane is approaching. It is generally a straight line and resembles a squall-line that occurs with a mid-latitude cold front. It is as much as 50 miles or even more before the first ragged rain echoes of the hurricane's bands and is usually about 100 to 200 miles ahead of the eye, but it has been observed to be as much as 500 miles ahead of the eye in the largest hurricanes.

**Preliminary Report.** Now known as the "Tropical Cyclone Report." A report summarizing the life history and effects of an Atlantic or eastern Pacific tropical cyclone. It contains a summary of the cyclone life cycle and pertinent meteorological data, including the post-analysis best track (six-hourly positions and intensities) and other meteorological statistics. It also contains a description of damage and casualties the system produced, as well as information on forecasts and warnings associated with the cyclone. NHC writes a report on every tropical cyclone in its area of responsibility.

**Prescribed Fire.** A management ignited or natural wildland fire that burns under specified conditions where the fire is confined to a predetermined area and produces the fire behavior and fire characteristics required to attain planned fire treatment and resource management objectives.

**Present Weather.** The type of weather observed at the reporting time. These conditions may include types and intensity of precipitation such as light rain or heavy snow, as well as the condition of the air environment such as foggy, hazy or blowing dust.

**Pressure Characteristic.** The pattern of the pressure change during the specified period of time, usually the three hour period preceding an observation. This is recorded in three categories: falling, rising, or steady.

**Pressure Falling Rapidly.** A decrease in station pressure at a rate of 0.06 inch of mercury or more per hour which totals 0.02 inch or more.

**Pressure Jump.** A sudden, sharp increase in atmospheric pressure, typically occurring along an active front and preceding a storm.

**Pressure Rising Rapidly.** An increase in station pressure at a rate of 0.06 inch of mercury or more per hour which totals 0.02 inch or more.

**Prevailing Visibility.** The visibility that is considered representative of conditions at the station; the greatest distance that can be seen throughout at least half the horizon circle, not necessarily continuous.

**Prevailing Winds.** A wind that consistently blows from one direction more than from any other.

**Prevention of Significant Deterioration.** A program, specified in the Clean Air Act, whose goal is to prevent air quality from deteriorating significantly in areas of the country that are presently meeting the ambient air quality standards.

**Primary Ambient Air Quality Standards.** Air quality standards designed to protect human health.

**Probability.** A chance, or likelihood, that a certain event might happen.

**Probability Forecast.** A forecast of the probability that one or more of a mutually exclusive set of weather conditions will occur.

**Probability of Precipitation.** (Abbrev. PoP)- The probability that precipitation will be reported at a certain location during a specified period of time.

**Probability of Tropical Cyclone Conditions.** The probability, in percent, that the cyclone center will pass within 50 miles to the right or 75 miles to the left of the listed location within the indicated time period when looking at the coast in the direction of the cyclone's movement.

**PROG.** Forecast (prognostication)

**PROGGED.** Forecasted

**Prognostic Discussion.** This Hydrometeorological Prediction Center (HPC) discussion may include analysis of numerical and statistical models, meteorological circulation patterns and trends, and confidence factors. Reference is usually made to the manually produced 6- to 10-day Northern Hemisphere prognoses for mean 500 millibar heights and mean 500 millibar height anomalies. Discussions may also refer to the method of operational ensemble predictions.

**Property Protection.** Measures that are undertaken usually by property owners in order to prevent, or reduce flood damage. Property protection measures are often inexpensive for the community because they are implemented by or cost-shared with property owners. In many cases the buildings' appearance or use is unaffected, so these measurements are particularity appropriate for historical sites and landmarks. These measures include relocation and acquisition, flood proofing, and buying flood insurance.

**Public Information Statement (Abbrev. PNS).** A narrative statement issued by a National Weather Service Forecast Office that can be used for:

1) A current or expected nonhazardous event of general interest to the public that can usually be covered with a single message (e.g., unusual atmospheric phenomena such as sun dogs, halos, rainbows, aurora borealis, lenticular clouds, and stories about a long-term dry/cold/wet/warm spell).

2) Public educational information and activities, such as storm safety rules, awareness activities, storm drills, etc.

3) Information regarding service changes, service limitations, interruptions due to reduced or lost power or equipment outages, or special information clarifying interpretation of NWS data. For example, this product may be used to inform users of radar equipment outages or special information clarifying interpretation of radar data originating from an unusual source which may be mistaken for precipitation (such as chaff drops, smoke plumes, etc., that produces echoes on the radar display).

**Public Severe Weather Outlook.** These are issued when the Storm Prediction Center (SPC) in Norman, Oklahoma anticipates an especially significant and/or widespread outbreak of severe weather. This outlook will stress the seriousness of the situation, defines the threat area, and provides information on the timing of the outbreak. The lead time on this outlook is normally less than 36 hours prior to the severe weather event.

**QPF Discussion.** This HPC forecast discussion is directed completely to explaining manual forecasts of areas in the contiguous 48 states expected to receive

$^1/_4$ inch or more precipitation during a 24-hour period. The manual forecasts are explained in terms of initial conditions and differences and/or similarities in the numerical model forecasts. General confidence in the manual forecast is expressed where it is appropriate and possible alternatives may be offered. This product is issued 3 times a day.

**Quantitative Precipitation Forecast.** (Abbrev. QPF)—A spatial and temporal precipitation forecast that will predict the potential amount of future precipitation for a specified region, or area.

**RADAR.** Acronym for *RA*dio *D*etection *A*nd *R*anging; a radio device or system for locating an object by means of ultrahigh-frequency radio waves reflected from the object and received, observed, and analyzed by the receiving part of the device in such a way that characteristics (as distance and direction) of the object may be determined.

**Radar Coded Message.** This is an alphanumeric coded message which will be used in preparation of a national radar summary chart. It is automatically produced by the WSR-88D's Radar Product Generator (RPG) in 3 parts (reflectivities, storm motion, and echo tops).

**Radar Data Acquisition (RDA).** An acronym for Radar Data Acquisition. The RDA is the hardware component of the NEXRAD system that consists of the radar antenna, transmitter, receiver, tower, and controlling computer. The RDA collects the unprocessed, analog voltages from the radar antenna and converts the signal to base reflectivity, base velocity, and spectrum width (in polar coordinate form). These "wide-band" products are transmitted to the RPG, which creates and disseminates end-user products. Also: The RDA is the origination point of the WSR-88D radar data that will be eventually used by the radar operator. This WSR-88D component group is made up of several subcomponents which generate and radiate radio frequency (RF) pulses, receive reflected energy from those pulses, and process this received energy into digital base data. The RDA is also the site of the first two of four data recording levels used by the WSR-88D to record and store radar data.

**Radar Meteorology.** Branch of meteorology that uses radars for weather observations and forecasts.

**Radar Mosaic.** A radar product that combines information from multiple radars to give a regional or national view of reflectivity or precipitation. An individual NEXRAD radar is limited to a range of about 200 miles. Typically, a mosaic product is produced for regions spanning several hundreds to several thousands of miles. Mosaic products are produced by vendors external to the NEXRAD system.

**Radar Product Generator (RPG).** The RPG is the computer in the NEXRAD system that receives polar-coordinate base radar data from the RDA and processes these data into end-user products. Algorithms are utilized for pattern-recognition, rainfall estimation, computation of VIL and other products. The RPG communicates these products to end-users. A specific subset of available products is always generated for the NIDS vendors for distribution outside of the NWS, DoD, and FAA. Other products are generated by the RPG upon request from a PUP.

**Radar Range.** Distance from the radar antenna. The WSR-88D radar has a range for velocity products out to 124 nautical miles and reflectivity products out to 248 nautical miles.

**Radar Reflectivity.** The sum of all backscattering cross-sections (e.g., precipitation particles) in a pulse resolution volume divided by that volume.

**Radiosonde.** An instrument that is carried aloft by a balloon to send back information on atmospheric temperature, pressure and humidity by means of a small, expendable radio transmitter. Radiosondes can be tracked by radar, radio direction finding, or navigation systems (such as the satellite Global Positioning System) to obtain wind data. See also rawinsonde.

**RAFC.** Regional Area Forecast Center.

**RAFS.** Regional Analysis and Forecasting System.

**Rain.** Precipitation that falls to earth in drops more than 0.5 mm in diameter.

**Rain Gauge.** An instrument for measuring the quantity of rain that has fallen.

**Rainfall.** The amount of precipitation of any type, primarily liquid. It is usually the amount that is measured by a rain gauge. Refer to rain for rates of intensity and the quantitative precipitation for forecasting.

**Rainfall Estimates.** A series of NEXRAD products that employ a Z-R relationship to produce accumulations of surface rainfall from observed reflectivity.

**RAOB.** Radiosonde Observation (Upper-Air Observation).

**Rawinsonde.** A radiosonde that is tracked to measure winds.

**RAWS.** Remote Automated Weather Stations.

**Reconnaissance Code.** An aircraft weather reconnaissance code that has come to refer primarily to in-flight tropical weather observations, but actually signifies any detailed weather observation or investigation from an aircraft in flight.

**Record Event Report.** This non-routine narrative product is issued by the National Weather Service to report meteorological and hydrological events that equal or exceed existing records.

**Recreation Report.** This National Weather Service product is used to relay reports on conditions for resorts and recreational areas and/or events. This report may also contain forecast information. Reports for recreational areas and resorts are often routine products, typically for a season, but possibly year-round.

**Red Flag.** This [sic] a fire weather program which highlights the onset of critical weather conditions conducive to extensive wildfire occurrences.

**Red Flag Warning.** A term used by fire-weather forecasters to call attention to limited weather conditions of particular importance that may result in extreme burning conditions. It is issued when it is an on-going event or the fire weather forecaster has a high degree of confidence that Red Flag criteria will occur within 24 hours of issuance. Red Flag criteria occurs whenever a geographical area has been in a dry spell for a week or two, or for a shorter period, if before spring green-up or after fall color, and the National Fire Danger Rating System (NFDRS) is high to extreme and the following forecast weather parameters are forecasted to be met:

1) a sustained wind average 15 mph or greater
2) relative humidity less than or equal to 25 percent and
3) a temperature of greater than 75 degrees F.

**Red Flag Warning.** In some states, dry lightning and unstable air are criteria. A Fire Weather Watch may be issued prior to the Red Flag Warning.

**Red Watch or Red Box.** Slang for Tornado Watch.

**Report.** A weather report is a statement of the actual weather conditions observed at a specific time at a specific site.

**River Flooding.** The rise of a river to an elevation such that the river overflows its natural banks causing or threatening damage.

**River Flood Statement.** This product is used by the local National Weather Service Forecast Office (NWFO) to update and expand the information in the River Flood Warning. This statement may be used in lieu of a warning if flooding is forecasted, imminent, or existing and it presents no threat to life or property. The statement will also be used to terminate a River Flood Warning.

**River Flood Warning.** This is product is issued by the local National Weather Service Forecast Office (NWFO) when forecast points (those that have formal gaging sites and established flood stages) at specific communities or areas along rivers where flooding has been forecasted, is imminent, or is in progress. Flooding is defined as the inundation of normally dry areas as a result of increased water levels in an established water course. The flood warning is based on the RVF product from the River Forecast Center (RFC) in Minneapolis, Minnesota. The flood warning normally specifies crest information. It usually occurs 6 hours or later after the causative event and it is usually associated with widespread heavy rain and/or snow melt or ice jams. It will contain the forecast point covered by the warning, the current stage (if it is available), and the established flood stage. It will also contain the forecasted crest from the River Forecast Center (RFC) in Minneapolis, Minnesota. From this forecasted crest, the NWFO will be able to determine which areas will be affected by the river flooding. This information will be included in the warning. Finally, the statement will include a site/event specific call to action.

**River Forecast.** An internal product issued by RFCs to other NWS offices. An RVF contains stage and/or flow forecasts for specific locations based on existing, and forecasted hydrometeorologic conditions. The contents of these products are used by the HSA office to prepare Flood Warnings (FLW), Flood Statements (FLS), River Statements (RVS), as well as other products available to the public.

**River Forecast Center.** Centers that serve groups of Weather Service Forecast offices and Weather Forecast offices, in providing hydrologic guidance and is the first echelon office for the preparation of river and flood forecasts and warnings.

**River Gage.** A device for measuring the river stage.

**River Observing Station.** An established location along a river designated for observing and measuring properties of the river.

**River Recreation Statement.** A statement released by the NWS to inform river users of current and forecast river and lake conditions. These statements are especially useful for planning purposes.

**River Statement.** A NWS product issued to communicate notable hydrologic conditions which do not involve flooding, i.e., within river bank rises, minor ice jams, etc.

**RMTN.** Regional Meteorological Telecommunications Network.

**Rocketsonde.** A type of radiosonde that is shot into the atmosphere by a rocket, allowing it to collect data during its parachute descent from a higher position in the atmosphere than a balloon could reach.

**ROSA.** Remote Observing System Automation. A type of automated data transmitter used by NWS Cooperative Program observers.

**RUC.** Rapid Update Cycle model. A numerical model run by NCEP that focuses on short-term forecasts out to 12 hours.

**Runoff.** In hydrologic terms, the part of precipitation that flows toward the streams on the surface of the ground or within the ground. Runoff is composed of baseflow and surface runoff.

**RVA.** River Summary, a NWS summary of river and/or crest stages for selected forecast points along the river.

**SafetyNET.** A satellite based part of the Global Maritime Distress and Safety System (GMDSS) for automatically disseminating safety information, including weather warnings and forecasts, to mariners almost anywhere on the world's oceans.

**Saffir-Simpson Scale.** This scale was developed in an effort to estimate the possible damage a hurricane's sustained winds and storm surge could do to a coastal area. The scale of numbers are based on actual conditions at some time during the life of the storm. As the hurricane intensifies or weakens, the scale number is reassessed accordingly. The following table shows the scale broken down by central pressure, winds, and storm surge:

| Category | Central Pressure (mb) | Wind Speed (mph) | Storm Surge (ft.) | Damage |
|---|---|---|---|---|
| 1 | 980 or > | 74–95 | 4–5 | Minimal |
| 2 | 965–979 | 96–110 | 6–8 | Moderate |
| 3 | 945–964 | 111–130 | 9–12 | Extensive |
| 4 | 920–944 | 131–155 | 13–18 | Extreme |
| 5 | > 920 | > 155 | > 18 | Catastrophic |

**Sandstorm.** Particles of sand carried aloft by strong wind. The sand particles are mostly confined to the lowest ten feet, and rarely rise more than fifty feet above the ground.

**Satellite Hydrology Program.** A NOHRSC program that uses satellite data to generate areal extent of snow cover data over large areas of the western United States.

**SAWRS.** Supplementary Aviation Reporting Station—the SAWRS program addresses the concerns of users who depend on weather observations for air operations. If the cooperator is collocated with a commissioned automated system, they ensure continuity during outage periods of the automated system. The requirement for a SAWRS arises from the FAA validated need for observations to satisfy FAR 121 or 135 operations or for the safe conduct of other aircraft.

**S-Band Radar.** These were in use as network radars in the National Weather Service prior to the installation of the WSR 88-D radars. They were 10-centimeter wavelength radars.

**Scattered (Abbrev. SCT).** A layer whose summation amount of sky cover is $^3/_8$ths through $^4/_8$ths

**Seas.**

1) This term is used in National Weather Service Marine Forecasts to describe the combination or interaction of wind waves and swells (combined seas) in which the separate components are not distinguished. This includes the case when swells are negligible or are not considered in describing sea state. or

2) Waves generated by the action of wind blowing at the time of observation or in the recent past. Seas become swell at some point.

**Secondary Ambient Air Quality Standards.** Air quality standards designed to protect human welfare, including the effects on vegetation and fauna, visibility and structures.

**SEL.** A watch cancellation statement issued to terminate a watch before its original expiration time.

**Service Hydrologist.** The designated expert of the hydrology program at a WFO.

**Severe Icing.** The rate of ice accumulation on an aircraft is such that de-icing/anti-icing equipment fails to reduce or control the hazard. Immediate diversion is necessary.

**Severe Local Storm.** A convective storm that usually covers a relatively small geographic area, or moves in a narrow path, and is sufficiently intense to threaten life and/or property. Examples include severe thunderstorms with large hail, damaging wind, or tornadoes. Although cloud-to-ground lightning is not a criteria for severe local storms, it is acknowledged to be highly dangerous and a leading cause of deaths, injuries, and damage from thunderstorms. A thunderstorm need not be severe to generate frequent cloud-to-ground lightning. Additionally, excessive localized convective rains are not classified as severe storms but often are the product of severe local storms. Such rainfall may result in related phenomena (flash floods) that threaten life and property.

**Severe Thunderstorm.** A thunderstorm that produces a tornado, winds of at least 58 mph (50 knots), and/or hail at least $^3/_4$ inch in diameter. Structural wind damage may imply the occurrence of a severe thunderstorm. A thunderstorm wind equal to or greater than 40 mph (35 knots) and/or hail of at least $^1/_2$ inch is defined as approaching severe.

**Severe Thunderstorm Warning.** This is issued when either a severe thunderstorm is indicated by the WSR-88D radar or a spotter reports a thunderstorm producing hail $^3/_4$ inch or larger in diameter and/or winds equal or exceed 58 miles an hour; therefore, people in the affected area should seek safe shelter immediately. Severe thunderstorms can produce tornadoes with little or no advance warning. Lightning frequency is not a criterion for issuing a severe thunderstorm warning. They are usually issued for a duration of one hour. They can be issued without a Severe Thunderstorm Watch being already in effect. Like a Tornado Warning, the Severe Thunderstorm Warning is issued by your National Weather Service Forecast Office (NWFO). Severe Thunderstorm Warnings will include where the storm was located, what towns will be affected by the severe thunderstorm, and the primary threat associated with the severe thunderstorm warning. If the severe thunderstorm will affect the nearshore or coastal waters, it will be issued as the combined product—Severe Thunderstorm Warning and Special Marine Warning. If the severe thunderstorm is also causing torrential rains, this warning may also be combined with a Flash Flood Warning. If there is an ampersand (&) symbol at the bottom of the warning, it indicates that the warning was issued as a result of a severe weather report. After it has been issued, the affected NWFO will follow it up periodically with Severe Weather Statements. These statements will contain updated information on the severe thunderstorm and they will also let the public know when the warning is no longer in effect.

**Severe Thunderstorm Watch.** This is issued by the National Weather Service when conditions are favorable for the development of severe thunderstorms in and close to the watch area. A severe thunderstorm by definition is a thunderstorm that produces $3/4$ inch hail or larger in diameter and/or winds equal or exceed 58 miles an hour. The size of the watch can vary depending on the weather situation. They are usually issued for a duration of 4 to 8 hours. They are normally issued well in advance of the actual occurrence of severe weather. During the watch, people should review severe thunderstorm safety rules and be prepared to move a place of safety if threatening weather approaches. A Severe Thunderstorm Watch is issued by the Storm Prediction Center in Norman, Oklahoma. Prior to the issuance of a Severe Thunderstorm Watch, SPC will usually contact the affected local National Weather Service Forecast Office (NWFO) and they will discuss what their current thinking is on the weather situation. Afterwards, SPC will issue a preliminary Severe Thunderstorm Watch and then the affected NWFO will then adjust the watch (adding or eliminating counties/parishes) and then issue it to the public by way of a Watch Redefining Statement. During the watch, the NWFO will keep the public informed on what is happening in the watch area and also let the public know when the watch has expired or been cancelled.

**Severe Weather Analysis.** This WSR-88D radar product provides 3 base products (reflectivity (SWR), radial velocity (SWV), and spectrum width (SWW)) at the highest resolution available along with radial shear (SWS). These products are mapped into a 27 nm by 27 nm region centered on a point which the operator can specify anywhere within a 124 nm radius of the radar. It is most effective when employed as an alert paired product with the product centered on alert at height that caused the alert. It is used to examine 3 base products simultaneously in a 4 quadrant display; and analyze reflectivity and velocity products at various heights to gain a comprehensive vertical analysis of the thunderstorm.

**Severe Weather Potential Statement.** This statement is designed to alert the public and state/local agencies to the potential for severe weather up to 24 hours in advance. It is issued by the local National Weather Service office.

**Severe Weather Probability.** This WSR-88D radar product algorithm displays numerical values proportional to the probability that a storm will produce severe weather within 30 minutes. Values determined using a statistical regression equation which analyzes output from the VIL algorithm. It is used to quickly identify the most significant thunderstorms.

**Severe Weather Statement.** A National Weather Service product which provides follow up information on severe weather conditions (severe thunderstorm or tornadoes) which have occurred or are currently occurring.

**Shear.** Variation in wind speed (speed shear) and/or direction (directional shear) over a short distance within the atmosphere. Shear usually refers to vertical wind shear, i.e., the change in wind with height, but the term also is used in Doppler radar to describe changes in radial velocity over short horizontal distances.

**Sheet Flow.** In hydrologic terms, flow that occurs overland in places where there are no defined channels, the flood water spreads out over a large area at a uniform depth. This is also referred to as overland flow.

**Short-Fuse Warning.** A warning issued by the NWS for a local weather hazard of relatively short duration. Short-fuse warnings include tornado warnings, severe thunderstorm warnings, and flash flood warnings. Tornado and severe thunderstorm warnings typically are issued for periods of an hour or less, flash flood warnings typically for three hours or less.

**Short Term Forecast.** A product used to convey information regarding weather or hydrologic events in the next few hours.

**Shower(s).** A descriptor, SH, used to qualify precipitation characterized by the suddenness with which they start and stop, by the rapid changes of intensity, and usually by rapid changes in the appearance of the sky.

**Significant Weather Outlook.** A narrative statement produced by the National Weather Service, frequently issued on a routine basis, to provide information regarding the potential of significant weather expected during the next 1 to 5 days.

**Sky Condition.** Used in a forecast to describe the predominant/average sky condition based upon octants (eighths) of the sky covered by opaque (not transparent) clouds.

| Sky Condition | Cloud Coverage |
| --- | --- |
| Clear/Sunny | 0/8 |
| Mostly Clear/MostlySunny | 1/8 to 2/8 |
| Partly Cloudy/Partly Sunny | 3/8 to 4/8 |
| Mostly Cloudy/Considerable Cloudiness | 5/8 to 7/8 |
| Cloudy | 8/8 |
| Fair (mainly for night) | Less than 4/10 opaque clouds, no precipitation, no extremes of visibility/temperature/wind |

**SKYWARN.** Highly trained volunteer storm spotters.

**Sleet.** Sleet is defined as pellets of ice composed of frozen or mostly frozen rain-drops or refrozen partially melted snowflakes. These pellets of ice usually bounce after hitting the ground or other hard surfaces. Heavy sleet is a relatively rare event defined as an accumulation of ice pellets covering the ground to a depth of $\frac{1}{2}$ inch or more.

**Sleet Warning.** Issued when accumulation of sleet in excess of $\frac{1}{2}$ inch is expected; this is a relatively rare scenario. Usually issued as a winter storm warning for heavy sleet.

**Slight Chance.** In probability of precipitation statements, usually equivalent to a 20 percent chance.

**Slight Risk (of severe thunderstorms).** Severe thunderstorms are expected to affect between 2 and 5 percent of the area. A slight risk generally implies that severe weather events are expected to be isolated.

**Sling Psychrometer.** An instrument used to measure the water vapor content of the atmosphere in which wet and dry bulb thermometers are mounted on a frame connected to a handle at one end by means of a bearing or a length of chain. The psychrometer is whirled by hand to provide the necessary ventilation to evaporate water from the wet bulb.

**Small Craft Advisory.** This is issued by the National Weather Service to alert small boats to sustained (more than 2 hours) hazardous weather or sea conditions. These conditions may be either present or forecasted. The threshold conditions for it are usually sustained winds of 18 knots (21 mph) (less than 18 knots in some dangerous waters) to 33 knots (38 mph) inclusive or hazardous wave conditions (such as 4 feet or greater). In the Great Lakes, this advisory relates to conditions within 5 nautical miles of shore. As a result, these will be only issued in the Nearshore Forecast. Along the coastal regions of the East Coast, Gulf of Mexico, and West Coast, this advisory relates to conditions out to as much as 100 nautical miles of shore (coastal waters). As a result, these will be only issued in the Coastal Marine Forecast. Mariners learning of this advisory are urged to determine immediately the reason by turning their radios to the latest marine broadcast. Decisions as to the degree of the hazard will be left to the boater, based on experience and size and type of boat. There is no legal definition for a "small craft."

**Small Craft Advisory for Seas/Swell.** Issued for combined seas of 7 feet or greater. (locally defined criteria).

**Small Craft Should Exercise Caution.** Issued for winds of 15 to 20 knots or combined seas of 6 feet. (locally defined criteria).

**Small Hail.** Technically used to refer to snow pellets or graupel.

**Small Stream Flooding.** In hydrologic terms, flooding of small creeks, streams, or runs.

**Smog.** Originally smog meant a mixture of smoke and fog. Now, it means air that has restricted visibility due to pollution or pollution formed in the presence of sunlight—photochemical smog.

**Smoke (Abbrev. K).** Smoke in various concentrations can cause significant problems for people with respiratory ailments. It becomes a more universal hazard when visibilities are reduced to $\frac{1}{4}$ mile or less.

**Smoke Dispersal.** Describes the ability of the atmosphere to ventilate smoke. Depends on the stability and winds in the lower layers of the atmosphere, i.e., a combination of mixing heights and transport winds.

**Smoke Management.** The use of meteorology, fuel moisture, fuel loading, fire suppression and burn techniques to keep smoke impacts from prescribed fires within acceptable limits.

**Snotel.** SNOw TELemetry. An automated network of snowpack data collection sites. The Natural Resources Conservation Service (NRCS), formerly the Soil Conservation Service (SCS), has operated the Federal-State-Private Cooperative Snow Survey Program in the western United States since 1935. A standard SNOTEL site consists of a snow pillow, a storage type precipitation gage, air temperature sensor and a small shelter for housing electronics.

**Snow.** Precipitation in the form of ice crystals, mainly of intricately branched, hexagonal form and often agglomerated into snowflakes, formed directly from the freezing [deposition] of the water vapor in the air.

**Snow Accumulation and Ablation Model.** In hydrologic terms, a model which simulates snow pack accumulation, heat exchange at the air-snow interface, areal extent of snow cover, heat storage within the snow pack, liquid water retention, and transmission and heat exchange at the ground-snow interface.

**Snow Advisory.** This product is issued by the National Weather Service when a low pressure system produces snow that may cause significant inconveniences, but do not meet warning criteria and if caution is not exercised could lead to life threatening situations. The advisory criterion varies from area to area. If the forecaster feels that it is warranted, he or she can issued it for amounts less than the minimum criteria. For example, it may be issued for the first snow of the season or when snow has not fallen in long while.

**Snow Core.** A sample of either freshly fallen snow, or the combined old and new snow on the ground. This is obtained by pushing a cylinder down through the snow layer and extracting it.

**Snow Flurries.** Snow flurries are an intermittent light snowfall of short duration (generally light snow showers) with no measurable accumulation (trace category).

**Snowpack.** The total snow and ice on the ground, including both the new snow and the previous snow and ice which has not melted.

**Snow Shower.** A snow shower is a short duration of moderate snowfall. Some accumulation is possible.

**Snow Squall.** A snow squall is an intense, but limited duration, period of moderate to heavy snowfall, accompanied by strong, gusty surface winds and possibly lightning (generally moderate to heavy snow showers). Snow accumulation may be significant.

**Snow Stake.** A 1-$^3/_4$ inch square, semi-permanent stake, marked in inch increments to measure snow depth.

**Snow Stick.** A portable rod used to measure snow depth.

**Sounding.** A set of data measuring the vertical structure of an atmospheric parameter (temperature, humidity, pressure, winds, etc.) at a given time.

**Space Environment Center (SEC).** This center provides real-time monitoring and forecasting of solar and geophysical events, conducts research in solar-terrestrial physics, and develops techniques for forecasting solar and geo-physical disturbances. SEC's parent organization is the National Oceanic and Atmospheric Administration (NOAA). SEC is one of NOAA's 12 Environmental Research Laboratories (ERL) and one of NOAA's 9 National Centers for Environmental Prediction (NCEP). SEC's Space Weather Operations is jointly operated by NOAA and the U.S. Air Force and is the national and world warning center for disturbances that can affect people and equipment working in the space environment.

**SPC.** Storm Prediction Center.

**Special Avalanche Warning.** Issued by the National Weather Service when avalanches are imminent or occurring in the mountains. It is usually issued for a 24 hour period.

**Special Fire Weather.** Meteorological services uniquely required by user agencies which cannot be provided at an NWS office during normal working hours. Examples are on-site support, weather observer training, and participation in user agency training activities.

**Special Marine Warning.** This is issued by the National Weather Service for hazardous weather conditions (thunderstorms over water, thunderstorms that will move over water, cold air funnels over water, or waterspouts) usually of short duration (2 hours or less) and producing sustained winds or frequent gusts of 34 knots or more that is not covered by existing marine warnings. These are tone alerted on NOAA Weather Radio. Boaters will also be able to get this information by tuning into Coast Guard and commercial radio stations that transmit marine weather information. Or a warning issued for 2 hours or less by the National Weather Service to warn boaters of any of the following that is not adequately covered by the existing Coastal Waters Forecast:

1) thunderstorm or non-thunderstorm winds of 34 knots or more (39 mph)
2) waterspouts, detected by radar or observed
3) tornadoes moving from land to water

**Special Tropical Disturbance Statement.** This statement issued by the National Hurricane Center furnishes information on strong and formative non-depression systems. This statement focuses on the major threat(s) of the disturbance, such as the potential for torrential rainfall on an island or inland area. The statement is coordinated with the appropriate forecast office(s).

**Spotting.** Outbreak of secondary fires as firebrands or other burning materials are carried ahead of the main fire line by winds.

**Squall.** A strong wind characterized by a sudden onset in which the wind speed increases at least 16 knots and is sustained more than 22 knots or more for at least one minute.

**Squall Line (Abbrev. SQLN).** A solid or broken line of thunderstorms or squalls. The line may extend across several hundred miles.

**Stair Stepping.** In hydrologic terms, the process of continually updating river forecasts for the purpose of incorporating the effects rain that has fallen since the previous forecast was prepared.

**Standard Atmosphere.** A hypothetical vertical distribution of temperature, pressure and density which, by international consent, is taken to be representative of the atmosphere for purposes of pressure altimeter calibrations, aircraft performance calculations, aircraft and missile design, ballistic tables, etc.

**State Forecast Product.** This National Weather Service product is intended to give a good general picture of what weather may be expected in the state during the next 5 days. The first 2 days of the forecast is much more specific than the last 3 days. In comparison with the Zone Forecast Product, this product will be much more general.

**State Weather Roundup.** This is a National Weather Service tabular product which provides routine hourly observations within the state through the National Weather Wire Service (NWWS). It gives the current weather condition in one word (cloudy, rain, snow, fog, etc.), the temperature and dew point in Fahrenheit, the relative humidity, wind speed and direction, and finally additional information (wind chill, heat index, a secondary weather condition). These reports are broken up regionally. When the complementary satellite product is not available, reports from unaugmented ASOS stations will report "fair" in the sky/weather column when there are few or no clouds (i.e., scattered or less) below 12,000 feet with no significant weather and/or obstructions to visibility.

**Stationary Front.** A front between warm and cold air masses that is moving very slowly or not at all.

**Station Model.** A specified pattern for plotting, on a weather map, the meteorological symbols that represent the state of the weather at a particular observing station.

**Station Pressure.** The absolute air pressure at a given reporting station. The air pressure is directly proportional to the combined weight of all air in the atmosphere located in a column directly above the reporting site. Consequently, the station pressure may vary tremendously from one location to another in mountainous regions due to the strong variation of atmospheric pressure with height. Vertical variations of pressure range up to 150 mb per mile whereas horizontal variations are usually less than.1 mb per mile.

**Storm.** Any disturbed state of the atmosphere, especially affecting the Earth's surface, and strongly implying destructive and otherwise unpleasant weather. Storms range in scale from tornadoes and thunderstorms to tropical cyclones to synoptic-scale extratropical cyclones.

**Storm Data.** This National Climatic Data Center (NCDC) monthly publication documents a chronological listing, by states, of occurrences of storms and unusual weather phenomena. Reports contain information on storm paths, deaths, injuries, and property damage. An "Outstanding storms of the month" section highlights severe weather events with photographs, illustrations, and narratives. The December issue includes annual tornado, lightning, flash flood, and tropical cyclone summaries.

**Storm Scale.** Referring to weather systems with sizes on the order of individual thunderstorms. See synoptic scale and mesoscale.

**Storm Surge.** A rise above the normal water level along a shore caused by strong onshore winds and/or reduced atmospheric pressure. The surge height is the difference of the observed water level minus the predicted tide. Most hurricane deaths are caused by the storm surge. It can be 50 or more miles wide and sweeps across the coastline around where the hurricane makes landfall. The maximum rises in sea-level move from under the storm to the right of the storm's track, reaching a maximum amplitude of 10 to 30 feet at the coast. The storm surge may even double or more in height when the hurricane's track causes it to funnel water into a bay. The storm surge increases substantially as it approaches the land because the normal water depth decreases rapidly as it approaches the beaches. The moving water contains the same amount of energy; thus, resulting in an increase of storm surge. Typically, the stronger the hurricane, the greater the storm surge.

**Storm Tide.** The actual sea level resulting from astronomical tide combined with the storm surge. This term is used interchangeably with "hurricane tide."

**Storm Total Precipitation.** This radar image is an estimate of accumulated rainfall since the last time there was a one-hour, or more, break in precipitation. It is used to locate flood potential over urban or rural areas, estimate total basin runoff and provide rainfall accumulations for the duration of the event and is available only for the short range (out to 124 nm). To determine accumulated precipitation at greater distances you should link to an adjacent radar.

**Storm Tracking Information.** This WSR-88D radar product displays the previous, current, and projected locations of storm centroids (forecast and past positions are limited to one hour or less). Forecast tracks are based upon linear extrapolation of past storm centroid positions, and they are intended for application to individual thunderstorms not lines or clusters. It is used to provide storm movement: low track variance and/or 2 or more plotted past positions signify reliable thunderstorm movement.

**Storm Warning.** A warning of 1-minute sustained surface winds of 48 kt (55 mph or 88 kph) or greater, either predicted or occurring, not directly associated with tropical cyclones.

**Stormwater Discharge.** In hydrologic terms, precipitation that does not infiltrate into the ground or evaporate due to impervious land surfaces but instead flows onto adjacent land or water areas and is routed into drain/sewer systems.

**Strike.** For any particular location, a hurricane strike occurs if that location passes within the hurricane's strike circle, a circle of 125 n mi diameter, centered 12.5 n mi to the right of the hurricane center (looking in the direction of motion). This circle is meant to depict the typical extent of hurricane force winds, which are approximately 75 n mi to the right of the center and 50 n mi to the left.

**Substation.** A location where observations are taken or other services are furnished by people not located at NWS offices who do not need to be certified to take observations.

**Sustained Wind.** Wind speed determined by averaging observed values over a two-minute period.

**Synoptic Weather.** Weather occurring over a wide region on time scales exceeding 12 hours.

**T. Temperature (Abbrev. TEMP).** The temperature is a measure of the internal energy that a substance contains. This is the most measured quantity in the atmosphere.

**Thunder.** The sound caused by rapidly expanding gases in a lightning discharge.

**Thunderstorm.** A local storm produced by a cumulonimbus cloud and accompanied by lightning and thunder.

**Tornado.** A violently rotating column of air, usually pendant to a cumulonimbus, with circulation reaching the ground. It nearly always starts as a funnel cloud and may be accompanied by a loud roaring noise. On a local scale, it is the most destructive of all atmospheric phenomena.

**Tornado Warning.** This is issued when a tornado is indicated by the WSR-88D radar or sighted by spotters; therefore, people in the affected area should seek safe shelter immediately. They can be issued without a Tornado Watch being already in effect. They are usually issued for a duration of around 30 minutes. A Tornado Warning is issued by your local National Weather Service office (NWFO). It will include where the tornado was located and what towns will be in its path. If the tornado will affect the nearshore or coastal waters, it will be issued as the combined product—Tornado Warning and Special Marine Warning. If the thunderstorm which is causing the tornado is also producing torrential rains, this warning may also be combined with a Flash Flood Warning. If there is an ampersand (&) symbol at the bottom of the warning, it indicates that the warning was issued as a result of a severe weather report. After it has been issued, the affected NWFO will follow it up periodically with Severe Weather Statements. These statements will contain updated information on the tornado and they will also let the public know when warning is no longer in effect.

**Tornado Watch.** This is issued by the National Weather Service when conditions are favorable for the development of tornadoes in and close to the watch area. Their size can vary depending on the weather situation. They are usually issued for a duration of 4 to 8 hours. They normally are issued well in advance of the actual occurrence of severe weather. During the watch, people should review tornado safety rules and be prepared to move a place of safety if threatening weather approaches. A Tornado Watch is issued by the Storm Prediction Center (SPC) in Norman, Oklahoma. Prior to the issuance of a Tornado Watch, SPC will usually contact the affected local National Weather Forecast Office (NWFO) and they will discuss what their current thinking is on the weather situation. Afterwards, SPC will issue a preliminary Tornado Watch and then the affected NWFO will then adjust the watch (adding or eliminating counties/parishes) and then issue it to the public. After adjusting the watch, the NWFO will let the public know which counties are included by way of a Watch Redefining Statement. During the watch, the NWFO will keep the public informed on what is happening in the watch area and also let the public know when the watch has expired or been cancelled.

**Ultraviolet Index.** This index provides important information to help you plan your outdoor activities in ways that prevent overexposure to the sun's rays. It was designed by the National Weather Service (NWS) and the Environmental Protection Agency (EPA). Unlike some countries' indices, the United States UV Index is not based upon surface observations. Rather, it is computed using forecasted ozone levels, a computer model that relates ozone levels to UV incidence on the ground, forecasted cloud amounts, and the elevation of the forecast cities. The calculation starts with measurements of current total ozone amounts for the entire globe, obtained via two satellites operated by the National Oceanic and Atmospheric Administration (NOAA). These data are then used to produce a forecast of ozone levels for the next day at various points around the country.

| Category | UV Index | Time to Burn | Actions to Take |
|---|---|---|---|
| Minimal | 0–2 | 60 min. + | Apply SPF sunscreen. |
| Low | 3–4 | 45 min. | Apply SPF sunscreen, wear a hat. |
| Moderate | 5–6 | 30 min. | Apply SPF 15, wear a hat. |
| High | 7–9 | 15–24 min. | Apply SPF 15 to 30, wear a hat and sunglasses. Limit midday exposure. |
| Very High | 10+ | 10 min. | Apply SPF 30; wear a hat, sunglasses, and protective clothing; limit midday exposure. |

**Urban Flooding.** Flooding of streets, underpasses, low lying areas, or storm drains. This type of flooding is mainly an inconvenience and is generally not life threatening.

**Urban Heat Island.** The increased air temperatures in urban areas in contrast to cooler surrounding rural areas.

**Very Windy.** 30 to 40 mph winds.

**Warning.** A warning is issued when a hazardous weather or hydrologic event is occurring, is imminent, or has a very high probability of occurring. A warning is used for conditions posing a threat to life or property.

**Watch.** A watch is used when the risk of a hazardous weather or hydrologic event has increased significantly, but its occurrence, location, and/or timing is still uncertain. It is intended to provide enough lead time so that those who need to set their plans in motion can do so.

**Weather.** The state of the atmosphere with respect to wind, temperature, cloudiness, moisture, pressure, etc. *Weather* refers to these conditions at a given point in time (e.g., today's high temperature), whereas *Climate* refers to the "average" weather conditions for an area over a long period of time (e.g., the average high temperature for today's date).

**Wildfire.** Any free burning uncontainable wildland fire not prescribed for the area which consumes the natural fuels and spreads in response to its environment.

**Wind.** The horizontal motion of the air past a given point. Winds begin with differences in air pressures. Pressure that's higher at one place than another sets up a force pushing from the high toward the low pressure. The greater the difference in pressures, the stronger the force. The distance between the area of high pressure and the area of low pressure also determines how fast the moving air is accelerated. Meteorologists refer to the force that starts the wind flowing as the "pressure gradient force." High and low pressure are relative. There's no set number that divides high and low pressure. Wind is used to describe the prevailing direction from which the wind is blowing with the speed given usually in miles per hour or knots.

**Wind Advisory.** Sustained winds 25 to 39 mph and/or gusts to 57 mph. Issuance is normally site specific. However, winds of this magnitude occurring over an area that frequently experiences such winds

**Wind Chill.** Reference to the *Wind Chill Factor*; increased wind speeds accelerate heat loss from exposed skin, and the wind chill is a measure of this effect. No specific rules exist for determining when wind chill becomes dangerous. As a general rule, the threshold for potentially dangerous wind chill conditions is about $-20°$F.

**Wind Chill Advisory.** The National Weather Service issues this product when the wind chill could be life threatening if action is not taken. The criterion for this warning varies from state to state.

**Wind Chill Factor.** Increased wind speeds accelerate heat loss from exposed skin. No specific rules exist for determining when wind chill becomes dangerous. As a general rule, the threshold for potentially dangerous wind chill conditions is about $-20°$F.

**Wind Chill Warning.** The National Weather Service issues this product when the wind chill is life threatening. The criteria for this warning varies from state to state.

**Wind Direction.** The true direction *from which* the wind is blowing at a given location (i.e., wind blowing from the north to the south is a north wind). It is normally measured in tens of degrees from 10 degrees clockwise through 360 degrees. North is 360 degrees. A wind direction of 0 degrees is only used when wind is calm.

**Wind Shear.** The rate at which wind velocity changes from point to point in a given direction (as, vertically). The shear can be speed shear (where speed changes between the two points, but not direction), direction shear (where direction changes between the two points, but not speed) or a combination of the two.

**Wind Speed.** The rate at which air is moving horizontally past a given point. It may be a 2-minute average speed (reported as wind speed) or an instantaneous speed (reported as a peak wind speed, wind gust, or squall).

**Windy.** 20 to 30 mph winds.

**Winter Storm Warning.** This product is issued by the National Weather Service when a winter storm is producing or is forecast to produce heavy snow or significant ice accumulations. The criteria for this warning can vary from place to place.

**Winter Storm Watch.** This product is issued by the National Weather Service when there is a potential for heavy snow or significant ice accumulations, usually at least 24 to 36 hours in advance. The criteria for this watch can vary from place to place.

**Winter Weather Advisory.** This product is issued by the National Weather Service when a low pressure system produces a combination of winter weather (snow, freezing rain, sleet, etc.) that present a hazard, but does not meet warning criteria.

**WMO.** World Meteorological Organization (UN).

# Selected Bibliography

*When Nature Strikes: Weather Disasters and the Law* is the first effort to discuss the range of areas of law in which weather plays a role. As a result, the sources consulted included a large number of Congressional documents, primary legal documents including court cases and legislation, newspaper articles, books on weather events, and meteorology and atmospheric sciences texts, as well as books and scholarly journal articles on law and policy. The totality of the materials consulted for this book, as well as other materials related to law and weather, is referenced and described in Marsha L. Baum, *The Law of U.S. Weather: Regulation, Liabilities, and Relief* (Buffalo: William S. Hein & Co., forthcoming), a comprehensive annotated bibliography of materials related to law and weather in the United States.

The following selective listing provides references to only a few of the books that will be of interest to the general reader. This list does not reference any of the many nonbook materials, including the multitude of Web sites, which can provide information for the person interested in further exploring the topics of this book. However, the notes for each chapter do provide the reader with citations for the specific sources such as court cases, articles, and Web resources selected and directly used in preparing *When Nature Strikes*.

## STORIES OF MAJOR WEATHER EVENTS

Barry, John M. *Rising Tide: The Great Mississippi Flood of 1927 and How It Changed America*. New York: Touchstone, 1997.

Burt, Christopher C. *Extreme Weather: A Guide and Record Book*. New York: W. W. Norton & Co., 2004.

Cooper, Christopher, and Robert Block. *Disaster: Hurricane Katrina and the Failure of Homeland Security.* New York: Times Books, 2006.

Drye, Willie. *Storm of the Century: The Labor Day Hurricane of 1935.* Washington, DC: National Geographic Society, 2002.

Egan, Timothy. *The Worst Hard Time: The Untold Story of Those Who Survived the Great American Dust Bowl.* Boston: Houghton Mifflin Co., 2006.

Gess, Denise, and William Lutz. *Firestorm at Peshtigo: A Town, Its People, and the Deadliest Fire in American History.* New York: Owl Books, 2003.

Horne, Jed. *Breach of Faith: Hurricane Katrina and the Near Death of a Great American City.* New York: Random House, 2006.

Laskin, David L. *The Children's Blizzard.* New York: Harper Perennial, 2005.

Ludlum, David M. *The Weather Factor.* Boston: American Meteorological Society, 1989.

Scotti, R. A. *Sudden Sea: The Great Hurricane of 1938.* New York: Back Bay Books, 2003.

Van Heerden, Ivor, and Mike Bryan. *The Storm: What Went Wrong and Why During Hurricane Katrina—The Inside Story from One Louisiana Scientist.* New York: Viking, 2006.

Zebrowski, Ernest, and Judith A. Howard. *Category 5: The Story of Camille, Lessons Learned from America's Most Violent Hurricane.* Ann Arbor, MI: The University of Michigan Press, 2005.

## DISASTER POLICY AND RELIEF MANAGEMENT

Comerio, Mary C. *Disaster Hits Home: New Policy for Urban Housing Recovery.* Berkeley, CA: University of California Press, 1998.

Cutter, Susan L., ed. *American Hazardscapes: The Regionalization of Hazards and Disasters.* Washington, DC: Joseph Henry Press, 2001.

Dyson, Michael Eric. *Come Hell or High Water: Hurricane Katrina and the Color of Disaster.* New York: Basic Civitas, 2006.

Farber, Daniel A., and Jim Chen. *Disasters and the Law: Katrina and Beyond.* New York: Aspen Publishers, 2006.

Haddow, George D., and Jane A. Bullock. *Introduction to Emergency Management.* 2nd ed. Burlington, MA: Elsevier Butterworth-Heinemann, 2006.

Nicholson, William C. *Emergency Response and Emergency Management Law.* Springfield, IL: Charles C. Thomas, 2003.

Resnick, Abraham. *Due to the Weather: Ways the Elements Affect Our Lives.* Westport, CT: Greenwood Press, 2000.

Steinberg, Ted. *Acts of God: The Unnatural History of Natural Disaster in America.* 2nd ed. New York: Oxford University Press, 2006.

## METEOROLOGY AND ATMOSPHERIC SCIENCES

Bryant, Edward. *Natural Hazards.* 2nd ed. New York: Cambridge University Press, 2005.

Cantrell, Mark. *The Everything Weather Book: From Daily Forecasts to Blizzards, Hurricanes, and Tornadoes.* Avon, MA: Adams Media Corp., 2002.

Cox, John D. *Storm Watchers: The Turbulent History of Weather Prediction from Franklin's Kite to El Niño*. Hoboken, NJ: John Wiley & Sons, 2002.

de Villiers, Marq. *Windswept: The Story of Wind and Weather*. New York: Walker and Co., 2006.

Ebert, Charles H.V. *Disasters: An Analysis of Natural and Human-Induced Hazards*. 4th ed. Dubuque, IA: Kendall/Hunt Publishing Co., 2000.

Fishman, Jack, and Robert Kalish. *The Weather Revolution: Innovations and Imminent Breakthroughs in Accurate Forecasting*. New York: Plenum Press, 1994.

Goldstein, Mel. *The Complete Idiot's Guide to Weather*. 2nd ed. Indianapolis, IN: Alpha Books, 2002.

Halford, Pauline. *Storm Warning: The Origins of the Weather Forecast*. Gloucestershire, UK: Sutton Publishing, 2004.

Lutgens, Frederick K., and Edward J. Tarbuck. *The Atmosphere: An Introduction to Meteorology*. 10th ed. Upper Saddle River, NJ: Pearson Prentice Hall, 2007.

Monmonier, Mark. *Air Apparent: How Meteorologists Learned to Map, Predict, and Dramatize Weather*. Chicago: The University of Chicago Press, 1999.

Sheets, Bob, and Jack Williams. *Hurricane Watch: Forecasting the Deadliest Storms on Earth*. New York: Vintage Books, 2001.

Tufty, Barbara. *1001 Questions Answered About Hurricanes, Tornadoes and Other Natural Air Disasters*. New York: Dover Publications, 1987.

# Table of Cases

# Table of Cases

# Table of Cases

# Table of Cases

# Table of Cases

# Table of Federal Statutes and Proposed Legislation

# Index

**About the Author**

MARSHA L. BAUM is Professor of Law at the University of New Mexico Law School in Albuquerque, where she is former Associate Dean for Library Affairs and former Director of the Law Library.